For Selwyn, sadly too late. And to
Sylvia who knows the affection with
which this dedication is made.

A Star Book
Published in 1987
e Paperback Division of
. H. Allen & Co. Plc
treet, London W1X 8LB

blished in Great Britain
ichael Joseph Ltd 1986

© Brian Freemantle 1986

bound in Great Britain by
rendon Ltd, Tiptree, Essex

BN 0 352 32126 1

THE STEAL

The effects of counterfeiting and industrial and technological espionage go beyond the obvious financial loss to the *bona fide* manufacturer. Deprived of income, research and development are stultified and in some cases abandoned, and I was told on numerous occasions during my researches into this book that Western technological progress has been positively retarded. The piracy of earlier centuries was defeated by concerted and combined international action. Backed as it is by governments, official intelligence agencies and organised crime, the modern version will not be.

The sales slogan of a Taiwanese counterfeiter—Golden Shine Corporation—epitomises the attitude. The company stationery boasts 'Your Game, My Game'. It is one that the pirates are winning.

T

C

by th
W
44 Hill

First p
by M

Copyright

Printed and
Anchor Br

IS

This book is sold subjec
by way of trade or othe
or otherwise circulated
consent in any form of b
which it is published a
including this conditi
subsequ

Contents

CONTENTS

Acknowledgments

In a four-month research journey that took me completely around the world I was given considerable assistance by enforcement bodies and intelligence agencies, but in almost every instance a condition of anonymity was imposed. At America's Federal Bureau of Investigation, for instance, only Assistant Deputy Director Philip Parker was prepared to be publicly identified. To those necessarily unnamed sources in the United States and their counterparts in England, Germany, Italy, Japan, Taiwan, Hong Kong, Thailand and India I extend my sincere gratitude for their time, patience and guidance.

There are, however, a great number of people whose assistance can be openly acknowledged.

I began my research in America, where I was given unfailing help by officials of the United States Customs Service. In particular, I would like to thank the Commissioner, William von Rabb, Roger Ubanski, Director of the Strategic Investigation Division and Ms Christine Fraser from the Public Affairs Department – all based at the Washington DC headquarters. In Los Angeles, I have to thank Agent in Charge Alan Walls and his deputy, John Charles; in New York, Patrick O'Brien, area director of general investigations.

Back in Washington, I greatly benefited from my Pentagon meeting with Dr Stephen Bryen, Deputy Assistant Secretary of Defence in the Department of International Economics, Trade and Security Policy. Across the Potomac at the Department of Commerce I gained an insight into the conflicts between two government departments from my interview with William Archey, the ebullient Assistant Secretary for Trade Administration – an insight that was extended with my encounter with Calman Cohen, Vice-President of the Emergency Committee for American Trade.

ACKNOWLEDGMENTS

Still in the American capital, I am indebted to Ray Lewis, Chief Librarian at the House of Representatives who, together with his efficient staff, aided my enquiries far beyond providing answers to the original questions and supplied me with a wealth of documentary material I was unaware existed. I was also very ably assisted by Dudley Freeman and his New York News Service.

At the upstate New York headquarters of IBM – Armonk was carefully chosen at the time as a site then out of range of any fallout that might be produced by a nuclear attack on Manhattan – Public Affairs Manager Lyle McGuire responded to every enquiry concerning the industrial espionage attacks on their products. So, too, did M. C. Reisch, from the Texas headquarters of the Bell Helicopter Company at Fort Worth.

From America I travelled to Japan. Before leaving England I attempted to arrange official meetings with Japanese government departments and trade officials to discuss the reputation the country has for industrial espionage and I renewed those attempts from the day of my arrival in Tokyo, where the published findings of my earlier investigations into the Russian KGB, America's CIA and worldwide drug trafficking have enjoyed widespread and considerable success.

I was shunted from person to person, from telephone extension to telephone extension, until I concluded that I was being avoided as a matter of policy. That impression was confirmed by some of the unattributable sources, who told me that no one in government or business wanted to risk the appearance of their names in a book as widely read as the accounts of my previous investigations had been. The subject was potentially too embarrassing. Throughout my enquiries it was made very clear that the Japanese resent as undeserved the worldwide criticism their conduct has earned them over the issue of industrial espionage. I regret that there was no one prepared to be quoted in support of that position, leaving me with the impression that resent it though they do, the Japanese are also deeply embarrassed by the criticism. I thank those who were prepared to talk to me anonymously and, on the record, here express my gratitude for his assistance to Laurent Dubois, Director of the Tokyo Bureau of the Union des Fabricants pour la Protection Internationale de la Propriété Industrielle et Artistique.

One of my first discoveries upon my arrival in the Taiwanese capital of Taipei was a copy of my book on the KGB, counterfeited by Mr Chen Ming Hwei. Mr Hwei never responded from his supposed publishing house at 615 Lin Shin N. Rd to my enquiries about possible royalties, not that I had really expected any answer. Jerry Fong, Deputy Executive Secretary of the country's Anti-Counterfeiting Committee, did at least say that the counterfeiting was unfortunate. So did Terry Chen, the Committee's Executive Secretary. For their further assistance, I thank both. Derek Cheng is a lawyer with the Taipei firm of Lee and Li and a frequent government prosecutor in Taiwanese counterfeiting cases whose guidance I found extremely useful.

In Hong Kong, I am indebted to Anthony Gurka, founder of Commercial Trademark Service (Hong Kong) Ltd; to Alan Wells, Paul Scholefield and Michael Pendleton, from the legal firm of Deacons, solicitors specialising in patent and trademark infringements; Ella Shuk Ki Cheong, the patents and trademark expert from solicitors Wilkinson and Grist, and Frank Knight, regional director of the East Asia Film Security Office of the Motion Picture Association of America. Hotel-bound because of Hurricane Hal, whose arrival in the archipelago was expected at any moment, I gained a fascinating insight into the scope of Triad involvement in counterfeiting – their control extends well beyond the immediate islands. My source has, alas, to remain anonymous, but I thank that person most sincerely.

Such is the violence and corruption that exists in the counterfeiting industries of Thailand that no one who talked to me would agree to have their comments properly attributed. I also took very seriously the warning that if I tried to visit a factory on the outskirts of Bangkok which was identified to me in detail as the major producer of fake Johnnie Walker whisky, the armed protectors would shoot to kill.

For the help I received in Bombay, I thank Captain Sudhir Malik and I am indebted for the time made available to me in New Delhi by Mohad Katre, Director of the Indian Central Bureau of Investigation.

In England, my thanks are due for the anonymous assistance I received from enforcement agencies; also, to those patient officials who briefed me at the Department of Trade in Victoria, London.

Of those people who can be publicly recognised, I am particularly grateful to Eric Ellen, Director of the Essex-based

ACKNOWLEDGMENTS

Counterfeiting Intelligence Bureau. Mr Ellen guided me before I embarked on my research trip round the world; on my return a colleague of his, CIB investigator Jack Heslop, took over. Another private detective from whom I obtained fascinating and intriguing information was Vincent Carratu of Carratu International, headquartered in the London suburb of Worcester Park.

Others whom I would like to thank are Robert Hay, Enforcement Coordinator for the Federation Against Software Theft; James Wolsey, Director of the Overseas and Anti-Piracy Division of the International Federation of Phonogram and Videogram Producers, and Dave Laing, Information Officer from the same organisation; Ms Anthea Worsdall, Secretary of the Anti-Counterfeiting Group, a countrywide organisation of preyed-upon British industries; Robert Birch, at the time of writing Director General of the Federation Against Copyright Theft Ltd; Harry Jones, of the Motor Manufacturers Association; Ian Taylor, coordinator of the British Publishers Association's campaign against worldwide book piracy, and David Fletcher-Rogers of the Dunlop Co. of Birmingham.

ng his invention that Webster's *Dictionary*
jective coined from Ovshinsky's name, to
Ovshinsky sued and won.
terfeiting and industrial and technological
the obvious financial loss to the *bona fide*
d of income, research and devictums of the
ting   e cases aban   buying pills or medi-
n prescription or by the packet, but singly from traders
vn streets. While appreciating that like most commercial
es pharmaceutical companies are motivated by profit, I
eir refusal to comment upon this evil industry and the

Book One

The seeds ye sow, another reaps;
The wealth ye find, another keeps;
The robes ye weave, another wears;
The arms ye forge, another bears.

'Song to the Men of England',
Percy Bysshe Shelley

Introduction

Japan's Emperor Hirohito posed for an official photogr
wearing a counterfeit Hermes tie

A New York Mafia family financed a British-run Acapulco factory whose fake perfume threatened the existence of the real Chanel company. In Taiwan, a pirate stole the trademark of a British wallpaper manufacturer and took the royal warrant as supplier to the Queen of England as well. Only days after the release of Band Aid's 'Do They Know It's Christmas', the song which initiated the pop world's international fund-raising campaign to relieve the famine in Ethiopia, a Singapore counterfeiter issued the single on a tape which included the appropriately titled 'Lay Your Hands on Me'. Kenya faced economic disaster when its coffee crop was destroyed by the use of a fake fungicide. Imitation parts came close to getting into America's space shuttle. Some were actually fitted into Boeing 737s and others into fighter training aircraft belonging to the Singapore government.

All are examples of the biggest ongoing theft in the world, the counterfeit business. American intelligence estimates its annual turnover to be in excess of $50,000,000,000, and rising. The International Federation of Phonogram and Videogram Producers alone claim that sound recordings valued at $1,200,000,000 were pirated in 1984. Singapore was the major producing country.

The cost cannot, however, be measured in purely financial terms. In 1949 Graham Greene posited the notion of adulterated vaccine in his brilliant novel *The Third Man*; today, in some Asian and African countries, this is no fictional ploy but reality – worse, the vaccine is not merely adulterated but completely fake. The same is true of birth control pills and antibiotics. Deaths have definitely occurred as a result of taking these products, but there is no way of assessing the numbers involved. The pharmaceutical deadly risks it takes with human lives ~~disasterously~~ by ~~~~

Counterfeiting is one aspect of multi-billion-dollar industrial and technological stealing. There is another.

Russia achieved an undoubted coup when it put Sputnik into space, but down to earth, it never achieved a matching initiative and now, together with the Eastern bloc, it still lags development years behind the West. Moscow recognises the fact and through its own intelligence agencies, and those of satellite countries, it has constructed a technology-gathering apparatus which was likened by one intelligence expert to a suction pump. Soviet intelligence has a genius with a James Bond-plus life style who has equipped whole hi-tech factories for them. He is still in circulation only because he managed to evade capture in South Africa and Europe by a matter of hours. Western intelligence agencies know the goddamned Richard Mueller is out there, somewhere, but they no longer know where or who he is.

America is the cradle of hi-tech. Under the presidency of Ronald Reagan a stringent effort has been mounted to block the technology transfer to the Eastern bloc, resulting in turf wars between different departments within the US government and provoking resentment from Western allies at what is seen as heavy-booted infringement of individual sovereignty.

Officially the Reagan effort is called the Technology Security Programme and by early 1985, according to Secretary of Defence Caspar Weinberger, it had already saved America $50,000,000,000 – the expenditure that would have been necessary to counter Soviet advances had various types of technology reached the Eastern bloc. And this interruption in the flow, again according to Weinberger, has cost the Soviet Union $13,000,000,000 to make missile, a shipborne surveillance radar, the Patriot ... ... missile, a towed-array submarine sonar system, an unannounced air-to-air missile, the improved HAWK surface-to-air missile and a NATO air-defence system. According to America's Central Intelligence Agency, the KGB and the military arm of Soviet intelligence, the Glavnoye Razvedyvatelnoye Upravleniye or GRU, got details of the US Minuteman silo enabling them to build a facsimile silo for their SS-13 and deploy early their first intercontinental ballistic missile. The general-purpose computer used throughout the Eastern bloc is the Ryad system. It is copied from the IBM 360 and 370 series. The Russian IL-76 Candid aircraft looks like the American C-141, and the IL-86 like the Boeing 747. There are features in the Soviet SA-7 heat-seeking shoulder-fired anti-aircraft missile identical to the US Redeye missile. According to Richard Perle, the ultra-hawkish US Assistant Secretary of Defence for international security, the Russians have created a microchip and technological centre in the city of Zelenograd almost entirely from secrets stolen from America's hi-tech powerhouse in Silicon Valley, an arrowhead area south of San Francisco.

Technological and industrial espionage is not, however, a war fought out strictly between the East and the West. There are subsidiary battles, fought just as determinedly. Hitachi, the Japanese electronics firm, budgeted $1,000,000 to steal the design specifications of IBM's 3081 computer – and still refuse to accept they were doing wrong. In Japan, the $15,000,000,000 Matsushita company is referred to colloquially as *maneshita*, which means one who copies. And they live up to the description. In 1983 Matsushita announced the development of a highly technical advance in semiconductors – the materials used as the basis for most modern electronic components – using lasers. The idea had been patented in 1970 by inventor Stanford Ovshinsky, President of Energy Conversion Devices, of Troy, Michigan, and was so combined international action. Backed as it is by governments, official intelligence agencies and organised crime, the modern version will not be.

The sales slogan of a Taiwanese counterfeiter – Golden Shine Corporation – epitomises the attitude. The company stationery boasts 'Your Game, my Game'. It is one that the pirates are winning.

CHAPTER ONE

The Shopping List

The Soviet shopping list for Western technology has an appropriate name. It is called the Red Book. A copy of the Red Book was obtained by West German intelligence, who made it available to Britain and America. Its official Soviet title is *Coordinated Requests for Technological Information*. It runs to twenty-seven chapters and is as thick as a city telephone directory. There is also a copy in the closed-to-ambassadors departments of the KGB and GRU in every Soviet embassy in Western capitals; the United States and England are singled out for particular attention because Moscow considers that these countries share the technological lead, particularly in microelectronics. High demands are therefore made of spies and agents placed in London and Washington DC.

The Soviet Union is a country obsessed by the need for conformity to norms and so a norm has been set for the Red Book. Soviet agents are expected to obtain four items a year from the lists in the constantly updated requirements book. Failure to meet the norm invariably results in disciplinary action: promotion comes early to an agent successful in obtaining prized technology.

The listings are comprehensive: included are the latest developments in Western research into artificial intelligence, robotics, robotic sensors, computer technology; they take in directed energy research in particle beams, high-energy lasers and microwaves, radar and infrared sensor discoveries, inertial component and systems integration for guidance and navigation, microelectrics and semiconductor experimentation, fibre optics technology and optoelectronics, power generation and propulsion, carbon-carbon technology, genetic engineering, telecommunication advances and transportation inventions covering aircraft design and technology, spacecraft design, ship improvements and aerodynamics and fluid dynamics. There is a separate chapter setting out the advances in weapon work to be stolen from the US.

The identity of the Soviet group which compiled and constantly adds to the Red Book is officially a state secret. Outside Russia, its title is known – the Military-Industrial Commission, usually shortened to VPK – but Western intelligence agencies remain unsure of its precise size although they are convinced some of its members hold ministerial and Politburo rank. Defence Minister and Politburo strongman Marshal Ustinov, who died in December 1984, was for a long time its chairman. The VPK's demands percolate down through a sieve of interested official bodies. Heaviest of all are the demands it makes on the KGB and the GRU. Orders are also placed through the Ministry of Foreign Trade, which is tasked with the job of purchasing the product through seemingly innocuous front companies and trade organisations established in the West. Other institutions expected to perform are the State Committee for Science and Technology and the USSR Academy of Sciences.

A report prepared by the CIA on the activities of the VPK states:

> In certain of the (technical) areas, notably the development of microelectronics, the Soviets would have been incapable of achieving their present technical level without the acquisition of Western technology. This advance comes as a result of over ten years of successful acquisition – through illegal, including clandestine, means – of hundreds of pieces of Western microelectronic equipment worth hundreds of millions of dollars to equip their military-related manufacturing facilities. These acquisitions have permitted the Soviets to systematically build a microelectronics industry which will be the critical basis for enhancing the sophistication of future military systems for decades. The acquired equipment and know-how, if combined, could meet 100% of the Soviets' high quality microelectronic needs for military purposes or 50% of all their microelectronic needs.

Further, by 1990, claim the Agency, Russia will have introduced two hundred new weapons systems, both strategically and tactically offensive and defensive. The systems include the SS-X-24 intercontinental ballistic missile, a Typhoon-class nuclear-powered ballistic missile submarine, the Blackjack B1 heavy bomber, SA-10, SA-X-12, SS-N-19 and SS-N-22 advanced surface-to-air and antiship missiles, a medium-lift space booster, a Saturn-class heavy-lift booster, a space plane and space shuttle, a large space station and a Potok communications satellite, code-titled 4 GHz. All include technology filched from the West.

Caspar Weinberger uses the word haemorrhage to describe the technological and industrial secrets drain from West to East. And President Reagan has not only made the staunching of that haemorrhage a prime objective of his own administration, but he also continues to try for Europe's commitment to the campaign as well. In January 1984 Weinberger signed a directive making technological security the responsibility of the Department of Defence, to the chagrin of the Department of Commerce and a large cross-section of American industry. To enforce that security, the International Transfer Panel was formed. It is served by two subpanels, one concerned with export control policy and the other with research and development.

Weinberger and the Department of Defence insist their security control is successful. Others are less sure. The doubters point out that Richard Mueller – or whoever he now is – remains at large.

CHAPTER TWO

The Red Pimpernel

The world's most successful technology agent has a face no one recognises, a name no one knows. American intelligence estimates there is $100,000,000 in Swiss numbered bank accounts to which he has access. There's a luxury villa in Switzerland, too, and others – in South Africa and Sweden and England – but he will not risk living in any of them because he knows they are watched. Budapest – secure behind the Iron Curtain – is safe, though. There is an apartment in the centre of the Hungarian capital, at Visegradenz 43. Here it was that he fled, in the last days of 1983. And it was at a Budapest clinic that he underwent the plastic surgery that gave him a new face. The new passport, to complete the identity change, came from the Hungarian secret service on express instructions from Soviet intelligence. And with the abolition of his ID, Richard Mueller ceased to exist.

His name, however, is still on the counter-espionage files of three continents and on the two indictments returned against him in America. But Richard Mueller was, of course, just another pseudonym as West German and American intelligence discovered when they tried to probe his background. Supposedly West German and born in 1948, there is no trace of his birth, parents, schooling or childhood. What is known is that in a fifteen-year period Mueller transferred $30,000,000 worth of American and European high technology to the Soviet Union, creating whole factories and gaining such a reputation that, according to one businessman briefly associated with him, he had access to government leaders at Politburo rank. The fear is that he still has it and that with his entirely new identity, he has returned to the West and is back in the job for which he has been so expertly trained.

12

THE RED PIMPERNEL

Intelligence files that have been made available to me suggest that Mueller was taught at Zelenograd, a hi-tech city six miles north of Moscow which is closed to foreigners. He underwent further and detailed instruction at the Moscow Institute of Precision Mechanics and Computer Technology. Finally, with the arrogant self-assurance of a latterday pimpernel, Mueller completed his technical studies at California's Caltech, on the very doorstep of the Santa Clara county home of American technological development, Silicon Valley.

By the early 1970s Mueller was ready, having established throughout the world a labyrinthine network of companies, the crossover and tangled construction of which came to resemble the intricate interior of the computers he intended to ship through them. Western intelligence agencies believe there are at least sixty and privately admit they have not identified them all. One was Microelectronics Research Institute Ltd, of South Africa. Another South African company was Sem Investments Pty. A third was Optronics Pty Ltd. In Zurich, Integrated Time Inc. is owned by Semitronics AG, registered in Zug. Mueller owned Semitronics. Dan Control was the name of Mueller's Swiss investment company. In West Germany, Mueller created Techimex and a subsidiary of Semitronics. In America, he set up an exporting company he called Semi-Con at Mays Landing in New Jersey and employed a man named Edward Breslin, a former American military intelligence officer, to run it. Canada was important to Mueller: there are no export-control licensing requirements between Ottawa and Washington, making Canada 'an open door' for diversion of technology to the Eastern bloc. In Montreal, Mueller formed USA Trade – a company only on paper. Its premises were, in fact, those of a freight-forward company called Kuehne and Nagel.

To run such a widespread organisation, Mueller needed help. So he went into partnership with another technology smuggler, a West German named Volker Nast. Together they constructed a smuggling network every bit as intricate as the elaborate system of companies on which it depended – and every bit as successful. Before it was broken, American intelligence calculate that $7,000,000 worth of semiconducting equipment was smuggled into the Eastern bloc.

Silicon Valley was the source, of course. There, Mueller and

13

Nast suborned the heads of two hi-tech firms: one was Robert
Johnson, President of Kaspar Instruments; the others were Gerald
Starek and Carl Storey, executives of 11 Industries. Both firms were
in Sunnyvale, California. Routing was from California across to
New Jersey on the East coast, then north to Montreal, with a
certificate attesting Canada as the 'end-user' of the equipment. In
Montreal that certificate was altered and the shipment switched to
Hamburg, addressed to Reimer Klimatechnik. Reimer Klimatechnik is an alias of Volker Nast. Sometimes the shipments
were again rerouted, to Semitronics in Switzerland; sometimes not.
Once safe in Europe, still undetected, the technology transfer was
virtually unstoppable. There exists in Europe an international
agreement under which TIR designated transport is exempt from
customs checks, the country of origin guaranteeing that nothing
illegal is being carried. Mueller organised his unhindered deliveries
through the TIR fleets of East Germany's Deutrans, Hungary's
Hungarocamion and Russia's Sovtransauto. The Moscow-based
Techmachimport company was a regular receiver of the shipments.
So, too, was the Soviet foreign trade company V/O Technoprom-
Import, whose offices are at Mosfilmovskaya St 35, Moscow.

Mueller made millions and spent millions. He furnished a luxury
villa on the outskirts of Hamburg with the contents of an English
country house. He bought another villa at Baarestrasse 57, in Zug.
He bought a Bentley and a Ferrari and negotiated with the stables of
Queen Elizabeth for studs for his thoroughbred horses. He
purchased a three-masted yacht called Tonga from Monaco's Prince
Rainier and cruised the harbours and fjords of the conveniently
neutral Sweden. While he did so, he was also househunting – a wise
provision for the future as events were to prove. He travelled
frequently to Cape Town, studying the real estate market while
liasing with a long-term GRU agent who supplied priceless
information during the Falklands War to Moscow.

Most frequent, however, were Mueller's trips behind the Iron
Curtain for which he could use any of the six passports he held. On
one visit he bought the Budapest apartment on Visegradenz St and
made additional transportation arrangements with the Mahart
company in the Hungarian capital. On another, he purchased an
interest in a Hungarian computer factory. But Moscow was the
Eastern European capital he visited most. In the winter of 1975 he
made two trips there with an American electronics expert, John

Marshall, who had just sold the Silicon Valley business called Advance Micro Devices. Marshall's introduction to Mueller came through Carl Storey, of 11 industries. Marshall wanted to establish himself as a consultant and Storey claimed Mueller was considering a semiconductor plant in Hamburg. When they met, Mueller said he was in business in Russia, providing equipment to make electronic watches. Recalling the Moscow visits, Marshall said, 'On both trips, the Soviets treated Mueller with special deference. Clearly he was someone they had had dealings with before and someone they wished to cultivate.'

Problems were about to arise, however, with Mueller's multi-million dollar enterprises. An employee of 11 Industries leaked to the American Department of Commerce that his company was smuggling out to the Soviet Union material governed by the Export Administration Act. There was confirmation from within the Soviet Union that semiconductor equipment from 11 industries and Kaspar Instruments was being used there. The subsequent absurdly inept reaction of the Department of Commerce formed the basis for the interdepartmental squabbling which continues to this day, although concerted efforts were made in Washington to convince me the rivalries have been resolved. From Washington, a Commerce official telephoned both businesses and naïvely asked them if they were trading with Moscow. Kaspar said no, just with Semi-Con in New Jersey. 11 industries denied doing business even with Semi-Con. The calls were made in April and it was not until three months later – during which time Mueller continued actively to trade and smuggle – that the Department of Commerce sent an investigator to California. Four investigators from the later critical Customs Department went as well. Shipping records showed the connection through Semi-Con with USA Trade in Montreal and Semitronics in Switzerland. Canada was positively identified in the documentation as the 'end-user'. But Customs detective Charles McLeod found in those same documents that the equipment had been converted for European mains voltage, making it impossible to use in Canada. There were even invoices – $175 a unit – for the conversion! Since the function of the Customs investigators was to assist the Department of Commerce, not initiate their own prosecution, they duly made their report to Commerce, pointing out that illegal transference would seem to be taking place. Commerce did nothing.

Mueller was active, of course. Immediately on receiving calls from the badly panicked officials of the two American firms, he flew to the United States – first to placate and then to establish a new, undetectable routing. He had one all ready to go into service. In Kansas City, Kansas, West German Frederick Linnhoff rented warehouse space and traded as Paul Allen of Allen Electronics. Like the now discarded USA Trade in Montreal, it was a company on paper only. In future, all the shipments from 11 industries and Kaspar Instruments were to go to Linnhoff. He would change the document description and value and ship the computer directly to Hamburg. It worked. It was later shown that one 'state of the art' piece of equipment from 11 industries reached East Berlin. A second – addressed to Volker Nast's Klimatechnik alias – was intercepted and replaced by sand. It went all the way to Moscow.

A second round of investigations proved more thorough, unravelling a new thread in the tangled skein of Mueller's operations. West German Jerry Gessner was European Sales Representative for Allied Materials, a Silicon Valley semiconductor manufacturing firm. He acted in the same capacity for 11 industries and Kaspar Instruments. Mueller also employed him. The routing arrangement, quite separate from those in Montreal or Kansas, was that Kaspar Instruments and 11 industries exported to Gessner. In Germany, working with Lother Haedicke who was the local representative for the American firm Honeywell, they reconsigned the shipments through Mueller's front companies to Moscow. These fresh disclosures had little effect in the long run, however, for none of the main culprits were caught. Indictments were issued, but Linnhoff fled to join Mueller and Nast in West Germany, where they were beyond any extradition provisions. Johnson, Starek and Storey were tried and found guilty of violations of the Export Administration Act. Each was fined $25,000 and additional fines of $10,000 each were levied against the two companies.

For Richard Mueller, the exposure of his network was an irritation, nothing more. There was the Hamburg house – which he had had surrounded by fully grown beech trees, helicoptered into place, because his wife Sieglinde particularly liked them – and there were the cars and the yacht. With Germany as his base, and increasingly from Sweden whose neutral status guarantees it immunity from most of the restrictive trading regulations with the

Eastern bloc, Mueller continued to trade. A particular target was Digital Equipment Corp. Based at Maynard, Massachussetts, it is one of the most technically advanced firms in the world and its computers are standard in Washington's Pentagon. It was those computers that the Soviets wanted above all others and they got them, by using the Cape Town company Microelectronics Research Institute as a front – a scam brilliantly organised by Mueller. The official documentation showed that MRI was owned by Sem Investments Pty. Nowhere did the name Richard Mueller appear. It does not feature on any documentation attached to Sem Investments, either. That is owned by two Swiss holding companies, Dan Control and Semitronics. Mueller owned both.

The equipment the Russians sought is called VAX-11/782. It can process data at more than 100,000,000 bits a second, which is three times faster than the best computers licensed for export from America. It is built to expand and to accommodate constantly updating software. It can be used directly in the computer-aided design and manufacture of high-speed silicon chips, to build circuits to make better computers. Valued at $2,000,000, it also has the capacity to control a globally effective combat and tactical guidance system. 'Put quite simply', I was told in Washington, 'it's the best there is.'

Horrified American intelligence now knows that between 19 May 1980 and 5 July 1983 Mueller succeeded in getting sixteen shipments out of America, using Microelectronics Research Institute: at least eight of those shipments involved VAX computers. How do they know? Because the records show that the shipments were officially approved by the Department of Commerce! Intelligence officials are now horrified by the fact that for two of the years in question, despite the brilliance with which Mueller created his company pyramid, the Department of Commerce knew of Mueller's connection with Microelectronics Research Institute in South Africa and with Semitronics AG in Switzerland. Also, their records had him listed as a technology trafficker from as long ago as 1974. Their mistake exposed, the government departments implicated did their best to evade the charge of bureaucratic bungling with a flurry of side-stepping and denials. Customs blame Commerce and Commerce, while conceding mistakes, say the connection was not recognised because the original information establishing the links went to the Treasury and the Department of Defence, not to them.

One intelligence source told me, 'We'll never fully know just how much the son of a bitch got away with. But from what we do know, it was enormous: absolutely enormous.' Certainly, it was enough to equip one entire semiconductor manufacturing plant at Zelenograd, possibly more, and with systems comparable with the most up-to-date available anywhere in the world.

Volker Nast was not the only trafficker in international technology with whom Mueller forged business links. His Swedish contact was Sven-Olaf Hakansson, who lived at Taby outside Stockholm and conducted business with the Soviets through a company called Sunitron. Company literature describes its function as being that of a technical and industrial consultancy. In addition, Sunitron imported and exported grinding and polishing materials, as well as trading in electrical and electronic equipment, instruments and motors. The multi-million partnership between Mueller and Hakansson stretched over six years, ending only with Hakansson's imprisonment and Mueller's flight for the fresh identity he now holds. Eleven of the sixteen shipments American intelligence later discovered to have been spirited out of the United States by Microelectronics Research Institute entered Europe through Sweden.

Before his arrest, Hakansson spoke openly of his activities and his association with Mueller.

Richard Mueller, like me, had been doing business with the Eastern states for many years. I took Mueller to be a clever and trustworthy businessman. I am a Swedish businessman, citizen in an alliance-free and neutral state and I do not take part in the USA's trade boycott of the Eastern bloc. My speciality is to sell advanced technology. I have nothing against making high technology available to the Soviets, even though I am not a communist. But I will not be mixed up in the transfer of equipment which is used by the Soviet military establishment. I do not control what my customers think when they order goods. The Eastern bloc is a choice market and Sweden has no blockade there. I sleep well at night since I have done nothing illegal in Sweden. We have a fine trade climate in neutral Sweden.

So fine, in fact, that Mueller and Hakansson planned to build a computer centre in Stockholm. It would have been a testing plant for equipment being transported to Moscow. Hakansson boasted of installing two entire VAX systems, as well as at least thirty other advanced computers, in the Soviet Union.

The Digital Equipment Corp. was not the only target for Mueller. Undeterred by the discovery of his last operation in Silicon Valley, he smuggled material from Hewlett-Packard, one of the oldest-established hi-tech firms in Silicon Valley. And from Sweden, itself, from a company named ASEA, a pioneer in high-voltage transmissions and robotics. Typically, the smuggling was layered and convoluted, to confuse detection. In 1979 ASEA signed a contract with the Soviet Union to build a steel rolling mill at Oskol, fifty miles south of Moscow. It was worth $70,000,000. Part of it included eighteen American-made Modcomp computers with the accompanying software. The contract was immediately put in danger in July of that year, when the Soviet Union invaded Afghanistan and Washington responded by greatly restricting exports from the country of strategic high technology. The Modcomp computers, made by Modular Computers Systems Inc. of Fort Lauderdale, Florida, were covered by the ban.

Moscow – and an official of the ASEA company – turned to Mueller and Hakansson to resolve the difficulty, which they did with their usual efficiency. Mueller placed the order with the British affiliate of Modular Computers through a company in Hanover, West Germany. The shipments went direct to Stockholm where they were transferred to Hakansson's company, Sunitron, and Sunitron shipped them to Moscow. On that occasion, the duo were paid twice – once by the Soviet Union and then again by ASEA. The ASEA payment of $750,000 went to Hakansson through a Swiss account and was authorised by Vice-President Bernard Brinkeborn, who has since resigned from the company and been charged with tax evasion and violation of foreign exchange regulations. Investigators later established that the Moscow firm of Metallurgimport paid a commission of $1,200,000 into one of Mueller's Swiss bank accounts.

By December 1982 Mueller, while maintaining his business

19

relationship with Hakansson, decided to switch his base to South Africa. It seems that the move was ordered from Moscow which, like governments in the West, is supposed to ban arms sales to the Pretoria régime. It doesn't: rather, it is active in supplying them, through people like Mueller. By so doing, Mueller ingratiated himself with the South African government whose denials that they used Mueller are disbelieved by the intelligence agencies of England and the United States. Those same agencies believe there was an additional reason for Mueller's transfer: that vitally important in-place spy, whose discovery was to be a disaster for Mueller.

Mueller's speculation in Cape Town real estate had ended with his purchase of a wine estate at Constantia on the outskirts of the city, for which he paid nearly $1,000,000. He worked hard to earn the reputation of a free-spending benefactor: he bought a bus for a local school and paid for the construction of a community centre.

There was one other purchase he made in advance of his transfer in 1982. Microelectronics Research Institute took over a former shoe factory in Cape Town with the intention, according to South Africans who worked there, of converting it to the country's first computer centre. But the intelligence agencies of America, England, South Africa and West Germany believe the installation was for testing the technology Mueller was smuggling out from America and Europe before shipping it on to the Eastern bloc. The factory was managed by Detlef Heppner who, until he entered Mueller's employ, was involved in the development of an electronic firing system for the West German Leopard tank. Another key employee was Manfred Schroeder, a computer technician later to be arrested and tried for his association with the trafficker. Before joining Mueller, Schroeder worked for the West German division of Digital Equipment Corp. Schroeder admitted to investigators that during his three years with Mueller he installed and repaired DEC equipment supplied to South Africa, West Germany, Sweden and to the Soviet Union. At least one of the DEC computers to reach Russia was the VAX 11/782 and a West German defence official calculates that one alone would have saved the Soviet Union five years of research involved in developing a matching system of its own. Certainly the strangers, who visited during some of the test sessions and who are now thought to have been highly qualified Soviet technicians and scientists infiltrated into the country to test the product for themselves, never appeared disappointed. It was not these infiltrations which were to bring about the collapse of Mueller's South African operation. It was his links with the GRU agent.

Until his arrest in New York in 1983, Dieter Gerhardt had worked for nineteen years as one of Moscow's key spies. At the time of that arrest Gerhardt held the rank of commodore and was the officer in command of the Simonstown naval base near Cape Town. As such, he provided intelligence of incalculable value to the Soviet Union. Within the mountains of the Cape peninsula is situated the vast underground listening post of Silvermine. Its equivalent in Britain is the GCHQ; in America, the National Security Agency. All the shipping movements in the South Atlantic and the Indian Ocean are monitored from Silvermine. Gerhardt had daily access to that monitoring and that meant Moscow did as well. During the Falklands War he communicated to Moscow every detail of British fleet manoeuvres for onward transmission to Argentina. British intelligence believes that the disastrous sinking of HMSs *Coventry*, *Sheffield* and *Antelope* could have been avoided if Argentina had not possessed such accurate intelligence. Formerly an attaché at the South African embassy in London, Gerhardt underwent training with the Royal Navy and is feared by military intelligence to have passed on to Moscow everything he learned about British frigate weaponry. Before his arrest, Gerhardt was for several months under intense surveillance from South African counter-intelligence officers who reported frequent meetings between the naval spy and Richard Mueller. The 1983 trial in Cape Town, at which Gerhardt received a life sentence and his courier wife Ruth a sentence of ten years for treason, was held completely *in camera*. But in the course of the trial, I understand, an espionage connection was claimed between Gerhardt and Mueller; there was even a suggestion that Mueller was Gerhardt's official 'Control', for the GRU. Mueller was not around, of course, to risk arrest. Warned before Gerhardt's seizure, he had already fled, leaving Sieglinde to move to Sussex, where he had bought her a £250,000 house against just such an eventuality.

Intelligence agencies in South Africa, England and Europe cooperated in an effort to trace Mueller's movements and when they did so it was too late because he was always several steps ahead. The combined investigation suggests that Mueller flew from Durban at the end of September 1983, direct to London. Aware that there would probably be an international alert out for him, he switched passports at Heathrow airport and flew straight out again, to Vienna. There it is believed he allowed himself just one night of rest before crossing to that luxury apartment on Visegradenz Street and the safe haven of Budapest. He could not yet afford to relax, however, with $2,000,000 worth of computer technology left behind in his Cape Town testing plant which he had no intention of abandoning. First from Budapest and then, as his trail grew colder, from Switzerland, it is known that he contacted lawyers in South Africa and West Germany. There were also frequent calls to the Swedish home of Sven-Olaf Hakansson. Mueller was setting up the most audacious diversion attempt of an audacious career.

Obedient to instructions both direct from Mueller or relayed through lawyers, Detlef Heppner and Mueller's other South African employees began dismantling the incredibly sophisticated electronic equipment at the premises of Microelectronics Research Institute; which included a complete VAX 11/782 system. There was so much that it filled a total of fifty-eight crates and boxes. Micor Shipping, a local transportation firm owned by Mueller's Sem Investments, transported the boxes to Cape Town harbour. There they were put into seven huge containers, which were then loaded aboard the Swedish-owned roll-on, roll-off freighter M/S *Elgaren*. On the evening of 20 October 1983 the master, Captain Ake Bruxelius, lifted anchor for the long haul northwards; his destination, Sweden.

By then, Mueller had begun commuting to Sweden, where he established contact with Hakansson. It is known that one of these trips took place shortly after the *Elgaren* sailed. Back in Switzerland, Mueller set about shuffling the ownership of the computer cargo, so as to baffle his pursuers. Optronics Pty purchased the equipment from Microelectronics shortly after the freighter sailed. While it was still on the high seas Optronics sold it on to Integrated Time Inc., the Zurich company which Mueller holds through Semitronics. On 31 October Mueller entered the Swedish consulate in the Swiss capital of Bern, openly producing his West German passport in the name of Richard Mueller, and filed a formal application to live and work in Sweden. It was granted.

Mueller then flew back to Stockholm and to a luxury house owned by Hakansson to await the arrival of the cargo he was sure had been safely spirited out of South Africa. But he miscalculated, for it was rumoured in the West German capital of Bonn that the *Elgaren* was carrying a probited cargo consigned to Sunitron. Victor Jacobson, a Swedish-born Customs attaché at the USA embassy there, connected Sunitron with Mueller and Mueller with South Africa, the *Elgaren*'s port of origin. Frantically, Jacobson tried to locate the whereabouts of the freighter but just missed it in Antwerp. So United States officials asked the West German authorities to board the vessel at Hamburg, next port of call. But Bonn refused to move on an informant's tip to Jacobson. The Customs attaché telephoned Washington to speak personally to the man at the top, Investigations Chief Roger Urbanski.

Urbanski sought help from the American Departments of Justice and Commerce. But it was only after direct intervention from the White House that Commerce could be persuaded to surrender the information it possessed, proving Mueller's involvement in technology diversion since 1975 and mapping out the structure of his companies pyramid so far as it was then known. Armed with the additional circumstantial evidence, the American Department of Justice made a formal request to Bonn. But in Hamburg the local court involved still refused to issue the necessary boarding warrants, on the grounds that the evidence was insufficient. Jacobson and other American officials shivered on the Hamburg dockside while the Hamburg court's refusal was appealed. The decision was reversed just seven minutes before sailing time and Jacobson roared out to the anchored freighter by launch to identify by torchlight the three containers which he now had official permission to seize. They were taken ashore and throughout that night and well into the following day German customs, watched by the apprehensive Jacobson, unloaded and tagged their contents. It took so long because the manifest was inaccurate and some markings had been ground off, making identification difficult. But once it had been made, the West Germans and the American contingent realised they were staring down at the most advanced computer manufactured in the world. But not all of it – under half, in fact, since the rest was still aboard the *Elgaren* now en route for Stockholm.

Jacobson, with more proof now, quickly won the cooperation of Swedish customs and flew out, sleepless, to Stockholm. They were waiting when the *Elgaren* docked at Helsingborg and the four missing containers, making up the complete computer system, were detained in a customs warehouse on 11 November 1983.

Still, Mueller and Hakansson did not abandon the hope of retrieving at least some of the cargo and getting it to its Eastern bloc destination. They are known to have held a series of crisis meetings on 12 and 13 November at Hakansson's fjordside house at Harsfjorden and from them emerged the idea of trying to establish in Sweden another phony computer centre like the one Mueller had set up with Microelectronics Research Institute in Cape Town. Hakansson approached an official of Radio Engineering Products Europe Inc. based in his home town of Taby. The innocent official agreed to rent out three hundred square metres of space. Hakansson's next move was to approach the Malmo agent to whom the VAX equipment had been consigned, Andersson and Jonsson Inc., and issue them with an order to collect and deliver the four crates detained in Helsingborg to a warehouse in Stockholm.

To move so openly not only required astonishing self-assurance but also implied an over-confident reliance on Sweden's unrestricted trading relations with the East. It might just have succeeded but for pressure being exerted on Stockholm by Washington. Sweden has a flourishing hi-tech industry but one that is heavily dependent on parts supplied by America and the US Department of State made clear to the then Swedish ambassador, Wilhelm Wachtmeister, how all too easy it would be to put a banning order on the exports of the companies involved. It was a warning Wachtmeister had no need to hear. He was told, further, of the investigations into Mueller's worldwide activities and of what West German customs found when they opened the three crates removed from the *Elgaren* in Hamburg. The pressure in Washington upon the ambassador was reinforced in Stockholm in meetings between officials of the US Department of Commerce and Swedish Foreign Trade Minister Mats Hellstrom and Cabinet Secretary Pierre Schori. On Tuesday 22 November, acting on orders from Hellstrom, Swedish customs raided the Helsingborg warehouse and forced the locked containers. Inside were the missing parts that made up the complete VAX 11/782 computer.

Two weeks later customs raided warehouses in Vastberga and Malmo, where five more containers belonging to Sunitron Inc. and Integrated Time Inc. were seized and computer parts discovered inside.

Still Mueller and Hakansson did not give up. They granted interviews with Swedish newspapers, claiming that their decision to establish the computer centre at Taby had been made a year earlier and that the shipment from South Africa was merely the equipment necessary to set it up. The Swedish government was unimpressed, however, and they designated the contents of the various containers seized as war material. In an official report made after a detailed and expert examination, War Material Inspector Carl Algernon said that the memory ability of the hardware they intercepted was more than that of six VAX 11/782 computers combined. The report said in part:

> This system, which had its principal application in a large number of military applications, has great computing capacity. The studied material contained, among other things, memory for data transport and data base handling, advanced graphic terminals and communication equipment. The system can be adapted to many different advanced applications, especially within computer support design for computer aided design (CAD) and computer aided manufacture (CAM) and different types of guidance systems.

Sven-Olaf Hakansson was arrested on 14 February 1984 on suspicion of serious tax evasion, currency violations and goods smuggling. On 20 June 1984 he was sentenced to four years' imprisonment. Richard Mueller once again escaped unscathed – his identity the only casualty – leaving behind him plenty for Western intelligence to investigate. Those investigations continue today. Western intelligence had already linked him with espionage, through his involvement with Dieter Gerhardt, but during their enquiries into the Hakansson smuggling empire Swedish customs discovered six thousand computer programmes, some encrypted. Examined by Swedish defence specialists, some were found to contain classified details of the new European fighter, the Tornado, which is the operational aircraft into the 1990s for the British, Italian and West German air forces. West German counterintelligence traced the stolen programmes back to the

Munich factory of Messerschmitt Bolkow-Blohm company. I understand the tapes contained constructional and operational data on the aircraft. As John Walker, Assistant Secretary for Enforcement and Operations at the US Treasury, assured politicians during a later enquiry on Capitol Hill, Mueller's organisation constituted 'the largest known criminal technology organisation in history'.

It was not, however, the first that the Soviet Union had set up to obtain technology. Another renowned trafficker is West German Werner Bruchhausen who, through a company called Continental Technology Corp. and its subsidiaries shipped $10,000,000 worth of hi-tech to Moscow between 1978 and 1980. It was obtained to order and was sufficient to equip a plant for the manufacture and testing of semiconductors. Volker Nast, acting independently of Mueller in the summer of 1980, tried to buy for Hungary a $47,000 Microwave Surveillance Receiver system, manufactured by Micro-Tel Corp. of Baltimore. The system receives, displays and analyses microwave signals; it has a primary military use and is governed by the US Arms Export Control Act. It was stopped by Customs at New York's Kennedy airport. Belgian Marc Andre DeGeyter handed over a cheque, which would have bounced, for $500,000 to an FBI undercover agent at Kennedy airport on 18 May 1981 for a computer programme called Adaptable Data Base system. Valued at $10,000,000, the system, according to technical experts, represented the highest level of sophistication then achieved for data base management. During his unwitting negotiation with FBI undercover men, DeGeyter openly admitted he was shopping for the Russians. And even after DeGeyter's arrest, the Russians did not give up on the Adaptable. Soviet diplomat Georgiy Veremey, attached to the Russian embassy in Washington, twice visited the trade exhibition display booths of Software AG who make the system. He later went to the company headquarters at Reston, Virginia, and tried to buy a bibliography of the firm's products that would have filled twelve boxes. When DeGeyter was arrested, the Soviet visa in his passport indicated he was being sponsored for a visit to Moscow by the Ministry of Internal Technology, Technical Machine Import. There were also telexes to a Russian named Bolshakov, at Techmachimport, in Moscow. Surprisingly DeGeyter was allowed to plea bargain. He admitted a misdemeanour under the Export Administration Act and a Commercial Bribery

Statute in the state of Virginia. He was jailed for four months, fined $500 and paid a $10,000 civil penalty to the US Department of Commerce. John Maguire, President of Software AG, described it as 'entirely incomprehensible'.

Greatest of all traffickers in illegal technology, however, was Richard Mueller and there are sections of British and American intelligence which fear that an unrecognisable Mueller has been reintroduced to the circuit because his expertise is too great to be wasted. In the meantime, for as long as it takes him to set up a new companies pyramid, other traffickers and organisations will fill the gap – not without some opposition, however. In America a programme was launched in October 1981 specifically to stop technology transfer to the East. Its codename is Operation Exodus. There is a matching programme in England, called Operation Arrow.

There is, too, an international effort to monitor the flow, through an organisation named COCOM.

CHAPTER THREE

Some Watchdogs Fight

Acronyms are the delight of bureaucrats. COCOM stands for the Coordinating Committee for Multilateral Export Controls. Based in Paris since its creation in 1949, COCOM is comprised of all the NATO countries – with the exception of Spain and Iceland, but with the addition of Japan. Spain, however, has applied to be admitted. COCOM's function is to block exports from member countries to the Soviet bloc of what is referred to as dual technology: that is, civilian technology that could have a military application.

Although it is an accusation ducked in Western capitals and in Washington, COCOM until the late 1970s was an organisation of minimal interest to the various governments who had created it. The period was, after all, one of détente. Now Pentagon hawks – and even doves – shudder to recall, for instance, that in 1972 President Nixon agreed the sale to Moscow of $20,000,000 of machines manufacturing the minuscule ball bearings necessary to perfect the performance of inertial guidance systems for ballistic missiles. In the next eight years the Russians made good use of this example of American error, developing the SS-18 multiple warhead rocket that practically made obsolete the US 1054 Minuteman and Titan missiles. This loss of initiative proved expensive for the United States. In order to make it good President Reagan had to finance research into a moveable tracked missile system, the MX, at a cost of $6,196,743,000,000! In Britain, the government of Harold Wilson concluded a trade deal under which Soviet inspectors were allowed into British factories ostensibly to examine goods Moscow was buying. I know that at least sixty-five Soviet technicians gained access through that agreement to some of Britain's most advanced technological installations, including

28

Rolls-Royce, Ferranti, Girling, International Computers, Swan Hunter, Vickers and Wilkinson Sword.

It was America that brought about the change of attitude towards COCOM and while every Western government believes that change is necessary, there is widespread resentment in London, Bonn, Rome and Paris at Washington's highhanded behaviour – its calm assumption that where it leads, its allies must follow. Nor is it only Europe that objects. So dismayed was William Root, the long-time chief of the American negotiating team, that he retired prematurely, complaining of his own country's arrogance. And an American ambassador responsible for the organisation had to intervene with midnight telephone calls to the Reagan administration to prevent talks with European allies collapsing.

For four years America insisted on being blindly followed and for four years Europe refused, which meant a four-year delay on what computer technology should be banned to the Eastern bloc. Different departments on Capitol Hill and within the Pentagon fought for the right to be final arbiter of the restriction list to be submitted to COCOM. American technology manufacturers protested that the uncertainty was inhibiting their research and development and European hi-tech firms and customers increasingly turned their backs on America. I have seen, for instance, a cable from US diplomats in Hong Kong to the Department of State in Washington, reporting on a meeting with local officials of the giant British multinational Cable and Wireless, in which American companies are described as 'unreliable last resort suppliers' because of the confusion over their licence to export.

The fiercest turf war of all was fought within the Pentagon. Combatants were Richard Perle, Assistant Secretary at the Defence department of the Office of International Security Policy and Richard DeLauer, Under-Secretary at the Office of Defence Research and Engineering. Perle argued strict controls and at one Capitol Hill enquiry, in an effort to convince Congressmen, he produced a slightly modified Apple II computer obtainable at any computer store throughout the world. Linked to two other computer devices and employing software designed by the Defence Nuclear Agency it was, said Perle, the system used extensively by the US Army and NATO to target nuclear weapons in Western Europe. Pressing his case, Perle said:

We are seeking to control the ease with which computers of this type are made available to the Soviet Union. Now we know very well that it is always going to be possible to buy computers in ones and twos and threes from commercial outlets and that we cannot put a hermetic seal around the Soviet Union and its allies. It is impractical and it won't work. What we think we can do in concert with our allies is reach agreement that these are not imported into the Soviet Union by the thousands and in particular so they are not imported into the Soviet Union tailor-made for the specific military purposes that we think they can usefully serve.

So between those who would argue that the problem is unsolvable because computers are commercially available and those who argue that we ought to stop all such trade in computers there is a middle ground. We are searching together with our allies to achieve that middle ground because the military consequences of failing to do so are inimical to our security.

DeLauer proposed a contrary argument. Overly strict controls, he insisted, could actually hinder both civilian and military development in the country. Too stringent restrictions discouraged private industries from investing in new technologies and prevented the members of NATO exchanging information. To those same Congressmen who had sat through Perle's Apple II demonstration, DeLauer said, 'To lock it (technology) away for the purposes of protecting it is counterproductive. It will slowly disappear. When you open the safe some years later, you will find it is no longer there. It is dust and as a consequence you kept it from being utilised in the most optimum fashion.'

There was technical support for DeLauer during the dispute from Lawrence Sumney, at one time Pentagon Project Director for a hi-tech system known as VHSIC, or Very High Speed Integrated Circuits. The multi-million dollar programme – the allocation for 1984 was $125,100,000 – seeks to develop two generations of integrated circuits with a very high data processing capacity for a wide range of military systems, including digital signal processors for radar, communications, missile guidance, electronic warfare and optical sensor systems. Sumney said that if the Pentagon's Policy Department won what he openly referred to as a 'turf battle' and restricted exchange of information on the undeveloped system, research on the project would come to a 'grinding halt'.

'Rubbish,' responded Perle. It is a word he often uses.

Perle dismissed this, together with Sumney's claim that the Policy officer argued from ideology, not expert knowledge, although he had to admit that no one in his office had technical training: he himself is an expert in international affairs, Dr Stephen Bryen's doctorate is in political science and the background of the other leading official, Donald Goldstein, is in intelligence. Nor would Perle admit the suggestion, made during a Congressional enquiry debate, that the Policy Office had caused the COCOM delay by trying to impose the US Military Critical Technologies List on European governments.

Lionel Olmer, Under-Secretary for International Trade at the Department of Commerce, told members of the permanent Subcommittee of Investigations of the Committee of Government Affairs that he thought American proposals to COCOM could have been put forward in Paris if the technical judgement had been left to Mr DeLauer.

'That's rubbish,' said Perle.

'One man's rubbish is another man's accuracy,' Olmer came back.

'That's complete rubbish,' insisted Perle. 'The fact is the Department of Defence in its approach to these computer negotiations have represented a departmental view.'

Dr Stephen Bryen is one who does recognise that COCOM was ineffectual until the Reagan administration took it up. He refers to it as a neglected backwater and says the American pressure – 'We're acting as a kind of Devil's advocate' – is for it to become a more modern organisation. Part of that modernisation would involve the creation within COCOM of a permanent military advisory group. Britain and France agree the need for it and Dr Bryen foresees the improvement will go through. America is also pushing to get all the COCOM members to harmonise their enforcement strategies. Penalties in Britain for anyone caught attempting to divert restricted material are fairly severe, says Dr Bryen. But in West Germany they are minimal – 'and that's bad'. Ideally, Dr Bryen wants COCOM to establish a computerised data bank of known diverters like Richard Mueller and

Werner Bruchhausen. 'Mueller would have surely got nailed if there had been some central coordination,' he says.

Dr Bryen admits, however, that difficulties exist with the Military Restriction List: 'what you end up with is virtually everything in the computer world is controlled, in one way or another. And that's too much. You really can't handle that sort of thing. What we've tried to do is control the high end and liberalise the low end.' He felt further declassifications were possible at the 'low end' and acknowledged that this attitude reflects a change on the part of the Policy Office from the time when Richard Perle and Richard DeLauer were rowing on Capitol Hill. It is a change brought about by their recognition of the impossibility of worldwide enforcement. 'It's not worth chasing personal computers.'

In January 1984 Secretary of Defence Weinberger appeared to try to resolve the infighting within his own department by issuing what is formally known as directive 2042.2. It ruled that Perle's office had the final say on technology transfer. Richard DeLauer did not, however, appear to read it that way. Asked by Congressmen, after the issuing of the directive, which office – Technical or Policy – had responsibility for advising Weinberger on technology transfer restrictions, DeLauer said at once, 'Both of us.'

To Perle was put the question, 'So is your shop and DeLauer's shop on equal terms here?'

'No,' Perle replied. 'I think I would have to say that the Office of the Under-Secretary of Defence for Policy [his own] has the final decision, which of course is always subject to appeal to the Secretary of Defence.'

That is certainly the way in which things have worked out in practice. In July 1984 an agreement was finally concluded between COCOM and the United States on the computers to be placed on the restriction list and William Schneider, jr, Under-Secretary of State for Security Assistance, Science and Technology assured politicians back in Washington that the negotiations on the American side had been conducted with 'a unified and reasonably interagency-agreed position on the numerous complex issues under discussion'.

While that may well have appeared to be the case from the distant vantage point of a Paris negotiating table, I remain unconvinced that unity was ever reached amongst the various departments in Washington. And what was supposedly achieved in France was a long time coming. Before it did, America's internal disagreements – and specifically the dogmatism of Perle's Policy Office – led to the departure in protest from the US negotiating team of its chief, William Root.

Root later explained before a Congressional enquiry that negotiations to update computer restrictions that had been in force for nine years reached a critical point in 1983. As in all international conferences and debates, America formulated its bargaining position before the negotiations began. But during those talks, Britain, France, West Germany, and the other NATO countries – supported by Japan – demanded there should be some compromise.

'The Allied suggestions for changes were, in many respects, reasonable and constructive,' insisted Root.

Richard Perle's Policy Office refused any change. So everyone else at COCOM refused to agree. Said Root, 'Our Allies are willing to cooperate, but they will not follow us blindly.'

The 1983 intransigence – later modified – was not the first hindrance to getting tighter controls agreed among the Western nations. According to Root, who was in an unequalled position to know, agreement was possible in 1979. But after the Soviet invasion of Afghanistan in that year Washington stiffened the restriction proposals already on the table in Paris. Once more Europe refused to follow America, regarding Washington's attitude as being politically instead of strategically motivated.

It was to these rigid, immediate post Afghanistan restrictions that the Defence's Policy Office insisted upon sticking in 1983.

But there were ambiguities. While Washington was unmoveable upon computers, it was prepared to allow Root and his team to negotiate with Europe for the controls on silicon, floating drydocks, space vehicles and technology for the production of superalloys. Said Root, 'Such flexibility is not synonymous with weakness.'

The European nations demanded rigorous examinations of embargoed lists so that their exporters might be in no doubt as to what could or could not be sent eastwards. Elaborating, Root said, 'They recognise that we are the strongest militarily. They recognise that we devote more technical and intelligence resources to the analysis of what should be controlled – and why – than we have available. But our proposals are not perfect. We should be grateful that they are not reticent about telling us so. Their criticism is constructive.'

Coming to the source of disagreements between America and Europe, Root said, 'We must do something about the arrogant US attitude which has been at the core of our ineffectiveness in COCOM computer negotiations.'

Something more tangible than humility was also needed, said Root, who had worked in the Department of State for thirty-three years. There was on the statute book a catch-22 written into the Export Administration Act. Officially, it is section 10(g). It requires the President to report to Congress if he overrides a Defence objection to an export. 'This would indicate that the commander in chief was not master in his own house,' said Root. 'There have been several instances when Defence views have prevailed even when it was generally believed that the President held different views.' Knowing the strength given them by that section, Defence cared little for the opinion of other agencies within the US government or for those of the chancelleries of Europe.

One catch-22 created another, said Root. 'The irony of this situation is that the resultant prevalence of Defence views on the details of cases and on the details of proposed item definitions for the control list has made it impossible to further the broader Defence objective of strengthening the basic controls. This is doubly ironic, because the basic objective of strengthening controls is shared by other agencies, the President and other members of COCOM.'

How little the Department of Defence cared for the views or attitudes of others, either at home or abroad, is shown by the fact that when in 1983 Root cabled the Department of State to which he was immediately responsible while at COCOM, requesting a revised negotiating position, the Pentagon refused to attend discussion meetings in Washington. Explaining the impression that created in Paris, Root said, 'The broader significance of Defence not being prepared to attend was to add to international perceptions that the United States was not going to budge and that the only way to reach agreement would be for the others to abandon their different views, no matter how well-justified they might be.'

34

Not only had America weakened its position in the North Atlantic Treaty Organisation by its attitude, but because of the disagreements the Soviet Union had continued to be able to obtain what should have been barred to it. In his letter to President Reagan in September 1983, indicating his intention to resign in protest, Root used the word 'arrogance' to describe America's attitude towards COCOM and Europe. Part of that letter insisted, 'Those who proclaim the loudest the need to strengthen these controls are doing the most to weaken them.'

Root reminded Reagan that in his televised address to the nation in September 1983 after the shooting down by the Soviets of the straying Korean airliner – the Russian Atoll missile was a copy of the American Sidewinder – the President had stressed the need to redouble efforts with Europe to stop the flow of military and strategic technology to the East. Root pointed out that 'Since that time we have, instead, been redoubling our efforts to convey to our Allies that their views do not count, that we know best and that they had better shape up. This is no way to obtain cooperation. It most certainly does not constitute efforts "with" our allies.'

After Root's departure and the much publicised reasons for it, there were officially leaked rebuttals from several of the combatants in the Washington turf war. Commerce Assistant Secretary Lawrence Brady, for instance, allowed himself to be openly quoted in the *Washington Post* of 17 September 1983, criticising the man who for twelve years had headed US teams negotiating East/West trade as having failed to recognise European changes in attitude towards export controls and being an impediment in the administration's efforts to strengthen COCOM. Richard Perle's adverse comments were quoted, too.

William Root, however, was not the only high level diplomat to complain about his own country's behaviour. The US ambassador to the Organisation for Economic Cooperation and Development (OECD) has the US oversight responsibilty for COCOM and in December 1983 Abraham Katz held the position. That month – a full sixteen weeks after Root had departed in disgust at the impossible position in which his country had placed him – the US team arrived to negotiate computer restrictions without any agreed position from which to talk, again due to objections from the Department of Defence. Katz describes the plight in which he and the US team found themselves as being 'a replay of the Perils of Pauline'. Dale Tahtinen, head of the US delegation, stretched the discussions into the evening and taking advantage of the time difference between the two continents, Katz worked throughout the night on the telephone, urging the Departments of State, Defence and Commerce to come up with some formula to avoid a diplomatic embarrassment. What they did come up with avoided the embarrassment, just, but the negotiating session was futile. Katz complained to Washington later in a cable still classified which he summarises: 'I have urged Washington to do what it should be doing. That is, develop negotiating positions before coming to negotiations.'

While the Pentagon were squabbling internally, there were simultaneous skirmishes being fought out just as determinedly between the Customs Department – which comes under the jurisdiction of the Treasury – and the Department of Commerce.

The dispute between these two departments is easier to analyse than the Pentagon turf war as it resolves more simply into a question of differing functions. Customs is a law-enforcing body. The purpose of Commerce is to encourage and facilitate American industry, particularly in exports. But in conjunction with that obligation to encourage export comes the requirement for Commerce, under the amended Export Administration Act of 1979, to ensure that embargoed material does not reach the Communist bloc. This area of its duties is covered by the Compliance Division within the Department's Office of Export Administration. Certainly, in the case of Mueller and others, Commerce failed lamentably to do that during the early 1980s. Indeed, after an enquiry in 1982 the bipartisan Senate investigation committee decided that Commerce was performing its enforcement responsibilities so badly that they should be transferred to Customs entirely. It did not happen but it was close. Instead Commerce got a greatly increased budget and manpower allocation to allow it to do its job properly, and William Archey was transferred from Customs to head trade administration.

Archey is a supremely confident man who pads around his office in stockinged feet and relaxes behind the closed curtains of his home conducting the Berlin Philharmonic orchestra playing on his stereo unit. While fully acknowledging the failures of the past, he takes pride in his department's achievements. In 1984

$227,000,000 worth of embargoed exports were blocked by running licensing checks on end-users – the sort of check that would have thrown up Mueller's MRI holding. A further $75,000,000 was prevented from leaving the country because the would-be purchasers were shown to be ineligible through an automated licence accounting and retrieval system known as LARS. Archey claims there is liaison between Customs and Commerce, because of a direct Presidential instruction, and that there is also contact – which I believe to be somewhat strained – between Commerce and the Department of Defence which, in addition to their own Military Control List, also have access to Commerce's Commodity Control List which covers 200,000 items. Archey believes American industry exaggerates the difficulty involved in getting export permission for those items, but has moved anyway to minimise delays. In 1984, for example, his department cut the number of days it took to process free world export licence applications from forty-six days in the first quarter to twenty in the last. The improvement was implemented – and streamlined in subsequent years – by what Archey calls a 'fast track' approach, literally changing the way the applications were considered. Hinting at the frictions which continue in Washington, Archey records that the Pentagon have declined his offer to copy 'fast track' processing of military applications. In a reference to the criticism heaped upon the department after the Mueller débâcle, Archey said in the summer of 1985, 'Over the past twenty-four months, we have come 180 degrees in terms of the rigor we apply to the review of Free World cases.'

Archey acknowledges the existence of turf battles and says that in the power struggle between the various departments Commerce has most to lose and least to gain. He adds that the repeated accusation levelled against Commerce as having failed to do its job is 'the biggest bullshit argument I've ever heard in my life'. It is bullshit again, he says, to claim that Commerce cannot simultaneously encourage exports and impose the necessary controls: never has Commerce ever done anything against national security in the effort for trade.

William von Rabb, the equally confident Commissioner for US Customs, considers that any turf war between his department and Commerce has been resolved. Von Rabb interprets Congress rulings to the effect that the authority for any overseas investigations should be vested in Customs and the two departments should cooperate within America. The difficulties, insisted the Commissioner, were brought about by Commerce not Customs. 'I don't understand Commerce,' he told me. 'I'm constantly confused by what Commerce is really trying to accomplish.'

Von Rabb openly admitted firing Archer: 'I removed him.' The Commissioner added, 'God knows how he ended up over at the Commerce department. He was basically removed because he didn't reflect the philosophical views of this administration. You draw your own conclusions: it's peculiar.' One obvious conclusion must be that, jostling for position and turf battles aside, cooperation between two departments the heads of which have such obvious and open reason for personal dislike is not going to be easy – which indeed makes the appointment peculiar. Von Rabb further criticises the length of time it takes COCOM to remove from the bottom end of its list technology no longer considered strategic and add to it developments which clearly are. He is apparently able to overlook the fact that in the case of computers delay was brought about by America.

Commerce do not appear to share von Rabb's view that Customs have exclusivity for overseas investigations. As the Mueller case illustrated, neutral Sweden is a conveniently open door for illegal shipments into Russia. The Swedish Datasaab firm installed an air traffic control system employing embargoed US equipment in Kiev and Commerce claims credit for an investigation which resulted in the parent company being fined $3,120,000 and being stripped of all US export privileges for an indefinite period. Austria is another neutral country through which technology is channelled. Commerce again claim credit for tracing through the Viennese firm of Xennon, owned by Austrian Gerd Walther, the transfer to the Soviet Union of integrated circuit manufacturing and computer-related equipment purchased through his Marlow Heights, Maryland, company by D. Frank Bazzarre. William Archey has also stationed investigators both in Vienna and Stockholm.

Liaison between all the departments involved in the power struggle is definitely better now than it was in 1981. But the bruises inflicted in that struggle are still tender, and they are not confined to the American capital. Considerable resentment has been created throughout Europe – in and out of COCOM – that will take a long time to die down.

CHAPTER FOUR

Some Watchdogs Bark

A word that causes much annoyance throughout Europe is extraterritoriality. That it should be something of a tongue twister is apposite, considering that the concept it represents is a convoluted one. Properly defined, it is the right or privilege of a state to exercise authority in certain circumstances beyond the limits of its territory. According to European complaints, improperly defined it describes the attempts of the US government to control equipment it considers strategically important incorporating American technology.

In July 1985 Liberal MP Paddy Ashdown openly protested in the British House of Commons that 'unwarranted American claims of extraterritorial jurisdiction' was making the country 'a technological satellite of the United States'; and in Bonn, the West German Minister for the Economy, Martin Bangemann, warned just as openly that his government 'will not tolerate' any further US attempts to restrict its trade policy. The chief European concern is that America's efforts to restrict trade with the East are more often dictated by political than strategic motives. Certainly, that was the way it looked in 1982 when President Reagan tried to stop Britain, France, West Germany and Italy from supplying the Soviet Union with the technology to construct a gas pipeline from Siberia to Europe. It is hard to interpret it in any other way after Dr Bryen's ready admission to Congress that the government's primary concern was over the amount of hard foreign currency the pipeline would enable the Soviet Union to earn. Access to technology was secondary. All four European countries advised their manufacturers to ignore the American pressure.

In France and Germany, I have heard that pressure likened to blackmail – not an unfair comparison to make, in the light of events. For Washington has made it clear to Stockholm that, grateful though it still is for Swedish cooperation over the case of Richard Mueller and the VAX computer, it will consider putting Swedish hi-tech firms on the export-banned list for parts unless Stockholm tightens its Eastern export controls. And to enforce the threat, licences were withheld until the Confederation of Swedish Industry complained to their government. Licences were again withheld in 1982 when the state-owned Austrian steelmaker Voest-Alpine entered into a $46,000,000 tie-up with American Microsystems Inc. to produce memory chips for Europe; nor were they granted until Vienna agreed to the controls Washington was demanding. For years Austria resisted American attempts to control re-exported American technology, but 'We developed the philosophy that if the American government applies rules, it's in the interest of our companies to follow them,' explained Ferdinand Lacina, Austrian Minister for Transport. Operation Arrow, the British bid to stem the flow of technology to the East, was only established by the Board of Customs and Excise after President Reagan had strongly lobbied Prime Minister Margaret Thatcher at the summit of world leaders at Williamsburg, Virginia, in 1983.

The special Arrow unit, based in the City of London, comprises twenty men, who work closely with United States Customs and both branches – MI5 and MI6 – of British intelligence. In both London and Washington I was repeatedly assured that the liaison between the two countries works well. But despite these assurances, there are frequent occasions when Board of Trade officials consider America oversteps the mark in its demands. One who helped me with my research on an unattributable basis said that Washington had been repeatedly warned not to make 'extravagant' claims and added, 'There's a great deal of heat generated from time to time. The Americans don't seem able to understand that other countries resent what they see as a positive intrusion upon their sovereignty.'

Resentment at Washington's attitude is particularly acute in West Germany which has the largest share of East/West trade, valued at $79,000,000,000 a year. Karl-Hermann Fink, head of the German Chambers of Commerce committee on trade with the East, protests, 'No one talking with an East bloc country can be certain of his ground because no one knows where US policy is going to end up.' In 1984 Bonn received 70,000 requests for clarification from West German exporters unsure what they were or were not allowed to trade. A $10,000,000 deal negotiated by the West German subsidiary of the American giant ITT, Standard Elektrik Lorenz, to provide electronic telephone exchanges in Hungary was cancelled because a dispute between Washington and Bonn over COCOM agreements could not be resolved. Hans Muehler, programmes manager for the West German company, said, 'European companies live from US microchips. No manufacturer is going to endanger his access to those chips by selling restricted technology to the East bloc.'

By 1986 America was in a position to exert further commercial pressure upon Europe, through the allocation of contracts for the $26,000,000,000 Star Wars research programme, officially known as the Strategic Defence Initiative. All the Western governments lobbied for involvement. Former British Secretary of Defence Michael Heseltine sought at least $1,000,000,000 worth of participation, but the discussions with his opposite number, Caspar Weinberger, stuck on the issue of the safeguards to be employed against technology leaks to the East. I understand the draft agreement proposes, without putting a figure to the extent of British involvement, that American officials examine all the records of British companies and research establishments which might conceivably participate to guarantee no third, subsidiary party involvement through which Moscow might gain access. This extreme caution seemed at odds with the offer President Reagan made during the run-up to the Geneva summit in November 1985 to *share* Star War technology with Soviet leader Mikhail Gorbachov.

International Computers Ltd, Britain's largest computer manufacturing company, complained in an internal report that Washington's attitude towards Europe was one of 'growing technological imperialism by the United States'. It was a grievance shared by hi-tech companies in every country I researched. Further, François Heisbourg, an executive with the French electronics firm Thomson CSF, claims that America has caused 'scandalous duplication' of NATO research and development into the VHSIC system – the very outcome that Lawrence Sumney had so feared back in the days of the debate over the COCOM restriction list. The refusal of the US Department of Defence to share VHSIC research with Europe has meant the establishment of independent research programmes in France and in Britain, each costing $500,000,000.

41

The VHSIC example illustrates what Lorenz Schomerus, a foreign trade expert in the West German Ministry of Economics, meant when he said: 'Our concern isn't so much that we won't be able to get technology X or Y for our products. Our concern is more that it might lead to an overall division of high technology products between Europe and the United States.' Nor is this an exclusively European worry but one shared by American companies who fear their technological supremacy will diminish because of the divisions between Washington and Europe. According to W. Clark McFadden, spokesman for the Industry Coalition on Technology Transfer, whose 3000 member firms employ 4,000,000 people and enjoy worldwide sales of $250,000,000,000:

> No subject has been more frustrating to US high technology than foreign availability. [He adds:] Adequately adjusting for foreign availability could probably do more to simplify and rationalise existing US export regulations than any other issue. The positive balance of trade contribution in the high technology sector continues to grow. Productivity in the high technology sector is increasing at a rate six times faster than US business in general: and the inflation rate in the high technology sector during the 1970s was only one third of the national average . . . the majority of our nation's research and development is conducted by high technology industry. This technological innovation has preserved the US qualitative edge in weapons systems. Indeed, the US high technology industry supplies over two thirds of all Defence hardware purchase for our military services.

But the pattern is changing. In 1984 the American National Science Foundation judged that since the beginning of the technological boom which America led, its share of the world market had dropped from seventy-five to fifty per cent and that by 1990 it would have gone down to thirty per cent. Calman Cohen, Vice-President of the Emergency Committee for American Trade, is outspoken on behalf of an organisation composed of the Fortune 500 of top American companies.

> The system we have does not make sense. It does injury to US business and does injury to national security, which it is

supposed to protect. If you try to control everything – which is what America appears to be attempting – you control nothing. We do not have the exclusive patent on scientific ingenuity: scientific development breeds by discourse and exchange between nations, not by isolationism and protectionism.

That is a view shared on the other side of the Atlantic. Cyril Hillson, Research Director of Britain's General Electric Co., said, 'There is a climate now in the United States that the government is reluctant to share scientific information and this spills over into business. It's a pity we can't talk freely with those whom we feel are on the same side as us.'

Just how sharply that 'reluctance' can make itself felt was shown by an intervention of the Pentagon Policy Office under Richard Perle. In the summer of 1982 he demanded that researchers should withdraw over a hundred technical papers from a symposium put on by the Society of Photo-Optical Instrumentation Engineers, because Soviet scientists had accepted invitations to attend. Again, in July 1983, six papers were forcibly withdrawn from an Alaska conference on permafrost. Their subjects – unclassified – were pipeline construction, the performance of off-road vehicles and the maintenance of roads and airfields in permafrost conditions. Dr Bryen later explained that the Pentagon did not feel the Soviet Union should learn from America how to maintain their airfields in Siberia.

Although America's extraterritorial demands have created friction with Europe, the policy has shown results. In 1984 the US Department of Commerce ordered Digital Equipment Corp. to apply for individual licences for shipments to Europe and in January 1985 Briton Michael Ludlam was sentenced to two years' jail for shipping six US computers to the East. The first person in England to be convicted under the Operation Arrow progamme, he had dealt with the Bulgarian government-owned INCO trading company through an Austrian intermediary he knew as Hans Wirth. To begin with, he had taken orders for PDP-11 computers, manufactured by Digital Equipment Corp. Then came the requests for VAX. The six were shipped to Zurich, with Switzerland stated as the country of destination on the end-user certificate.

And the United States has conceded some relaxations since the 'ban everything' period of mid-1983, in an effort to ease the difficulties of American exporters. In 1984, overriding Pentagon objections, the Department of Commerce took off its control list a large number of hi-tech laboratory instruments which incorporated microprocessors. Commerce's valid argument was that the continued prohibition was ridiculous because in every case matching technology was available throughout Europe. Among the instruments declassified were air pollution monitors, humidity meters, petroleum test equipment and spectophotometers that determine the quantity and quality of chemical samples. At the same time, in Paris, COCOM dropped the US-imposed embargo on eight- and sixteen-bite computers which means that any Western country can now freely sell to the Soviet Union the Apple II computer that Richard Perle demonstrated to Congressmen on Capitol Hill, arguing its battlefield dangers.

CHAPTER FIVE

Truth, the Whole Truth and . . .

US Secretary of Defence Caspar Weinberger is a hawk, the man whose 'don't go soft on the Russians' letter on the eve of the Reagan/Gorbachov summit in November 1985, angered and embarrassed the American negotiating team in Geneva. The letter, from Weinberger to the President, was leaked to the *New York Times*.

Secretary Weinberger is a man aware of the power of the press and he believes the Soviet Union is, too. He accuses the KGB of a massive – and successful – disinformation campaign to drive Europe away from Washington through disputes over the handling of new technology.

Certainly the KGB attach great importance to disinformation. In 1972 the Politburo created an entirely new, KGB-linked division, the International Information Department, headed by Leonid Zamyatin who accompanied Gorbachov to the Geneva summit and who, in 1986, was posted to London as Soviet ambassador. The KGB's previous disinformation section – Department A of the First Chief Directorate – was elevated in importance and continues to work independently. Western intelligence categorise disinformation against the West under the title 'Active Measures'. Weinberger insists that Moscow's current campaign to isolate America from its allies is on a grander scale than anything previously attempted. He quotes an assessment produced by the Department of State: 'These often clandestine efforts by the Soviets and their surrogates to influence political and public opinion in the non-Communist world have grown in boldness and intensity reflecting what appears to be an increased use of Active Measures as a policy instrument by the Soviets and their allies.' Specifically targeted, according to CIA intelligence reports, are Sweden, Austria, Spain, Germany and

Japan. The reason, according to Weinberger, is that America is successfully staunching what CIA Director William Casey has referred to as the 'technological haemorrhage'.

An early example of Zamyatin's work was circulated in May 1982, just before the Versailles economic summit. Drawn up to the format of a document issued by the Department of Commerce on what appeared to be official stationery, the three-page fake was dated 18 February 1982 and distributed in Brussels. It purported to contain the recommendations of a 'Special Presidential Working Group on Strategic Economic Policy' and discussed the Siberian pipeline dispute between Washington and the rest of Europe. There never was any such document and its purpose was to exacerbate already strained relations.

On 24 October 1984 another forgery surfaced. Again supposedly from the Department of Commerce, it appeared to be signed by the Deputy Secretary and was addressed to West German firms. It asked for an itemisation of articles they produced or traded that were on the COCOM restriction list and for an indication of 'the presumable (sic) volume of sales to the Warsaw Pact countries and to Australia, Finland and Switzerland . . . Do you have any idea of what is the volume of your High Technology (sic) articles sales through Western Europe and other channels that in the end turn up in Eastern bloc countries.' According to American intelligence, who first identified the forgery, the intention was to create trouble with European governments by suggesting that a department of the American administration was prepared to go behind their backs and, further, by implementing the idea that America was prepared to use COCOM to gain trade advantages over Europe.

Judging from the amount of disinformation Moscow spread about on COCOM that year, its measures were at last beginning to have some effect. Since its creation in 1949 the organisation had been virtually ignored by the Soviet press. But on 27 January 1984 the Ministry of Defence newspaper, *Red Star*, disclosed the existence of COCOM and described it as an 'economic NATO'. The writer was General Major A. Gurov, a doctor of economics and a man on whom the CIA have files as a leading commentator on military expenditure and its effect on the civilian economy. In April 1984 the Central Committee newspaper, *Sotsialisticheskaya Industriya* (Socialist Industry), published an article entitled 'Instrument of Transatlantic Dictate'. It claimed that COCOM was a Cold War creation and that the United States had led and orchestrated it from its inception, 'exerting unprecedented pressure on its partners, prohibiting even insignificant trade operations with Socialist countries' and showed unaccustomed wit in asserting that the philosophy of American trade was that 'everything except chewing gum has potential military utility'. The article claimed Western Europeans as the victims of 'economic terrorism', having lost hundreds of thousands of Common Market jobs through US dominance, and even went so far as to identify the industries affected as hi-tech.

In another disinformation exercise, a particularly successful one according to American intelligence, the KGB again attacked COCOM with the state-owned press as their chosen weapon. *Izvestia* published an article in August 1984, supposedly based on criticism that had been published in West German newspapers and magazines. Under the headline 'FRG Chafes at COCOM Curbs on Trade', the article said that West Germans believed 'COCOM is nothing more than an appendage of the US embassy in Paris' and that it pulls 'the noose of dependence even more tightly around the necks of its Atlantic allies'. It then set out what the American intelligence community and the US Department of State believe to be the official Soviet line on the organisation, hammering home the points already made in the *Sotsialisticheskaya Industriya* article: COCOM 'is the product of the Cold War . . . a tool in Washington's hands'. The US-inspired list of banned goods is 'becoming longer and longer'. America is 'working towards the total paralysis of East-West trade and is almost ready to classify even pacifiers as strategic goods'. Washington's 'arbitration is inflicting irreparable damage on the FRG's economic interests'.

In September 1984 an article by two writers from the Russian Novosti Press Agency was published as a feature in the London *Times*.

> The US drive to embargo electronics for the Soviet Union has a subsidiary purpose. These restrictions, in fact, allow the US to exercise control over the technological development of their NATO allies . . . Western European countries . . . must assess for themselves the possibilities and the prospects of cooperation with the Soviet Union . . . they ought to consider

the damage that electronics embargo might do – not to the Soviet economy ... but to their own economic health and independence.

It was an undoubted coup for the Soviet intelligence that the article should have made it into print with an English newspaper of record and, via *The Times*, into cuttings libraries all over the country. Shortly after the Novosti article made its accredited appearance, it was revamped in the *Guardian* – only this time the source was not identified. *The Times* quoted: 'The latest restriction seems to be that any company using American computers must have permission from Washington before it moves a computer from one building to another', of which the unattributed *Guardian* version was, 'It means, for example, that the Inland Revenue must get permission from Washington before it moves a computer from one building to another.'

To combat forgery and disinformation, the CIA has created a special department. There have been occasions when, fearing damage to relations with a European country, members of that department have personally travelled from Washington to convince officials and ministers that what has offended them *is* disinformation. It is a campaign in which President Reagan himself has taken a direct hand. In one of his weekly radio broadcasts, he warned of 'propaganda and disinformation meant to mislead Western governments and their citizens and subversion, forgeries and covert action ... The Soviets, communist-bloc nations and surrogates elsewhere rely on a huge apparatus, including the KGB, to spy on us and influence our public opinion.'

It is official American policy for the CIA, FBI and other arms of US intelligence to collect and expose technological disinformation which, from extensive meetings in Washington, I know to cause particular concern in the administration. I also know, from meetings in London, Bonn, Paris and Rome, that disinformation though it might be, it finds many – too many – receptive ears because for once Soviet lies seem remarkably close to the truth for a large number of Europeans.

CHAPTER SIX

Prunes, Silicon and the KGB

Until the late 1960s, prunes were the product of Santa Clara county, the arrow head peninsula running south from San Francisco: half the world's supply were produced from the plums grown there. There were plenty of apples and apricots, too. So likely names were obvious for hi-tech products which replaced the fruit orchards in the Valley of the Heart's Delight, as it was then called by the local chamber of commerce, and they too flourished in the kindly climate, making instant millionaires of their developers and earning the valley a new sobriquet. The twenty-five mile long strip threaded from Palo Alto to San Jose along Route 208 is now known as Silicon Valley.

Other such hi-tech concentrations have since sprung up round the world: Russia has Zelenograd, the United Kingdom has Silicon Glen in Scotland and Taiwan has Hsinchu. But Santa Clara county was where, in 1961, the marketing began of the invention that was to revolutionise twentieth-century industry and technical development. Properly, it is the integrated circuit memory chip but that memory is etched on to a non-metallic silicon (Si) – the element that renamed the valley which the world leaders in hi-tech have made their home. The much preyed-upon IBM is there. Hewlett-Packard was one of the original companies. Steven Jobs attended lectures at Hewlett-Packard, borrowed equipment from founder William Hewlett and, with a friend, Stephen Wozniak, created an illegal electronic device which could be attached to telephones to provide free telephone calls. Wozniak used it once to call the Pope, in Rome, and almost got connected by saying he was Henry Kissinger. Later Jobs and Wozniak combined their electronic expertise again and in the garage and bedroom of Jobs' parents' home made a prototype of the first personal computer and registered a company to manufacture it. Called 'Apple', it has since become more preyed-upon than IBM.

For twenty years Silicon Valley epitomised the American Dream of instant success rewarding the entrepreneur prepared to work at a bright invention. Mercedes were the most common cars along Route 208 and the jacuzzi and pool-backed homes at Mountain View and Cupertino and Sunnyvale were priced at $300,000. The skiers flocked to their cabins at Lake Tahoe or kept yachts in Santa Cruz harbour. Bellarmine and St Francis were the two favoured private schools. It was the good life and no one wanted it to end. Nor has it, not completely. But by 1985 all the companies then established there were admitting a recession, because so many had started up that the supply of silicon chips exceeded demand. There was, naturally, a knock-on effect for the associated industries who used the chips. Alone amongst those customers with an interest in the valley, there was one who eagerly looked forward to the sackings and lay-offs and the inevitable financial hardship these would bring.

The most important Russian consulate in the world is at 2790 Green St, in the Pacific Heights district of San Franciso. It is a squarely constructed red brick building with a breathtaking view of San Francisco Bay and an all-important but incongruous hut built on to its flat roof. The technically expert occupants of that hut get the best view of all but they don't have a lot of time to admire it, because that hut contains the most up-to-date listening and monitoring equipment – some of it stolen from the United States – and with it the Soviets eavesdrop on telephone conversations in Silicon Valley. Pacific Heights residents have complained in vain at the daily collapse of their television reception. The fault is neither in their equipment nor in the transmission, but due to a factor beyond the TV technician's control – overload at the precise moment when the operators in that hut on the roof transmit. The intelligence word is 'dump' and the consulate employs state-of-the-art technology to dump the day's espionage haul in an encoded and much abbreviated form. Called 'spurt' transmission, it is an American brainchild developed with the help of scientists at Britain's GCHQ listening post at Cheltenham in Gloucestershire.

To receive the 'spurted' intelligence, the Russians orbit a receiving satellite over San Francisco.

When the activities of Green Street were first publicly announced in 1984 by Robert Wasserman, a police chief at the neighbouring town of Fremont, the then Vice-Consul Gennady German called the police investigation 'senseless' and insisted the accusations were 'groundless'. Since then I have received repeated assurances of their validity from three separate American intelligence agencies, one specifically concerned with communications espionage. The assistance I received in California was given on the condition that I refrained from identifying any particular agency. But one official I dealt with estimated that more than half of the 120 Soviet personnel attached to the consulate were involved in espionage. 'Bona fide officials bring their wives, who actively operate,' my informant assured me. 'And they're specialised. We believe at least twenty-five not just to be KGB or GRU but to be trained scientists and technology specialists within those organisations.' At the time of writing, two KGB operatives attached to the San Francisco consulate – opened in 1972 in return for similar American facilities in Leningrad – are Anatoli Mishkov and Vladimir Lomovtsov.

Through the incontrovertible evidence produced by its various intelligence agencies, Washington knows of the activities of the San Francisco consulate and in November 1983 moved to hinder it. Silicon Valley – together with other hi-tech areas in San Diego and Seattle – were declared closed areas to Soviet diplomats, journalists and businessmen. But the Green Street consulate still had its hut on the roof – and something more, control of the intelligence agencies of its Warsaw Pact satellites. I know there to be bulging files in CIA and FBI archives in Washington DC showing those intelligence agencies to be wholly controlled by and subservient to the KGB. Yet, incredibly, the ban issued by the Department of State was not extended to exclude them. It was an oversight that Moscow has made the most of ever since, just as it has contrived to exploit the financial difficulties of some of the Silicon Valley high livers.

Among the listening posts so obligingly left to the Soviets by their accommodating hosts, the Poles are the best. The Polish intelligence service is called the *Sluzba Bezieczenstwa* or SB. Through it Soviet intelligence – using the San Francisco consulate and its vital satellite communication facility – have orchestrated two of the most damaging hi-tech espionage coups in the last decade. One analyst in Washington DC told me, 'The damage is incalculable: literally. Were it not so important, we'd stop trying to estimate it.' At the time of writing, three years after the discovery of the espionage, he and other analysts are still making the effort. 'It could take years longer,' he told me.

A prime mover in the Silicon Valley 'heists' was James Durward Harper, his case history a classic example of how Eastern bloc intelligence make use of financial hardship. Particularly worrying for US counterintelligence is the thought that, given the current crisis in Silicon Valley, there could be many more James Harpers. An accomplice of his was a former consultant to the British National Enterprise Board who, deep into the FBI's world-spanning investigation, was only identified as the Big Man. William Bell Hugle had managed to evade an earlier FBI probe into hi-tech dealing with the Eastern bloc by moving to England for a year, where he worked with the Scottish Development Board. Safely back in California in 1980, Hugle met Sir Keith Joseph when he was the Conservative Minister for Trade on an official visit to the West Coast in the hope of encouraging Silicon Valley companies to establish outlets in England.

It was Hugle, once managing director of a company called Hugle International Inc. at Sunnyvale, who was the middleman linking the hard-up Harper with the eagerly buying Polish intelligence agent whose alias – the Minister – better fitted a spy novel than reality. His real name is Zdzislaw Przychodzien. A Polish defector later confirmed Harper's own admission that he originally asked for $1,000,000 from the Poles. What he got was $250,000, divided up amongst secret bank accounts in Switzerland, the Cayman Islands, maybe even London. In exchange, Poland and the KGB got the secrets of the US Minuteman intercontinental ballistic missile and the country's ballistic missile defence system research and development programme. Those secrets, according to John Cunningham, an executive of the Ballistic Missile Defence project office, provided the Warsaw Pact with 'a windfall' of intelligence about the capabilities of NATO strategic forces, together with plans stretching into the 1990s for defending those capabilities. Cunningham was one of the experts who described the value to Moscow as 'beyond calculation'.

American intelligence know for certain that Moscow did receive the information. During his spying career, which spanned an astonishing eight years, Harper travelled frequently to Switzerland, Vienna and Warsaw and later told his interrogators of a 'wydzial' or specific intelligence unit, masterminded by a KGB official who would present a shopping list – culled from the Red Book – to be filled. Obedient to the shopping list, Harper amassed documents weighing up to one hundred pounds, of which he only ever handed over a part. When that consignment – concerning the Minuteman missile – was delivered in Warsaw, the KGB flew in a team of scientists specially to examine them and subsequently Przychodzien's 'wydzial' received a commendation from Yuri Andropov, later Soviet leader but then Chairman of the KGB.

Harper, Przychodzien's source, started out as an engineer who equipped an electronic workshop in a house in the Silicon Valley township of Mountain View. He never worked with classified materials, nor did he hold a security clearance. But Ruby Schuler did and Harper cultivated, and subsequently married, her because of it. She was a secretary/bookkeeper and an executive secretary for Systems Control Inc. (SCI), and SCI had numerous contracts with the Ballistic Missile Defence Advanced Technology Centre at Huntsville, Alabama. Schuler died before Harper was arrested. But before she did so, she told a friend, 'There was a reason Jim and I got married that only he and I know. I can't tell you or anyone else and I never will.' The reason was that Harper had suborned her into being a spy and married her in the belief that if they were ever arrested she could not then give evidence against him. Their joint venture began in 1975, when Harper sold his first batch of secrets obtained from Schuler for a total of $12,500. He never attempted to conceal his sudden affluence, but boasted to friends of having made $100,000 tax-free as a power supply consultant at the Solectron Corp. which has offices in Sunnyvale, San Jose and Miltipas, all Silicon Valley townships. The purchasers that time round were two Poles to whom he was introduced by Hugle. It was not till some time later, at the Intercontinental Hotel in Vienna, that he met the man known as the Minister. Zdzislaw Przychodzien was, in fact, a lieutenant colonel in the SB who used the Polish Ministry of Machine Industry as a cover for his espionage activities. During one of those European meetings,

Harper also met Przychodzien's superior, Sergei Gromotowicz, and, together with Hugle, the four of them organised their affairs on a proper business footing. Harper later boasted, 'I'll never have to work another day.' The Minister agreed that payment should be made in US dollars. The arranged split was a third for Hugle, a third for Harper and a third for Harper's source, his mistress Ruby Schuler. Harper set out what he had available and later made a tape recorded admission of how he did so. 'I gave him at that time a copy of the front page, the title page, the table of contents and one chapter of all the documents I had available at that time. The Big Man [Hugle] assured the Minister (Przychodzien) I could be trusted and the Minister said he was very interested ... The three of us, the Minister and the Big Man and myself went to my room and set up another meeting in Vienna.'

Throughout his subsequent espionage career, Harper toured extensively in Europe. The Hotels Continental and Alpla-Palmiers were the favourites in Lausanne, Switzerland. It was always the Intercontinental in Vienna, where he was given the telephone numbers of Dietrich and Elizabeth Svoboda if there were ever a need for contact. Arrangements were made for him on arrival at Warsaw airport to ensure that his passport did not receive any sort of entry stamp which might later have alerted US Customs or investigators and in Poland Harper stayed at Przychodzien's villa in the township of Zalesie Gorme, about twenty kilometres outside Warsaw. On some of these trips Ruby Schuler accompanied him, able to learn at first hand what was on the KGB Red Book list from agents who frequently accompanied Przychodzien at briefing meetings.

For the KGB, the high point of Harper's career was the moment at which he handed over the Minuteman material. By then he had been hiding it for some time and it had become disordered. As he later explained, 'I had a hell of a time putting it back together.' Russian scientists, flown in from Moscow to complete the task, were, according to Przychodzien and Gromotowicz, extremely excited by the documents which they 'had been unsuccessfully seeking all over the world'. Harper said in his admission: 'He [Przychodzien] went back out and talked to them again and a while went by and he came back in with a big envelope with $100,000 in it. They just decided you didn't have to worry about the missing pages. I said OK, fine. So I got this big envelope with $100,000 in it and proceeded to count it and got about a quarter of the way through it and said, "Oh hell with it, it has to be there." I can eyeball it, and it's all one hundred dollar bills.'

Meetings continued in Europe, where from time to time Harper's Red Book shopping list was updated with requests. To make contact more convenient, Harper also met with Poles – one who was to feature in the second espionage coup for Russia – in Mexico. By now, 1981, Harper was a trusted spy for the KGB. He was proud they had faith in him: 'I have always delivered,' he boasted. Certainly, he was diligent, making the most of his opportunities when he was taken after hours into the Systems Control Inc. offices at Palo Alto by his mistress and allowed access to what he wanted. Later FBI forensic experts found Harper's fingerprints on a large number of recovered documents. The full list of the material that Harper supplied to Moscow included, in addition to the Minuteman information, sighting systems, lasers and one of the most sophisticated radar systems ever designed by Silicon Valley scientists. It was an impressive haul and at his trial it earned him a life sentence.

Throughout the investigation and the indictment issued against Harper, William Bell Hugle was positively identified as the middleman who made the introduction to Przychodzien. No charge was made against him.

His link with Przychodzien was already a matter of public record before the Harper trial. In 1974 Hugle International Inc. went bankrupt and among the claims filed against it was one for $648,000 on behalf of a firm listed as UNITRA ECE, a Polish exporter. One of the officials of that company was Czeslaw Szuniewicz; the other was Zdzislaw Przychodzien. UNITRA said the money they were attempting to recover was for 'product design and process specifications'. What those designs and specifications were for was not specified. Lawyers acting for the creditors could find no record in the files of Hugle International Inc. of the $648,000 payment.

During the FBI investigation into Harper and Hugle, the name of a Polish intelligence officer other than Zdzisław Przychodzien and Sergei Gromotowicz emerged. It was that of Marion Zacharski and it was already on record from FBI investigations into what had until then been considered the biggest case of technological espionage ever encountered in Silicon Valley.

William Holden Bell was the spy, a Silicon Valley technologist who was jailed for eight years for his treachery.

Zacharski was allowed to live in America as a representative of the Polish-owned American company Polamco. He lived in the same Playa del Rey apartment complex as Holden Bell who, as a bankrupt, had been isolated by the KGB as a susceptible subject likely to respond to pressure. Holden Bell had to file for bankruptcy because of his ineffectual management of foreign business trips for the Hughes Aircraft Co., where he was Radar Operations Manager for Europe and the Middle East. After he had been sentenced, Holden Bell explained to Congressmen the KGB method of recruiting Silicon Valley spies. For his was a classic case.

> He [Zacharski] slowly became my best friend ... he was interested in what I did and enlisted my aid in making contacts in industry for the possible sale of Polamco machine products. He suddenly delivered $4000 to me for my very minimal effort in that regard.
> He expressed an interest in having Polamco hire me as a consultant after I retired from Hughes Aircraft Co. In order to impress him I showed him a sample of some work I had done of which I was quite proud. Although I showed it to him on the tennis court he took it to his apartment for reading. It was a classified secret.

His story was also a perfect illustration of how Silicon Valley secrets are obtained. The advertising of non-existent posts, followed by the pumping of applicants from rival companies is the way in which competing American companies spy on each other.

Holden Bell was hooked. 'My financial burdens, of course, were resolved overnight ... At this time the apartments were being converted into condominiums at the cost of over $80,000. Zacharski asked me if I were going to buy one, as his company was buying his. He knew I didn't have the funds. In view of my prospective employment by Polamco, he thought he could help me. Subsequently, he appeared at my door handing me envelopes of cash. With this money I paid the IRS (taxes) and made a down payment on the condominium. I signed a receipt for the money and concealed the source from my wife.' Obtaining a signature to that receipt is another piece of tradecraft in Eastern European espionage practice; from the moment he had signed, Holden Bell was open to blackmail, unable to refuse any demand made of him.

He was given a camera, taught how to photograph top secret documents and instructed to rendezvous with his contact in Innsbruck, Austria. Right up until the last moment, even en route for Austria, Holden Bell tried to dodge the reality of his situation: 'I was rationalising and kidding myself that the persons I would meet were representatives of Polamco, that this was just the kind of industrial espionage that goes on all the time.' The pressure intensified in Innsbruck. Holden Bell was handed $5000 by two men, one of whom he remembers as Paul. 'Under the guise of discussing methods of payment to me, they took great care to describe where I lived and shopped in frightening detail. They also showed me pictures of my family, my wife and my young boy and told me that there were only six persons involved. They told me that if anyone caused a problem, they would be taken care of.'

For his European meetings – there was another in Lintz and another in Geneva – Holden Bell was given Jackson as a code name and the impression he was dealing with experts. 'They knew exactly what they wanted – right down to the company identification numbers. They even asked if I could go to work for a different American company, DARPA, to get what they wanted.' DARPA is the acronym for the Defence Advanced Research Projects Agency, an organisation directly funded by the Department of Defence.

Back in Silicon Valley, the spying became regularised. Payment to Holden Bell was in gold coins. 'It was always the same. He [Zacharski] would come to my door when I was alone, hand it to me with a smile and walk away, or place it in my tennis bag as we walked to the tennis courts.' As he gathered experience, so he became more professional and was fully inculcated into the tradecraft of spying. There was a planned delivery trip to Mexico City: 'I was to carry an airline bag and respond to a code phrase "Are you interested in the Aztec exhibit?" By replying, "No, I'm interested in the Mayan calendar" I was shown a key chain with a black medallion bearing a silver P for Poland, which my contact would display. I never went. The FBI interviewed me first. I told them everything. There is little left of my life now but I feel I am freer in prison than I was with Zacharski.'

Holden Bell made a telling point in talking to investigating

Congressmen when he said: 'In light of all my financial and
personal problems and my friendship with Zacharski, all of which
the company [Hughes] were aware of, my security clearance surely
$hould have been rejected or should have been reviewed. In
California, you must renew your driver's licence every three years.
My clearance was twenty-eight years old.'

In the closing months before his arrest by the FBI, the KGB –
through their Polish intermediaries – were pressing Holden Bell to
provide what details he could about the Cruise missiles that were
subsequently placed in England at Greenham Common, in
Berkshire, and in other European locations. The KGB pressed
Holden Bell for details of a part of Cruise technology identified to
him as a video correlator. He also knew, from his contact with the
Poles, that the KGB were trying to recruit a spy in the Boeing
Aircraft company which works on a number of top secret US
defence contracts. I was assured by an FBI investigator, quite
independently of my enquiries into the Holden Bell case, that on
one occasion when a visiting group of Soviet engineers toured the
Boeing premises they wore specially treated shoes to pick up metal
filings for later examination and analysis.

Holden Bell was arrested because FBI surveillance on Zacharski
established their relationship. That arrest, however, was too late
to prevent secrets of incalculable value reaching the Soviet Union.
The Pole possessed no diplomatic immunity and was put on trial,
at which he was sentenced to life imprisonment.

The cases of Harper and Holden Bell are copybook technology
espionage episodes and as such are the subject of lectures both in
the FBI and CIA training colleges. CIA Director William Casey, a
taciturn man, overcame his reticence to issue a public warning in
1982:

> The KGB has developed a large, independent, specialised
> organisation which does nothing but work on getting access to
> Western science and technology. They have been recruiting
> about a hundred young scientists and engineers a year for the
> last fifteen years. They roam the world looking for technology
> to pick up. Back in Moscow there are four to five hundred
> assessing what they might need and where they might get it –
> doing their targeting and then assessing what they get. It's a
> very sophisticated and far-flung operation.

One arm of that far-flung operation is concealed within a bona fide student exchange scheme. Western, in practice mainly English and American, students are limited to reading the humanities in Russia. Invariably, Soviet students in Europe and America seek to read the sciences and technologies. In San Francisco, I was told by a senior intelligence operative that the supposed Soviet undergraduates accepted to study for a first degree on the West Coast are easily recognisable for the postgraduates they are simply by their age.

During an enquiry into the extent of Eastern bloc theft of Western technology, American senators were provided with a fascinating insight by a Jewish immigrant who spoke to them from behind a screen to protect his identity and used the pseudonym Joseph Arkov. A trained Soviet engineer, 'Arkov' had worked for some years in the Soviet Union in a research institute trying to perfect highly sophisticated cameras for military use. The Russian preference was for technology from the West – Japan and America were particularly favoured – rather than that developed within the country. He said: 'There is no patriotism in department stores.'

Arkov further testified:

> In my work in the second research institute, I had the assignment of copying Western and Japanese high technology. One of my tasks, for example, was to develop a system design for the production of colour television cameras for video tape recorders. In this pursuit, my superiors made no attempt to be deceptive about what they wanted me to do. I was not to conduct any original research and development. I was given television components produced in Japan and I was told to copy them ... Once they (the Soviets) know what makes a given piece of machinery work, they find that they do not have the technical know-how and equipment to produce the product themselves. That is why they want Western high technology machines that will enable them to produce the products. And the Western products they desire the most are those produced in the United States. That is why they want American high technology machines with which they can produce the components for high technology products.

An enormous effort is put into obtaining every available technical journal and magazine. Arkov and other defectors with whom I spoke assured me that through false names and addresses and 'front' companies in Western capitals, the KGB and the GRU subscribe to all authoritative publications. Arkov explained:

> In a military refresher course following my graduation from college I was part of a group that was shown films of US military equipment such as tanks, artillery and amphibious vehicles. One film showed the internal layout of one such vehicle. The blueprints revealed their publication date, a time only two months prior to the date of the refresher course. That indicated to me that the Soviets had obtained and made informational use of the design of the vehicle before it went into production. In addition, one of my duties in the research institute was to read American technical journals and US government publications. A special team of English-speaking Russian linguists was employed to provide us with prompt translations into Russian of the journals and documents.

Another licit source which the Soviets make thorough use of is the trade fair. Arkov again:

> In my engineering jobs in the Soviet Union I frequently was assigned to attend trade fairs where Western nations, including the United States, displayed their high technology equipment. I was seen as a potential buyer. But, in fact, I was not there as a would-be consumer. I had not been sent to the trade fair to buy anything. I was there to obtain information about Western technology concerning aircraft and missiles as well as other technical areas. I discovered many valuable technical ideas at trade fairs and reported on them to my supervisor back in the Soviet Union. Aside from learning and inspecting the wares displayed in trade fairs, Soviet visitors have been known to steal products and their components. I know a man in Russia who had been assigned as a security guard at a trade fair in Moscow. This assignment was the turning point of his career. In league with the KGB the man used his position as security guard to steal several pieces of high technology equipment. He was rewarded very handsomely for his thievery. Not an especially intelligent man he could never have earned on his own the Ph.D degree he subsequently was awarded. He was then made director of a

department in a research institute, a position for which his training, experience and ability left him totally unqualified.

It was from Arkov that American intelligence gained their knowledge of Soviet exploitation of the student exchange system. Frequently, Arkov insisted during interviews, supposed Russian students are in fact men who have already obtained a Ph.D in their chosen subjects. 'The Soviets considered college-age students to be too young and unpredictable to be trusted to attend universities in the United States. Equally important, we had not yet advanced far enough in our studies and knowledge to obtain the high level of information Soviet authorities desired,' he said.

From my enquiries into the case of Harper and Przychodzien I can positively identify five men ostensibly attached to the Ministry of Electronics at Usieuicha 24/2, Moscow, as being involved in the KGB and GRU technology stealing programme. They are Alexander Rublsov, Alexander Ivanov, Leonid Dymov, Vasily Kurdin and Gennady Verklovenko. Up until 1982, liaising with them via the nightly 'dump' from the San Francisco consulate in Green Street, was Stanislav Nosov, described on Department of State – and FBI – files as a commercial counsellor, and Yuriy Palov, listed on those same documents as a vice-consul concerned with science, technology and education exchanges. Palov, in fact, was the man through whom Moscow manipulated the student exchange.

By 1983 the Reagan administration had moved against this blatant piece of abuse. The Department of State announced they would ban visas to people whom they suspected of wrongful use of the facility. William Schneider, Under-Secretary of State for Security Assistance, Science and Technology, said when the ban was announced: 'We have found a considerable amount of activity where the actual purpose of (a foreigner's) coming to the United States has been concealed and is (industrial) espionage. The numbers are significant enough to be having an important impact on the military power of the Soviet Union.'

Notably, the ban was extended beyond Soviet citizens to include other Eastern bloc nationals. The Department of State also made it clear that visas which were granted to Eastern bloc technicians to visit a specific factory or site would be restricted to that location and not be a general permit for those people to 'wander about the country'.

The new edict went some way towards controlling information lost through infiltration, but it left untouched the problem of espionage from the inside. Money had been one reason for Harper becoming a spy. Another, equally important, motivation was the feeling that he had been pushed aside by the Hughes Aircraft Co. Christopher Boyce, too, was a disgruntled employee – of the TRW Systems Group, headquartered in the town of Redondo Beach which is just south of Silicon Valley. Boyce took out his grudge against TRW by linking up with a schoolboy friend called Andrew Dalton Lee, who managed to combine technology espionage with smuggling heroin from Mexico. Payment from the Soviet embassy in the Mexican capital financed the purchase of drugs which he trafficked in the United States. In exchange, Moscow received detailed information on a US satellite it knew to be orbiting over Russian missile test sites. The spy-in-the-sky system was called Rhyolite and the Russians had first learned of its existence through child sex pervert Geoffrey Prime, a Russian linguist at GCHQ.

The hi-tech companies of Silicon Valley are very aware of the dangers facing them from aggrieved employees. IBM have consciously set themselves the goal of becoming the most caring as well as the biggest hi-tech company in the world. The president's door is open to the lowliest clerk who is not satisfied his grievance has been settled through the intermediary complaints procedure established to do just that. Employees expect as right advantageous stock holding: twelve employees of Televidio in Sunnyvale became millionaires overnight when it went public in February 1983. Apple gives every employee a personal computer. Every Friday the ASK Computer Systems Co. in Los Altos gives a party at which the president drinks beer from a plastic beaker alongside the office boy. Ironically, the system is copied from the Japanese practice of binding a worker to his company with strong ties of loyalty – ironically, because the hi-tech predators are not exclusively from the Eastern bloc. A Japanese company was caught carrying out one of the biggest larcenies on record and although there was a $300,000,000 compensation payment, I understand them still to believe they were unfairly accused.

CHAPTER SEVEN

The Crown Jewels ...

The codeword was Adirondack, after the American mountain chain, and once the investigation got under way it built up a momentum that hit Tokyo like an appropriate avalanche. IBM regard it as a salutary lesson to any country which tries to steal its secrets. Hitachi believe they were set up and that it was not the theft of technological expertise that was at issue, but American irritation at the trade-debt imbalance with Japan. The facts illustrate the fierce worldwide rivalry between computer manufacturers – a rivalry on which 'consultants' trade to make themselves fortunes.

Barry Saffaie was just such a consultant. He also called himself Barry S. Tabrizi, a lie just like his claims to have a doctorate in engineering from the University of Southern California and a bachelor of arts degree from the University of California at Los Angeles. As Tabrizi, he formed Silicon Valley Consultants in Sunnyvale, California. As Saffaie, he simultaneously worked as a manager for National Advanced Systems, a subsidiary of National Semiconductors and based in Silicon Valley. Besides manufacturing their own computers, National Advanced Systems marketed the products of Hitachi in America.

Hitachi is the fourth largest company in Japan – after Fujitsu, IBM Japan and Nippon Electric Co. – and manufactures software which can be utilised in IBM machines. In technical jargon, the two are 'compatible'. In a case of several paradoxes, Hitachi was formed in 1910 by Namihei Odaira specifically to manufacture Japanese technology and reduce the country's reliance upon Western invention. The founder's original intention was apparently espoused by his successors. The most innovative of the Japanese hi-tech companies, it has filed 35,000 patents and employs 16,000 people exclusively on research and development. In 1980 Chairman Hirokichi Yoshiyama told an interviewer: 'Having come this far, Japan must make serious efforts to break with the past patterns of relying on technology developed by someone else or of copying other developed countries. I take every opportunity to stress the importance of discarding technical developments based on someone else's and of embarking on development of our own.' Events that took place within a year of this assertion would indicate that he had not stressed the view sufficiently strongly or that his workforce had not been listening.

In November 1980 a forty-five-year-old Haitian-born computer scientist named Raymond Cadet resigned from IBM's computer laboratory at Poughkeepsie in New York State. IBM are highly security-conscious and are only too well aware of the secrets that an employee can take with him to a rival company. Cadet was given the exit interview the company insists every departing employee should undergo and signed a statement to the effect that he was taking no confidential material with him. That was another lie. When he left Poughkeepsie, Cadet took with him ten of the twenty-seven volumes making up the workbooks for a new generation of computers IBM were developing. The computers were called 308X and their codename was Adirondack. The first – the 3081 – became operational in October 1981.

For seven months Cadet worked for a computer firm near Washington, then he changed jobs. On 1 June 1981 Saffaie took him on at National Advanced Systems. From what I have learnt of the case, I do not believe Saffaie did so because he was aware of the stolen Adirondack handbooks – they were an unexpected bonus. The initial reason was that Cadet was a comparatively up-to-date ex-employee of IBM and NAS were anxious to know of research developments in a company whose software was interchangeable with that of Hitachi.

If a rival can obtain details of improved technology, it can reverse engineer – take them apart to see how they work – manufacture the mainframes and software without the possible year-long research and development delay and get its compatible, probably cheaper, product on to the market within months. Which is why there are in Silicon Valley almost as many consultancy firms monitoring product development as there are companies innovating that development.

In the summer of 1981 the man with two names and phony doctorates shuttled across the Pacific from his $233,000 homes in Los Gatos and Palm Springs, California, briefing Hitachi on what he knew. Also, he sold them the handbooks.

Saffaie was not the only consultant trying to keep Hitachi abreast of IBM development. Another was Maxwell Paley, who actually worked for the company for twenty-one years, rose to head its Advanced Computing Systems laboratory and now advises other companies through the San Jose firm of Palyn Associates. In 1981 Paley offered to provide Hitachi with an informed study of IBM's new computer developments, legally based on published material. The man to whom that offer was made was Kenji Hayashi, a senior engineer in the Hitachi computer designing department who regularly visited California on fact-finding trips. Initially, Hayashi was excited by Paley's offer. But the enthusiasm did not last long. Immediately after his return to Japan, Hayashi cabled:

WE HAVE ALREADY GOT ADIRONDACK WORKBOOK THAT IS SIMILAR TO YOUR COVERING (INDEX). BUT WE HAVE ONLY VOLUMES 1, 3, 4, 8, 9, 10, 11, 12, 15, 22. IF YOU HAVE ANOTHER VOLUME, LET ME KNOW. WE CONSIDER AGAIN. . . . PLEASE KEEP CONFIDENTIAL.

To Paley, well aware of the security screen behind which IBM attempts to conceal its latest developments, it was obvious that Hitachi possessed stolen documentation. Subsequently, he was to be criticised for not warning a valued client. But, believing that Hitachi 'weren't fighting fair', he chose to warn IBM instead, alerting IBM Engineering Vice-President Robert Evans with the words, 'I think one of my Japanese clients has got your crown jewels.'

IBM, which spends a minimum of $50,000,000 a year protecting its secrets, moved at once to recover the jewels. The firm's general counsel, Donato Evangelista, was nominally in charge of the operation, but Richard Callahan was entrusted with its execution at street level. A Marine captain in Korea, Callahan is a former FBI agent, counterintelligence expert, Treasury investigator and agent of the Bureau of Narcotics and Dangerous Drugs. He joined IBM in 1973 as their chief investigator and has earned an awesome reputation within the company as a counter-espionage agent.

65

Callahan's first task was to confirm the accuracy of the tip-off, a task he entrusted to Paley who – in exchange for a $150,000 retainer – sent the following cable:

'I made a contact and was told information you requested is under rather strict security control. But can be obtained.' Paley suggested a Tokyo meeting, to which he was accompanied by Callahan and a colleague from Palyn Associates, Robert Domenico. They stayed at the Imperial Hotel, where on 2 October 1981 Paley and Domenico met with Hayashi. The Japanese gave Paley a five-page list of handwritten questions about the operating systems of the 3081 machine, valued at $6,000,000. On Callahan's instructions, Paley then offered Hayashi an index of the entire set of Adirondack workbooks. Court records show that Paley warned Hayashi that Palyn Associates did not steal confidential material but that they possibly knew someone who did. And then he asked Hayashi to produce the books Hitachi already possessed. The purpose of this was to be able to see the workbooks for themselves and for Callahan to be able to guarantee that they were in fact stolen.

IBM documents are marked with four different levels of confidentiality. The lowest, 'for internal IBM use only', governs such things as internal telephone books; 'IBM confidential' is usually ascribed to maintenance manuals; 'restricted confidential' covers routine analysis and 'registered confidential' marks sensitive product designs and plans. On 6 October Hayashi showed Paley volumes 8, 11 and 22 of the workbooks, each of which was marked 'IBM confidential'. Hayashi told the American consultant that Hitachi wanted the missing volumes 'very badly'. He then returned the index, now coded to indicate the order of priority in which Paley should procure the rest of the workbooks: 'A' was highly desirable, 'B' less so and 'C' stood for an updated version of one of the books already in Hitachi's possession. Hayashi disclosed the existence of Saffaie, whom he described as someone with 'IBM friends', but said Hitachi wanted additional conduits of information. And what they wanted most of all, added Hayashi, was the opportunity to examine for themselves IBM's most advanced disc drive memory before its general commercial distribution.

Later, in their rooms at the Imperial Hotel, Callahan identified the three workbooks as genuine and realised the company faced a frightening case of industrial espionage. Back at the Armonk headquarters, the few IBM officials involved in the leak held a conference to decide whether to pursue the case through the civil or the criminal courts – not that the issue was ever in any real doubt since at Armonk, I was assured, the policy in major cases of stealing is always to initiate criminal proceedings. Once given the go-ahead, Callahan moved swiftly. He knew that there already existed in Silicon Valley an undercover FBI investigation. Codenamed PENGEM – Penetration of the Grey Electronics Market – it was targeted at the transfer of technology to the Eastern bloc and was fronted by a sham consulting agency in San Jose called Glenmar Associates. With Callahan as their liaison officer, two of the FBI agents staffing it had undergone technical training at IBM to enable them to appear technically proficient. IBM also provided ID and work record details in case a suspicious client tried to check them out. When Callahan notified Glenmar of the IBM leak, the FBI agreed to take charge of investigations, stipulating that in the interests of preserving Glenmar's cover Paley should not be told of it.

The genuine consultant contacted Hayashi when the Japanese flew to New York on one of his regular visits, offering to set up a meeting with the IBM informant from whom he was getting all the 3081 details. Las Vegas was the agreed venue and in November Paley and Callahan flew to the Nevada gambling resort, booking into rooms at the Hilton which the FBI had already bugged with video and sound recording devices. Callahan had never attended any of the Tokyo meetings at the Imperial Hotel, so in Las Vegas he was introduced to Hayashi as Richard Kerrigan, a lawyer who had worked for Paley in the past. The introductions over, Paley withdrew. Later that day, Callahan presented Hayashi to Alan Garretson, the FBI agent in charge of the Glenmar Associates operation and one of the men whom IBM had trained. Callahan gave Hayashi to understand that Al Harrison, Garretson's pseudonym, might be able to provide the information the Japanese sought. With the cameras and tape machines recording everything, Hayashi itemised the Hitachi requirements. To avoid any later court challenge, Garretson was careful to warn the Japanese that what he wanted would have to be obtained illegally and that if caught the thief 'could be put in jail for stealing'. An indication that Hitachi knew that well

enough comes from another tape recording, of a telephone
conversation between Callahan and Jun Naruse, the Hitachi
memory systems technician chosen to examine the promised IBM
memory device. The telephone call from Naruse to Callahan was
for assurance that everything had been properly planned and there
were no potential difficulties. If there were, Naruse warned, 'it's
real trouble for Hitachi'.

A 3081 computer was already operational in the Pratt and
Whitney Aircraft plant, the engine division of United Technologies at Hartford, Connecticut, and that was the model chosen for
Naruse's inspection. There was a 5 a.m. rendezvous in the lobby of
a Hartford hotel at which an FBI-briefed employee handed over
high security identification badges to the aircraft plant, receiving in
return an envelope apparently stuffed with money.

'How much did you have to pay?' asked Naruse.

'Plenty,' said Garretson.

Both Garretson and Naruse carried cameras. Inside the computer room, Garretson warned the Japanese to avoid any background identification. After taking all the technical photographs
he needed, Naruse asked Garretson to photograph him actually
hugging the machine. Back at the hotel, Naruse handed Garretson
an initial payment of $3000. On 18 November, at Santa Clara, he
gave the FBI man a further $7000 for maintenance manuals of the
memory mechanism.

Requests for more and more IBM information flooded into
Glenmar Associates and Palyn Associates. As a supposed lawyer,
Callahan warned Hayashi that his IBM sources were growing
increasingly frightened at the demands that were being made. Part
of Callahan's letter read: 'As you well know, they risk disgrace
and perhaps imprisonment if they are caught taking the IBM
information you have been asking for. They are only willing to risk
the consequences if the money rewards are great enough.' In
reply, Hayashi wrote: 'From the point of us, cost should depend
on how we can use it. Except the rare case [a magnetic head and
platters used to read and write data on to the disc drive, for which
he'd offered $10,000] our requesting information will be published
in the future. Then timing is the best or most important as to
decide the value.' To explain himself more fully, Hayashi drew a
chart the declining line of which indicated the diminishing value of
the information. There was, however, the possibility of a

consultancy contract between Hitachi and Glenmar if Glenmar could lay hands on a microcode which updated the performance of one of IBM's older machines. Hayashi assured Callahan: 'Our top management will understand your potential if you locate it by the end of January.'

On 7 January 1982 Garretson telephoned Hayashi in Tokyo to say he had obtained the code: the price he was asking, $12,000. On 18 January Hayashi brought a Hitachi software expert named Isao Ohnishi to a meeting with Garretson and during that meeting Hayashi explained the establishment of a secure and hidden money chain. Hitachi intended to fund Nissei Electronics, an affiliate, which would in turn transfer the money to NCL Data Inc., a firm based in Santa Clara whose president was an American. Named Thomas Yoshida, he would pay Glenmar.

In a later letter to Garretson, Hayashi wrote: 'I have destroyed your letter yesterday. Please destroy my letters after you recognise the essence.' And the essence took some recognising, once the two fell to haggling over prices and negotiations grew more and more complex. On the list of requests was the source code for an IBM MVS/SP Version II. Hayashi offered between $50,000 and $100,000; Garretson asked for $250,000. Hayashi protested that was too high. Meetings continued between the Japanese and Garretson, in Silicon Valley and also in Honolulu. Another Hitachi request was for every design document and component applicable to the 3081. Hayashi took to calling the efforts to fill this order the 150K project, a reference to the $150,000 the Japanese were prepared to pay for it. Presented with the copious shopping list, Garretson said the price would be $700,000. Hayashi countered by saying Hitachi did not need the complete list after all. Some items were being obtained through reverse engineering and the source microcode for the MVS/SP Version II had been obtained from someone else. For the rest, Hitachi's top offer was $300,000. Garretson bargained on and finally the price was agreed at $525,000.

The FBI were determined to establish at what level within the Hitachi management structure the stealing of IBM material was known. They got their chance to find out when Hayashi said in April 1982 that his company was interested in hiring as consultants IBM executives who were close to retirement. Garretson gambled, telling Hayashi the executives were so high-ranking that they would need assurance from Hitachi managers of seniority that such a transfer would be effected discreetly. To provide that assurance, Hitachi flew out Kisaburo Nakazawa who was general manager of Hitachi's Kanagawa factory. That factory produces the company's mainframe computers. The Japanese met Callahan and Garretson on 23 April 1982 in San Francisco. FBI affidavits record Nakazawa assuring the two Americans he was aware of the risks that had been involved in their obtaining the IBM secrets, which he further assured them had been very useful. Nakazawa further said that he was authorised to spend up to $1,000,000, especially for 'hiring as private consultants current IBM executives'. Any information provided by those executives would 'be kept in a locked room with selected access',

In May Garretson told Hayashi he had succeeded in obtaining all the IBM material Hitachi had ordered. The agreed price of $525,000 was wired into Garretson's Washington account from the fund held by NCL Data Inc. On 22 June, the day chosen for the handover of the IBM secrets at Glenmar's offices, Thomas Yoshida drove the collection car – a Volkswagen – and Ohnishi and Hayashi were passengers. Only Ohnishi and Hayashi went into the Glenmar building, where the IBM material waited in its boxes. Excitedly, Hayashi, who had sought the souvenir photograph of himself hugging the IBM machine in Hartford, ripped an IBM label off one of the cartons and stuck it in his wallet, another souvenir. There was to be a further memento that he did not anticipate. At that moment the FBI agents formally identified themselves and arrested Yoshida, Hayashi and Ohnishi. All were photographed as they were led away handcuffed.

At the time they announced the Hitachi arrest, the FBI also disclosed that matching charges – for conspiring to transport stolen material out of the United States – were being made against employees of Mitsubishi Electric Corp., a second Japanese company. Japan was stunned. The then premier, Zenko Susuki, called it 'very shocking'. Katsusada Hirose, the Ministry of International Trade and Industry official in charge of data processing, said the incident was 'regrettable, especially at this time when we are trying to promote cooperative relations of the two countries in various fields of technology'. Although denying any wrongdoing – both companies claimed they considered they were dealing legally with bona fide consultants – Hitachi President

Katsushige Mita and Mitsubishi President Nihachiro Katayama both publicly apologised, a tradition in Japan. Both companies temporarily suspended computer advertising and by the end of the week of the arrests in Silicon Valley, Hitachi's stock on the Tokyo exchange had dropped sixteen per cent.

In the West, all those reactions were viewed as the product of an understandable embarrassment – a misconception which was almost instantly exposed. The backlash was led by the national press, with its huge audience, and was triggered – so I have been assured by Japanese sources who asked to remain anonymous – by those pictures of Hayashi, Ohnishi and Yoshida being led in handcuffs from the offices of Glenmar Associates. 'That was an unthinkable humiliation in Japan,' said my Tokyo informant who was involved in the case. 'People who murder get treated like that, not someone proving loyalty to his company by trying to gauge what a competitor is doing. And the very legality could not be absorbed by the Japanese mind. In Japan, the sort of undercover operation created by Glenmar Associates would only have been considered for a narcotics case.'

There was a widespread assumption that the American government had created the incident artificially to show Tokyo its irritation at the imbalance of trade figures between the two countries. That argument was refined to the point of asserting that the Glenmar Associates sting had been set up in response to IBM – and Washington – fears that Hitachi was making too deep an inroad into the accepted world supremacy of the American company. Certainly, Hitachi seemed to be presenting a serious challenge, having responded enthusiastically to a government mandate to increase exports. It was among the leaders of those Japanese hi-tech companies who had captured more than fifty per cent of the world market for the most popular computer chip, the 64K dynamic RAM. Silicon Valley's Hewlett-Packard purchased from them; in Japan itself, they surpassed IBM sales. They had forged a European outlet through Olivetti and were moving into small business and personal computers. There was, besides, a history of the Japanese government trying to give its computer industry a competitive edge over IBM. In the 1960s the government denied to IBM's Japanese subsidiary the tax advantages it allowed its own hi-tech companies and in 1971 the Ministry of International Trade and Industry organised the latter into three joint research-and-development groups which were funded to compete with IBM. Out of that funding, Hitachi and Fujitsu Ltd were allocated $100,000,000 to devise IBM compatible machines and by 1981 Hitachi had succeeded.

One of the country's leading national newspapers, *Asahi Shimbun*, said of the Glenmar Associates seizures: 'Even among some Americans there can be heard voices that this was a highly political action against Japan.' Another source told me:

> Their reversal of attitudes – from apparent loss of face to belligerent defence – was astonishing. What was even more astonishing was that the Japanese employees of IBM Japan became those who appeared humiliated. The drop in morale was staggering: Japanese were ashamed to admit they worked for IBM. It took a concerted effort to reverse that attitude: IBM lapel pins were made and employees encouraged to wear them, as badges of pride, not shame.

There were cases of IBM users in Japan switching to Hitachi machines and the newspapers greatly publicised the decision of the American Social Security administration to buy two Hitachi computers – for $7,000,000 – rather than the more expensive IBM models.

Indictments in the Hitachi case were returned against seventeen people, nine of whom – including Kisaburo Nakazawa – were in Japan. When they failed to appear for arraignment, bench warrants were issued in San Jose. But the US government never pressed extradition proceedings. It also accepted the submission in the Mitsubishi case that the Japanese employees did not 'knowingly and wilfully' intend to break the law. Lawyers acting for Hitachi and for Hayashi, Ohnishi and Yoshida argued forcefully that the sting had been orchestrated not by the FBI but by IBM as an operation intended to eliminate a competitor and that the whole case should be thrown out of court. During those pre-trial hearings, the closed court had access to some of the thirty-five hours of video tapes and more than sixty hours of audio tapes, which included the scene of Hayashi embracing the IBM machine in Hartford and discussions about theft and risk. When the court ruled against the case being dismissed, the lawyers worked to minimise open court disclosure of those films and tapes. So the bargaining began.

Hitachi instructed its lawyers to enter a no-contest plea on condition that its accused employees were not put on trial. In Washington, the Department of Justice refused what they considered too easy an escape but came back with an offer of its own: if guilty pleas were entered, there would be no jailing. More discussions followed in Tokyo between Hitachi and their legal representatives. The conclusion was that loss of face having been only narrowly averted once already, Hitachi could not afford to risk it again by allowing the recordings to be made public. It had to accept the Washington compromise. In court, Hitachi was fined $10,000, the maximum; Kenji Hayashi was also fined $10,000 and placed on probation for two years; Isao Ohnishi was fined $4000 and put on probation for two years. Thomas Yoshida pleaded no contest to charges of assisting in the conspiracy.

Whatever the reaction in Japan, IBM considered they had been publicly vindicated – but not yet compensated. From civil court documents, I know that IBM estimated their loss at somewhere between $750,000,000 and $2,500,000,000 and having disposed of the criminal hearings, their lawyers initiated proceedings to recover some of that cost. This time the negotiations were conducted entirely in secret and a condition of the final settlement was that they should – like the settlement – remain undisclosed. It was, in fact, a complicated agreement. Under it, Hitachi agreed to pay $300,000,000 over a period of years as a licensing agreement for the use of the stolen material. IBM was accorded the legal right to examine Hitachi products for any evidence of patent infringement, that right to be exercised if considered necessary not just by purchasing Hitachi equipment on the open market and 'reverse engineering' it but by on-the-spot investigation in Hitachi factories and plants. Should IBM consider that their products were again being pirated, Hitachi agreed to the complaint being probed by an independent panel of arbiters. Further, should that panel find against them, then the Japanese company agreed to be bound to withdraw the product from the market. At Armonk, I was assured that the examination agreements were invoked to guarantee no future infringement and in Tokyo an unattributable source described to me the financial settlement as 'brilliant' because it encouraged Hitachi to develop technology of its own. A further part of the secret settlement dealt with the legal fees incurred – $2,000,000 – which it was agreed Hitachi should pay in full.

The terms and conditions of the civil settlement that closed the case were so unusual that a year later the American Department of Justice initiated an anti-trust investigation, to establish whether it gave IBM the sort of unfair advantage in an open market that they had been accused of seeking when the arrests were originally disclosed in Tokyo. No conclusion was ever returned by the Department of Justice. The IBM/Hitachi settlement remains in force and IBM anticipate no change to it. But the judgement it enshrines remains in dispute. The IBM view, according to a high-ranking official, is that

> Hitachi got caught with their hand in the cookie jar, where their hand shouldn't have been. We were conscious of the loss of face dilemma – that the Japanese don't like admitting that they made a mistake – and we didn't want any prosecution to boomerang on us, saleswise. But our secrets and our technology were of paramount importance. It was a warning to them and to all our competitors.

The Japanese feeling is still that they were wrongly led into an illegal situation and that what they became involved in is a daily or a weekly occurrence among the proliferation of consultancies in the hi-tech, hi-competition milieu of Silicon Valley. From the tapes I have heard of the Hitachi case, it is a difficult argument logically to support.

With another Japanese company, there is not even the benefit of doubt.

CHAPTER EIGHT

. . . And the Golden Eggs

If the Adirondack workbooks were the jewels in the IBM crown, then Stanford Ovshinsky was justified in regarding his Energy Conversion Devices as a basketful of golden eggs. Certainly, he deserved them after the lean years of struggling with a revolutionary computer-improving invention. By 1983 he believed his company, with an original staff of two, to be *the* world leader. He estimated it would eventually have a turnover of $10,000,000 a year, which is a lot of golden eggs. Japan's Matsushita company thought so too, which is why they stole them.

Stanford Ovshinsky is a maverick inventor, a man with no academic qualifications whose breakthrough concept was later acknowledged by Sir Neville Mott of England's Cambridge University when he publicly accepted the shared 1977 Nobel Prize for Physics. To the layman, a device for improving computers sounds complicated but as with most inventions the underlying idea is simple. Indeed, there is perhaps a sense in which Ovshinsky's lack of formal education dictated it should be. The son of an immigrant Lithuanian scrapdealer, Ovshinsky was born in Akron, Ohio. Paradoxically, he found school boring but learning fascinating; so he educated himself. After high school he attended a trade school and graduated to become a machinist. For a while he ran his own shop and then joined a firm manufacturing car parts as their research director. It was work which made him curious about the brain: he imagined a connection between the switches that turn machines on and off and the way in which brain cells motivate a human being. The connection is a far from obvious one, but as Ovshinsky later explained to an interviewer, 'I wanted to understand how you encode memory: how you transfer it.' Ovshinsky further likened the human brain to the semiconductor which makes computers and videos work. But the traditional computer semiconductor is a silicon chip – a solid component, whereas human brain cells are amorphous. Ovshinsky started trying to make an amorphous semiconductor, using materials known as chalcogenide glasses.

In 1960, together with his biochemist wife Iris, Ovshinsky founded Energy Conversion Devices Inc. in West Maple Road, Troy, Michigan. There he experimented with chalcogenide glasses like tellurium, germanium and oxygen. By 1970 he had his invention. It was a method for storing and retrieving information by reversibly changing a layer of material between amorphous and crystalline states upon exposure to a small amount of light, such as a laser beam. On 22 September 1970 he patented his invention, receiving the number 3,550,441, and announced his discovery with a fanfare of publicity that later got him criticised within the industry as a showman. Initially, his hi-tech colleagues disdained the invention despite the fact that it was cheaper than the traditional semiconductors and had a far greater memory capacity. That initial disdain contributed to the slow commercial development of the invention. Ovshinsky explained: 'We lacked adequate funds to develop the technology ourselves; also we experienced a phenomenon, common to most new technologies, which can be characterised as "technology acceptance lag".'

To overcome that acceptance lag, Ovshinsky exposed his idea throughout the world to as wide an audience as he could. There were two comprehensive articles in the *Scientific American*; *Fortune* magazine wrote about it and the paper he wrote himself for the *Physical Review Letters*, entitled 'Reversible Electrical Switching Phenomena in Disordered Structures' and ignored when it first appeared in 1968, became one of the five most cited in what is the leading journal for American physics. The United States National Academy of Sciences convened a committee to study amorphous materials and publicly praised Ovshinsky's research.

By the time its 1974 edition was published, Webster's *Dictionary* included the word 'ovonic', defined thus:

adj: (after S. R. Ov[shinsky], 1922, US inventory + [electr] onic) designating, of, or utilising various glassy, amorphous materials that undergo electronic or structural changes and act as semiconductors when subjected to voltage, light, etc.; used in computer memory elements, electronic switches, etc.

The year 1974 was also significant for another event in Ovshinsky's calendar – a visit to Japan where he held discussions with officials of Matsushita. The Japanese company have an American corporation – Matsushita Electric Corp. headquartered in New Jersey – and trade worldwide its Panasonic, Quasar, National and Technics products. It was not Ovshinsky's first visit to Japan. Since 1964 he estimates he has been to the country over forty times. The purpose of the 1974 visit was to hear from Matsushita whether it would link up with his firm through a licensing agreement and develop the system. Matsushita was an obvious choice for Ovshinsky, as Japan's largest electronics firm, valued at $15,000,000,000; but the meeting was disappointing, for Matsushita turned down the idea. Undeterred, Ovshinsky continued to look for partners, eventually linking with the Sharp Company – the full title is Sharp-ECD Solar – with which he started up a Japanese affiliate under the chairmanship of Professor Edwin Reischauer, former United States Ambassador to Tokyo.

Other associations developed, too. Ovshinsky entered into an agreement with Standard Oil of Ohio to build an $80,000,000 amorphous solar cell plant. With the American Natural Resources Company of Detroit, he entered an agreement to commercialise an amorphous thermoelectric device capable of generating electricity from waste heat sources, like smokestacks, with no moving parts but equipped with an amorphous storage battery. As Ovshinsky recalled in 1983: 'I thought our commercialisation lag was over.' So it was, but in a way he had never imagined. For in April that year Dr Shigeru Hayakawa, managing director of Matsushita's $600,000,000 research and development division, announced at a New York press conference that the company had developed 'for the first time in the world' a laser-induced erasable optical memory system. This Japanese system, boasted Mr Hayakawa, had a recording capacity 1000 times greater than that of an 8-inch 1-Mbite floppy disk or 150 times that of a full-scale computer disk unit. He further claimed that the invention was the product of ten years of research. In the announcement, the words 'crystalline' and 'amorphous' were used. At the press conference, the phase change between the two was described as 'a new trick'.

77

Ovshinsky and his $21,000,000 company started a Jack and the Beanstalk battle against the $15,000,000,000 Japanese giant. It is an analogy prompted by Ovshinsky's later explanation to Washington politicians. He said: 'The United States has been the goose that has laid such golden eggs in high technology and small companies such as ours should not be allowed, I believe, to become victims to such large, powerful and unscrupulous companies, no matter what country they come from.' Matsushita, he said, 'feels it is beyond the laws of its own land and feels it is beyond the laws of the land of the United States as well'.

When the lowly 'Jack' decided to fight the giant by using the laws of the United States, the discoveries were startling. Perhaps the most startling of all was that Matsushita was not only geared to market through Panasonic products utilising Ovshinsky's work, but that company executives had blatantly inked over by hand Ovshinsky's original patent to fool the US Patent Office into granting them a duplicate patent. Dated 26 August 1974, the Japanese application deleted the words 'amorphous state and crystalline state', which appeared on line three of Patent 3,550,441, and substituted the phrase 'a low optical density state and a high optical density state'. Initialled by Matsushita executives Takeo Ohta and Mutsuo Takenaga, the alterations were dated 14 August 1974 – the very year in which the Japanese company had turned down Ovshinsky's offer of a licensing agreement. And because the description did not match precisely any previously recorded invention, Patent 500,468 was granted.

There were more revelations to come. There was the $10,000,000 patent infringement case brought against Matsushita on 19 July 1982 by the Silicon Valley firm of Stanford Institute Research International, headquartered in Menlo Park. The Institute accused the Japanese company of making, selling and using television cameras utilising the system patented in 1968 by SRI, the first of its kind to convert colour television cameras from three tubes to one thus enabling a cheaper product. There was the case initiated on 11 March 1983 by Papst Mechatronics Corp. of Middletown, Rhode Island, and brought before the United States International Trade Commission under the amended Tariff Act of 1930. The Japanese firm involved were accused of importing axial flow fans – used to cool video, computer and electrical equipment – in contravention of the Papst patent and of selling them cut-price.

Speaking of his own suit, Ovshinsky used the word 'arrogant' to describe Matsushita's attitude and actions. 'To me it should be beneath their dignity to steal from us. To do this in such flagrant disregard for what is well-known throughout the world about our work, very much so in Japan, meant a total disregard of both Japanese and United States' public opinion, scientific opinion, laws, everything. Just pure arrogance.' Further, Ovshinsky publicly declared his view of the case as a blot on the honour of Japan – always a sensitive point with the Japanese and I understand it was this accusation in particular that was responsible for the subsequent settlement agreed by the corporation. Certainly, Ovshinsky played on this aspect of the affair for all it was worth – using the press and the media unremittingly to humiliate Matsushita into a face-saving compromise. His fear was that the corporate giant would wait him out, embroiling him in protracted litigation against the time when the Ovshinsky patent would expire. But Ovshinsky's experience as a publicist won the day and in December 1983 Matsushita agreed to pay $3,000,000 to Energy Conversion Devices as part of a settlement also conceding Ovshinsky royalties as well as the right to be consulted before any further products employing his invention should go into production.

Ovshinsky considers his fight to have been well worth undertaking. And justified, comparing official statistics of the American and the Japanese government. Between 1960 and 1980, Japanese hi-tech industries invested $10,000,000,000. During the same period, US companies invested $300,000,000,000. Says Ovshinsky: 'Every country is fighting for "technology leadership" and that is why the US cannot lose the battle, because if you lose that battle in these days, you are not really an industrialised country any more.'

CHAPTER NINE

The Worldwide Trawl

The technology net that the Soviet Union casts in the United States has a particularly fine mesh. Both FBI and CIA sources have suggested to me that some 800 KGB and GRU agents – each with as many cells as they can cultivate – are in active operation in the country. But the Soviets do not confine their activities to the US. Just as other hi-tech predators trawl American expertise, so the Soviets cast their net elsewhere.

Vyacheslav Grigorev was one of five Soviet agents expelled from Britain in April 1985. He worked in London for Aeroflot, the Soviet airline, and Britain's counterintelligence organisation, MI5, know that his assignment was to obtain a particular laser gyroscope developed by British Aerospace. It was the expertise involved in developing this invention that the then Minister of Defence Michael Heseltine quoted in his efforts to secure British contracts for America's Star Wars programme.

Earlier, in September 1984, the Russians had sent an official delegation to the Farnborough Air Show for the first time. Forty Russians attended, bringing with them their wide-bodied 11-86 passenger jet, the Mi-26 – the world's largest helicopter – and a short takeoff An-27 transport plane. An intelligence official described the episode to me as 'something resembling scenes from the Keystone Cops'. He said,

> The Russians were supposed to be getting orders, of course. But at least twelve – maybe even fifteen – of their delegation were KGB and GRU, specifically tasked with obtaining as much technology information as they could. At the end of the show, I doubt there was an available brochure, instructional booklet, illustration or pamphlet they hadn't obtained. The

amount of photographs they took of every exhibit – not so much the exteriors of aircraft but every possible detail of engines and engine parts – was incredible. But it didn't end there. The British were watching them, watching the aircraft and the exhibits. And the Americans were doing everything they could to get close and identify the amount of Western technology that had been modified and utilised on the Russian exhibits.

Ten of the twenty-five Russians expelled from Britain in September 1985 were identified to British counterintelligence by Soviet defector Oleg Gordievsky as being agents responsible for obtaining all available technology on the revolutionary Ptarmigan secure battlefield communications system, the most advanced and sophisticated in the world. Also on the Red Book shopping list were the 'over the horizon' radar system developed by Marconi and the sonar system utilised by the British Nimrod surveillance aircraft.

In 1983 another Soviet defector, Vladimir Kuzichkin, named Anatoli Chernayev – officially a third secretary at the Russian embassy in Kensington – as a technology spy. Chernayev, protesting his innocence, was expelled. In April of the same year Valeri Nikolayevich Ivanov was expelled from the Soviet legation in Canberra after Australian counterintelligence uncovered evidence of his hi-tech spying. KGB linguist Vladimir Fedorovich Mikunov – fluent in French, English and Mandarin – was posted in 1983 to be the technology gatherer in Singapore, one of the Far East's most notorious counterfeiting countries. The GRU's technology agent there was Yevgeniy Ignatyevich Kutusov.

From Singapore, Moscow extended its trawl throughout Asia.

Yevgeniy Fedorivich Khritonov – officially a first secretary – and Ernest Yevgeniyevich Obminskiy, a counsellor, and Mikhail Mikhailovich Shapovlov, a trade counsellor, made up the KGB's hi-tech team in Bangkok. In Jakarta, the function was performed by Kolos Borisovich Trigubenko, whose KGB cover was that of an embassy counsellor, and Boris Petrovich Bezsmertnyi who was a GRU Red Book 'purchaser', although his official cover was that of military and naval attaché. Vladilen Aysyukov, First Secretary at the Soviet Embassy in Manila, is in fact a KGB career officer who received specific education at Moscow's Lebedev Institute – a leading scientific establishment – to enable him to carry out his intended function. At the same establishment, the KGB's Vyacheslav Andreyevich underwent technical training. He is now Deputy Trade Representative at the Soviet legation in Kuala Lumpar. Captain Yuri Guzenko, ostensibly the military attaché, is another competitor for his Red Book rewards on behalf of the GRU.

Western – and particularly American – intelligence organisations, acting in concert, charted the creation of the hi-tech cells throughout Asia. In March 1983 they also monitored the expulsion from France of forty-seven Russians, fourteen of whom they identified to President François Mitterand's administration as agents assigned to scientific information gathering. I know from conversations in Paris, London and Washington that the Mitterand expulsions came after positive evidence had been produced to the French President by the DST, the French counterintelligence service, of the activities of those fourteen. The expulsions – the greatest in terms of numbers since the 1971 exodus from Britain of 105 Russians – did not sour relations with Moscow. Mikhail Gorbachov, the Soviet leader, later paid what was diplomatically described as a 'productive visit' to the French capital, home of the COCOM organisation. It did, however, harden the Mitterand attitude towards this sort of espionage. In November 1985 Henri Conze, Deputy Director for International Affairs at the French Defence Ministry, felt confident enough of the new hard line to say, 'We are much more restrictive than COCOM on the transfer of security-related technology.'

This is exactly the response that Washington seeks to inspire by quoting, as I have in the preceding paragraphs, the intelligence networks Moscow has established to steal technology secrets. Washington has had minimal success. Among some enforcement agencies in the US, there is particular anger directed towards London. 'Bullshit' was one word used to describe to me the belief that a special relationship exists between the governments of President Reagan and Margaret Thatcher. The term 'bullshit' came from an American official but the British reaction, when the word was repeated in a question, was that 'it's America wallowing in it, not us'. Certainly, US Customs Commissioner William von Rabb singled out Britain – together with West Germany, despite its initial reluctance to cooperate over the Mueller case – as an example of outstanding cooperation in the efforts to stem the flow of strategic information to Moscow. He pointed to the accord achieved at the Williamsburg summit and used the word 'spectacular' to describe the working relationship between the two countries.

It was two days later, in another part of America but from an equally high-ranking US government official, that I heard the word bullshit. According to him, the American complaint was that cooperation was virtually one-sided, with Britain benefiting substantially but America practically not at all. The official told me, 'We have problems; major problems. Britain won't help us at all. There hasn't yet been an official protest but we've made it clear that we expect better cooperation. We are just not getting what we should.' Quoted to me as an example of one way benefits was a case in which US Customs and the FBI cooperated to their fullest extent in providing documentary evidence of a money trail in which a $2,000,000 ransom for a non-reported or admitted kidnap was laundered through Switzerland into the United States to buy arms for the IRA. Few US laws – apart from those involved in the surreptitious transfer of the money from the United States back into Ireland – had been broken, yet the American enforcement authorities voluntarily supplied information without which the case would never have been fully understood. In return, Washington asked for evidence from London and Dublin that they might effectively conclude their own investigations. 'We can't get it from either. We've done everything to help them but they're very reluctant to help us. We went out of our way. It's very much a one way street.'

The official with whom I was talking conceded that the quoted case did not come under the aegis of Operation Exodus or the Export Administration Act. It was symptomatic, he insisted, of London's attitude in general, however. 'When we go to them for help, they scream extraterritoriality.' The result, he claims, is an increasing reluctance on the part of some US agencies to accede to London's requests for assistance. 'I back off,' admitted the high-ranking official. 'When the request first comes in, I say "To hell with them" because here we go again. It really bothers me: it's just a major problem we have.'

A further cause of annoyance between Washington and London – although again not specifically to do with the transfer of security-related technology – is the British involvement in the shipment of arms to Iran, a country prohibited from receiving any US war material since the seizing of the fifty-two American hostages in the last year of Jimmy Carter's presidency.

> We can't get anything out of England on Iran. England seems to be the country through which most of the stuff goes, to Iran and Iraq and Libya: it goes there and then gets diverted. The British won't help us at all on that. It's not COCOM, so they have no obligations to and I guess they're trying to develop good relations with those countries. We've had cases we just have not been able to prosecute because of the reluctance.

When the complaints were put to British officials, one Whitehall executive countered:

> America is not the world's policeman and the world's laws are not those of America ... While on the surface there would seem to be a lot in the American argument, there is also an attitude *beneath* the surface which mustn't be forgotten. While feeling every sympathy for what happened over the Iran hostages, it *was* an American situation, not a British or a European one. Providing the proper 'End User' certification is complied with, there is no reason why a registered and bona fide arms dealer in Britain or Europe should not enter into some aspects of trade with countries with whom Washington has no trading links.

Teheran's representative in London is Colonel Rassekh Ahmadi. He deals in military parts and equipment through an organisation called International Management Services and IMS is an entirely owned subsidiary of the Ministry of Defence.

Of course, my Whitehall source is right: there are other arguments and perhaps not so very deep below that 'surface'. One is that US firms frequently abuse the spirit if not the letter of COCOM regulations by forming subsidiary relationships with countries not governed by COCOM – Sweden and Austria are the two favourites – and then trading with the prohibited countries while the ban-observing Europeans lose the business. British MP Paddy Ashdown cites the case of a British firm called Plasma Technology Ltd, which was precluded from displaying microchip technology at the Canton Trade Fair because of COCOM restrictions. When he arrived in China, President David Carr found that a Swedish-American company had already sold that same technology to the Chinese. In April 1984 a CIA report claimed 'the Kohl government continues to interpret COCOM regulations narrowly in its own best interests' and met with a sharp rebuttal. The West German government not only rejected it as 'riddled with falsehoods' but said that, on the contrary, the effect of Washington pressure applied through COCOM was to give America a continued and unfair lead in technology development.

An English source told me that technological agreement between America and Europe would never be completely amicable. 'Washington try to make this simplistically into an East/West problem, like there was a definitive line drawn on a map. Which there isn't. For every Soviet spy or agent trying to discover a Western secret, there are about ten Western spies or agents, trying to find the same information. For a Western company!' And there is the evidence to support that contention.

During the presidency of Jimmy Carter, the Freedom of Information Act became law in America. Under that law, the general public can file for access to government documents. What a former CIA deputy director, Admiral Bobby Inman, described as a 'cottage industry' has evolved to make these applications, specialising in accessing those documents which identify government contractors for clients who are keen to learn of the work in which those contractors are involved. These researchers call themselves brokers – the FBI and CIA term is 'access professionals' – and are also expert at probing the US Patent Office, at which complete details of technological processes must be filed before a patent can be granted. American intelligence knows that the Eastern bloc makes extensive use of access professionals through front organisations. But they know, too, that the most extensive use of all is made by American companies spying on their rivals to keep abreast of technological developments. Nor is this practice confined to America, as a Whitehall official explained: 'Every country in Europe has its access professionals; it's a factor of commercial life with which everybody lives. It's sometimes extremely difficult to be sympathetic to the American attitude.'

I expect further difficulty to arise between Europe and Washington over a programme being evolved by Patrick O'Brien, Investigations Director for US Customs, based in New York. O'Brien is creating a 'Most Wanted' list of technology smugglers throughout the world; so far, there are ten on the list and Richard Mueller and Volker Nast are among them. Under US law, O'Brien believes – and is supported in that belief by the necessary district attorneys – that there is the jurisdictional authority to initiate Grand Jury hearings and obtain indictments against all ten because the majority of the illegal shipments leave America through New York's Kennedy Airport. O'Brien told me: 'We are going to track them down, wherever they are in the world. The message is going to be, you are never going to be free of us. They know who we are and we know who they are. We are going to wear them down, being fugitives.'

The catch is that good relations – such as they are – between America and Europe may also be worn down in the process. For the ten Most Wanted smugglers all live in Europe where the American laws involved do not apply. Extraterritoriality, again.

I have discussed the Most Wanted list with the appropriate authorities in three European capitals and in each saw it dismissed as legally unworkable. In Bonn, I was reminded that there is no legislation in the constitution which permits another country to extradite a German national and that, although the government regretted it, a number of German nationals featured on the Most Wanted list. In London, comparisons were actually drawn between Soviet treatment of so-called allies under the Warsaw Pact and American treatment of NATO partners allies – the argument being both superpowers impose their laws from above. 'There are times,' said the official, 'when it's difficult to distinguish between the two attitudes.'

Expanding on his argument, the official echoed the view I heard expressed in West Germany that the biggest difficulty facing European governments – and therefore, by inference, facing COCOM – is that of formulating some comprehensible idea of American policy. For substantiation, the official quoted two incidents which America itself invokes to justify its restrictive exports policy. In the Soviet Union, a truck plant bordering the Karma River was built over a period of seven years employing $1,500,000,000 worth of legal automotive technology imports from the United States and from Europe. In 1981, after the invasion of Afghanistan, the CIA determined that a large number of the military vehicles in use there had been manufactured at the Karma Plant and Washington frequently quotes this as a prime example of 'dual use' danger – the permitting of an export to the Eastern bloc for civilian use only to discover it being used for military purposes. The Whitehall official went on to say:

> A favourite cliché in Washington is Monday morning quarter-backing: making game plans after a football defeat from which it would have been easy to have avoided that defeat. Washington pushed the Karma development: if it can't anticipate the danger of dual use – even though it was initiated in the time of détente – then how can it expect Europe to create some cohesive policy?

The second example better illustrates the confusion to which European countries can be subjected. In January 1985 intelligence reports confirmed that twenty-two US-built helicopters had been diverted through a circuitous routing that involved Antwerp, Rotterdam, Hong Kong and Japan before finally reaching North Korea. US helicopters are not on any banned list, since they are not considered to be dual use vehicles. But North Korea itself is on a banned list because of the Korean War. So Commerce's Office of Export Enforcement stopped the shipment of fifteen additional helicopters that had been ordered and in February placed the German firm, Delta-Avia Fluggerate GmbH, on a black list denied any further export privileges. 'The absurdity of it all,' explained my Whitehall informant, 'was that the helicopters could have been legally ordered and shipped to Moscow – without any objection from the Pentagon, US Customs or US Commerce – and re-exported to North Korea. There's further absurdity. How, logically, can it be argued that a truck is a vehicle that can be dangerously put to a second military use but that a helicopter is not!'

Despite the frictions, America continues to believe in its working relationship with its allies. Caspar Weinberger quotes the existence of a secure teletype link between Washington and COCOM's Paris headquarters, there to speed information exchange, and says that America is encouraging discussions to promote mutual understanding within COCOM of member nations' procedures for export licensing and control. There is ongoing discussion, also, on how to tighten industrial security. Weinberger further quotes a memorandum of understanding between Washington, the United Kingdom, France and Canada for the joint development of the Terminal Guidance Warhead for the Multiple Launch Rocket System (MLRS). That development, Washington believes, will not only strengthen politically the involved nations but enhance within those nations an understanding of the need for technology security.

By 1 February 1985, under US pressure, COCOM had agreed new controls on robotics hardware and software, spacecraft, certain advanced technology printed circuit boards and their manufacturing equipment and advanced aero-engine technologies, including air traffic control systems. Weinberger calls 'gruelling' the negotiating sessions needed to reach those agreements and says they 'resulted in a more realistic appraisal of products and technology which, if exported to the Eastern bloc, would enhance the military build-up underway in those countries'.

Conscious of the prolonged and near-abortive negotiations over the control list for computers which brought about the premature retirement of the head of the negotiating team and obliged the intervention of a US ambassador, Washington was also discussing in 1985 the posting at the Paris headquarters of COCOM of a liaison officer from the US Department of Defence. The purpose of this would be to create what Weinberger calls 'more efficient communications' between the Pentagon and the American team.

Because of the US efforts to strengthen controls in COCOM, the office of Richard Perle is confident that Russia and its satellites have virtually no hope of obtaining advance signal processing systems, FFT processors, array processors, spectrum analysers, image processors or acoustic holographic analysers. Having revitalised the moribund COCOM, Washington has turned to nations not part of the organisation to continue its technology blockade of the Soviet Union. Bilateral agreements are being negotiated at the time of writing with countries in the Pacific Basin and Asia. A cooperation arrangement has already been concluded with India.

'Viewed against 1981, when nothing was happening to stop the flow of technology to the East, what we have already achieved is a spectacular success,' said Customs Commissioner von Rabb. 'The Russians are sweating.'

CHAPTER TEN

The Second Time Around

China possessed a highly-developed civilisation at a time when the now industrialised West still dressed in animal skins. Halted by a Cultural Revolution which positively stultified culture, it is today in a technological Stone Age of its own. China is nonetheless determined to achieve a second hi-tech renaissance and will use every available means – technology espionage, for instance. An FBI agent in California told me: 'We know they're out there, working hard. Sometimes they win, sometimes we do.'

To date the FBI's biggest win – and the sheer scale of the organisation they uncovered is an indication in itself of how seriously the Chinese are now competing – occurred in 1984 when the Bureau smashed in Newark, New Jersey, a $1,000,000,000 spy ring the leader of which, according to American sources, had 'close family ties' with the highest level in the Beijing government. He was thirty-nine-year-old Da-chuan Zheng who, before his arrest, succeeded in smuggling $25,000,000 worth of military hi-tech back to mainland China. Assistant US Attorney Andrew Ruotolo said the ring was working from a $1,000,000,000 shopping list to provide China with the most sophisticated military equipment available. American sources believe its emplacement would have been on along China's border with the Soviet Union. It would have been used, according to Ruotolo, in night border skirmishes and to detect mortar and missile fire. Advanced mini-calculators and several computers, each valued at $25,000, were among the defence items – available only to American and NATO forces – that Zheng obtained.

Zheng travelled to America accompanied by his sister-in-law, Jing-li Zheng. Using for cover her position as representative for a Shanghai magazine, she acted as his interpreter. The remainder of the ring were naturalised US citizens, specifically chosen by the Beijing government for their advanced education in computers and engineering. Dr Kuang-shin Lin, thirty-eight, was described by scientific colleagues as 'absolutely brilliant'. A computer genius who made his home in Lincroft, New Jersey, he held a doctorate in computer science and two master's degrees from the State university at Stonybrook, Long Island. At the time the FBI and Customs investigators broke up the ring, Lin was working as an engineer at AT&T's research laboratories in Lincroft, New Jersey. Before that he had been employed as an electronics engineer at Bell Laboratories in Homdel, New Jersey, where he had access to the most developed of their hi-tech research. Fourth member of the ring, Allen Kwong Yeung, was a graduate of Cornell University who owned what one agent described as a 'cover' restaurant in upstate New York, at Cortland. When the Bureau moved in, Yeung was working on an advanced degree at Syracuse University. Apart from his restaurant, Yeung also ran the Eastar Trading Co. His partner in this venture was David Tsai, a computer programmer for the Chase Manhattan Bank who made his home at Flushing, in the Queens borough of New York, available to Zheng and his sister-in-law as a 'safe house'.

Customs agent Arthur Stiffel identified the Eastar Trading Co. as the 'front business' through which the ring shipped their hi-tech spoils to Hong Kong, for final rerouting to Beijing. But before the front could be exposed for what it was, it needed an elaborate sting operation to be set up, with undercover agents posing as sellers of equipment that would jam radar on B-52 bombers and detect ground-to-air missiles. A Customs official told me: 'Considering that they appeared to want the equipment to guard their borders with the Soviet Union, it is something of a paradox that there was a similarity between agents from Beijing and agents from Moscow. For what they want, money is no object.'

This is not the only occasion when mainland China has been caught engaged in technology espionage. At the end of 1983 a company partially owned by the Chinese government was fined, for infringement, although to minimise embarrassment a plea-bargaining arrangement was reached. The firm concerned was Chipex Inc., an electronics corporation with offices in San Jose, California. Chipex is owned by Hua Ko Electronic Co. of Hong Kong, which in turn is owned by TeleArt Ltd of Hong Kong and

Hua Yuan Co. The Hua Yuan Co. is the Hong Kong trading division of China National Light Industries Corp. of Beijing.

It took US Customs, the Department of Commerce and the FBI two years of investigation to unravel the onion-skin layers of the operation, which was involved in shipping silicon wafers from California to China. Under the bargaining arrangement, Chipex were allowed to plead guilty on one count of illegally exporting US technology, which prevented any disclosure of its labyrinthine methods of getting the hi-tech to Beijing. I know, however, that once again the British Crown colony of Hong Kong was the entry point and repeatedly, during discussions with enforcement officials particularly charged with preventing embargoed hi-tech from reaching Beijing, the British were accused of failing to liaise with US authorities. 'We don't get the cooperation we need or expect from London and we don't get the cooperation we should from places where London is supposed to have some sort of influence,' a Customs agent complained. 'There are occasions when it seems that Hong Kong actually *takes* its guidance from Britain's attitude, that it couldn't give a damn.'

There does exist a legal hi-tech trade between the West and China: in 1984 Beijing was calculated to have spent nearly $450,000,000 on Western-made computers. But Western suppliers find almost without exception that the customary after-sale service has declined and that the country incurs high and unnecessary repair costs because of failed or faulty Chinese maintenance. The Chinese reluctance to admit they need any sort of after-sales help was openly acknowledged in the Beijing *People's Daily* in April 1985. In a self-critical article, the paper admitted: 'Many users buy their computers in a hurry without first making the necessary preparations and end up leaving their machines idle.' There was, further admitted the influential newspaper, 'a serious wastage problem ... even according to optimistic estimates, only fifty per cent of computers are in effective operation.' That figure should be set against the ninety-eight per cent of computers 'in effective operation' in the more highly industrialised, supplying nations.

Maintenance difficulties have also been conceded by Li Yuxiang, Director of the General Office of Computer Industry Administration, which is a division of the Ministry of Electronics Industry. To combat them, the China Computer Technical Service Corp., another government agency to which three thousand people are attached, has established forty-one training centres throughout the country. By the end of 1986 they expect to have an additional ten in operation and hope to have computer service personnel in place in each of China's twenty-nine provinces. At the moment the critical *People's Daily* reports that in the most heavily populated country on earth there are only twenty thousand people with the ability to maintain the computers upon which the government have declared their future development depends.

Beijing is also pressing for complete Chinese hi-tech self-reliance. In March 1985 the Central Committee of the Chinese Communist Party declared that an official aim and the *China Daily*, the English language newspaper published in Beijing, reflected the official attitude when it reported that China intended a 'massive push in scientific and technological research quickly to narrow its technology gap with developed nations'. A Californian Customs agent who referred to the *China Daily* statement told me: 'It means that for a long while yet it won't just be Soviet hands in that damned cookie jar.'

Book Two

Who steals my purse steals trash ...
But he that filches from me my good name
Robs me of that which not enriches him,
And makes me poor indeed.

Othello, William Shakespeare

CHAPTER ELEVEN

Band Aid, Live Aid ... and Pirate Aid

A usually dishevelled Irish pop singer named Bob Geldof conceived the idea of bringing together all the leading names in the British recording industry, making a hit single and devoting the millions to alleviate the 1984 – and continuing – famine in Ethiopia. He called it Band Aid. The idea was a phenomenon in a business of phenomena. Band Aid's 'Do They Know It's Christmas?' begat 'We Are the World' sung by a group comprised of every leading pop star in America, which called itself USA for Africa. And that led in July 1985 to the most amazing and star-studded concert in the history of pop, the satellite linked performances in London's Wembley Stadium and Philadelphia's JFK Stadium of every major pop musician in America and England. It was called Live Aid. Some of the beneficiaries live very well indeed.

At the time of writing it is estimated that £80,000,000 has been raised to fight the African famine. On top of that, more money still was generated by the recordings and the concert: an additional £5,000,000, at a conservative assessment. I had a figure of £10,000,000 suggested to me – money which has gone to line the pockets of the pirates who accurately predicted the money-making potential of the pop world's efforts and made their biggest individual killing marketing the stolen recordings. And killing is the apposite word. Bob Geldof used it, when we talked. 'That's what's happening, because of the rip-off,' he said. 'Every time someone buys one of these tapes, it's killing a child in Africa whose life might have been saved if the money had been properly directed.'

The stealing of the charity recordings highlights a predominantly Asian-based counterfeiting activity that the recording industry calculates to cost them $1,200,000,000 a year worldwide in terms of lost sales. To fight the piracy is also expensive: in 1984, the last year for which the statistic is available, the recording industry spent $4,000,000. Nesuhi Ertegun, Turkish-born President of the International Federation of Phonographic Industries, describes in cataclysmic terms the dangers facing the recording industry in which he has devoted a lifetime – spent largely in America, first as founder of Atlantic Records with his brother Ahmet and then as chief operating officer of WEA, the international outlet for the huge Warner Communications. Says Ertegun, 'If something isn't done about it, piracy and private copying are going to put us all out of business and in ten years there will be no recorded music left to tape.'

Singapore, which under the leadership of Premier Lee Kuan Yew earned itself an international reputation as the glittering economic jewel in a tarnished Asian crown, is the worst culprit for record piracy in the world – as the government well knows. Some people I interviewed even accused it of connivance. In 1985 Singapore counterfeiters stole recordings from America alone valued at $220,000,000. That assessment comes from the International Intellectual Property Alliance – composed of the trade organisations of US publishers, film producers and computer manufacturers – in a report prepared for an American review of those countries hoping to enjoy in 1986 a trade benefit system run by America and officially known as the Generalised System of Preferences (GSP). The total value of the 'intellectual' theft committed by Singapore's pirates was $358,000,000, and that in one year alone. The report summarised its findings on an island country of 2,500,000 people with the statement 'Singapore is truly the world capital of piracy.'

It was certainly from Singapore that the stealing of the pop world's attempts to stem the Ethiopian tragedy was organised. And the chief organiser was a multi-millionaire Indonesian-Chinese named Joseph Gondobintoro. It was Gondobintoro whose myriad companies reproduced the Live Aid concert, some in eight-volume cassette packs, others in well-designed long-playing record cases containing twelve LPs. Although any accurate figure has been impossible to establish, the worldwide monitoring of the International Federation of Phonogram and Videogram Producers suggests that Gondobintoro succeeded in selling 'well over' a million of his composite packs. Saudi Arabia was a huge purchaser, exceeded only by Nigeria where Gondobintoro has a manufacturing plant. Libya was another ready customer and so were Greece, Egypt, India and Pakistan.

The cynicism of Singapore's supposed official awareness of Gondobintoro's activities is matched – topped, even – by that of his Indonesian homeland. Upon those illegal cassettes which have been seized the authorities have found a stamp showing that the Indonesian government – which has no legislation forbidding such counterfeiting – imposes and receives a tax on every one.

Two of Gondobintoro's companies are Orly International Pte Ltd and Panwell (Pte) Ltd. They share the same Singapore address at 108 Robinson Road. Panwell – a company with a $15,000,000 capitalisation – has a factory which imports from South Korea the wax necessary for the manufacture of counterfeit records. Orly International is the export facility through which Gondobintoro ships either counterfeited or blank tapes and record wax to his company in Nigeria – Pancos Industry Nigeria Ltd at 27 Allon Avenue Ikeja, Lagos 49, Marina Block B. Gondobintoro is also the sole agent in Indonesia for Maxell blank tapes and Teac equipment.

Gondobintoro was not the only Singapore counterfeiter of the pop efforts to raise millions for the African famine. Geldof's original Band Aid single was stolen by a company registered on the island as Supreme and owned by a Chinese named John Aw. The International Federation of Phonogram and Videogram Producers orchestrated a publicity campaign to embarrass the government of Lee Kuan Yew. The effect, however, was not a move against the pirates but against the retail outlets, several of which were fined. Another of the pirate companies is Sound Technic (Pte) Ltd, active in blank tape and recording wax production. In 1982 one of Sound Technic's directors, Ng Teow Chye, established a cassette tape factory in Nigeria.

Neither Supreme nor Sound Technics are as big a pirating organisation, however, as Rainbow Sound Enterprise whose registered address is 6-C Golden Wall Flatted Fty Y, Jalan Rajah, Singapore. Producers of pirate labels Concert, AMQ and AMB, they were identified to me by investigators as consistently holding in 1981, 1982 and 1983 second place in the counterfeiting league behind Gondobintoro, whose labels include King, Billboard, Joker and Queen. Proprietors of Rainbow Sound Enterprise are

Tan Siew Hong and Chong Loy Seu. Chong Loy Seu is also a partner in another firm, Japantax.

An indication of the scale of the Singapore operation comes from Ertegun. 'Pirates in Singapore refuse orders for less than a containerload, which is 180,000 cassettes.' The majority of these containers are addressed to Nigeria, a one hundred per cent pirate market which has been cornered by the Singapore manufacturers. In 1984 – the last year of available statistics – 35,000,000 tapes were bought by Nigeria at a loss to the American industry alone of $120,000,000. The total that year was 50,000,000 illegal tapes exported worldwide from Singapore.

Some were straight 'lifts' – copies of an existing hit. Others – like the tapes of Band Aid, USA for Africa and Live Aid – were the product of what is known in the industry as bootlegging: the creation of a long-playing cassette or record which did not previously exist, for the simple reason that it could not. Geldof explains that because so many of the international artists who agreed to appear were separately contracted and legally bound to record companies and management agencies, a specific undertaking had to be given that no tapes or LPs would be produced. A streetwise man with no illusions, Geldof accepted that they would inevitably be stolen; he actually appealed at the Live Aid performance for the copiers to make a contribution – which they did not, of course. When Gondobintoro's bootlegging was exposed he changed the cover of the cassette – attractively designed so that the shape of Africa was created from an actual photograph of the packed Life Aid audience into the rough outline of a guitar body – to suggest that all proceeds from the sale were going to the African famine victims after all. 'Fucking rubbish,' was Geldof's response, a man so honest that sometimes it is easy to wish he would lie a little. 'Everything being earned by the Singapore pirates is going where it's always gone, into their own fucking pockets.'

The pirates have even created their own protection society to fight, as they invariably do, the rare cases of piracy brought against them under the archaic and hopelessly outdated legislation empowered under the Imperial British Copyright Act of 1911, locally amended in 1914 by the Copyright (Gramophone, Records and Government Broadcasting) Act of 1968. Called the Sound Tape Retailers' Association, it is funded by a $200 levy raised on each of the hundreds of retailers selling the pirated tapes. Exacted monthly, it goes to create a fighting fund against prosecution. A legal advisor to the Association has been Laurence Wee. His father, Wee Chong Jin, is the Chief Justice of Singapore. The report of the International Intellectual Property Alliance talks of Singapore being 'a haven for piracy' and continues:

> The government has not only condoned the theft of foreign works for consumption domestically (attempting to justify it on educational, scientific and development grounds) but has looked away as its pirates have exported millions of dollars of pirated works throughout the world. Pirates in Singapore are well-organised and are thought to be linked to a network operating in other Asian countries, including Malaysia and Pakistan.

In 1984, it has been established, 13,220,408 blank tapes – valued at $16,720,000 – were imported for pirating for the domestic market alone. Ninety per cent of that local market bought pirated instead of legitimately produced tapes. The American record industry assesses the lost sales to be $50,000,000 domestically and $170,000,000 worldwide. Singapore's export market produces statistics which are even more staggering. The International Federation put at 540,000,000 the number of pirated sound recordings in 1984, worth $1,200,000,000. Sales of $350,000,000 were monitored in Asia and Australasia; the same amount was recorded in Africa, the Middle East and the Mediterranean. The $125,000,000 counterfeited tape trade in Nigeria made it the biggest customer in Africa. Saudi Arabia, by spending $108,000,000, topped the league in the Middle East. America is a huge pirate purchaser, with sales of $320,000,000: in that year, the Anti-Piracy Unit of the Recording Industry Association of America reported the seizure of $78,000,000 worth of illegal sound and video recording equipment being used by US pirates. In Western Europe, $130,000,000 of pirate recordings were sold. Spaniards spent $28,000,000, heading the illicit market, but Italy was a big spender at $16,000,000: the specially packaged LP set of the Live Aid performance was seized entering through the port of La Spezia. Piracy is big business in Greece, with an annual turnover of $11,300,000: in February 1985 George Mikrellis was jailed for six and a half years for cassette piracy. Mikrellis was a former director of the Greek Copyright Protection Society, the country's anti-piracy organisation.

Singapore is not the only country of recording pirates, just the biggest. Turkey has a pirate recording industry; so does Japan, Taiwan, South Korea, Malaysia, Indonesia, Thailand, Malaysia, Egypt and Brazil.

In 1979 Japan achieved the distinction of being the second largest market in the world for records and prerecorded tapes, a distinction it has held ever since. In 1983 – the last period for which the figures are available – sales of record singles and LPs reached 63,400,000 and there were 78,200,000 tapes sold. Unique to Japan is the use of 'karaoke' tapes. These are available in bars, restaurants and taxis and consist of the backing music only to songs sung by internationally known groups: the idea is to allow the customer the fun of performing in the stars' place. It is not illegal, although under international convention it is a form of counterfeiting. More obvious counterfeiting flourished, until a bill was passed in the Diet in June 1984. Ideal conditions were provided by record shops in every major city throughout the country. By renting out tapes, they enabled the customer to record on to a blank tape at home, rather than buy a normally priced cassette. And if he or she did not want to be bothered to go home, the shops had high speed duplicators on which the customer could make their copy without having to leave the store. While indigenous Japanese recordings had legal protection against this form of abuse, the law did not cover recordings of Western origin. The only recourse left to producers involved was to injunct dealers supplying the sound copy system and, eventually, legal protection was added in the amendment to the country's copyright law which came into force in January 1985. What the record industry cannot satisfactorily halt is the huge amount of private copying carried on at home. As long ago as 1983 a survey indicated that 800,000,000 LPs a year were being counterfeited in Japan in this way.

The United States' Generalised System of Preferences has been proven internationally to be the most effective weapon with which to fight worldwide piracy. The purpose of the report brought out by the International Intellectual Property Alliance was to demonstrate to the ten worst counterfeiting countries that unless there were reforms the system of trading preferences would be changed by an impatient American Congress.

Chief beneficiary of the system is a country which does not officially exist, an absurd reversal of the situation that obtained until President Richard Nixon's historic visit to Peking when the Communist China of Mao Tse-tung was the enemy denied official recognition and the nationalistic régime in Taiwan of Chiang Kai-shek was the real China. With the international normalisation of relationships after the death of Mao, Peking – or, more properly, Beijing – became the city to which the West posted its ambassadors, transferring them from Taipei. Compounding the stupidity of this curious head-in-the- sand diplomacy, those diplomatic connections which still exist between Taiwan and the West cannot be acknowledged. There is no Taiwanese embassy or consulate in London, for instance. But there is an organisation called the Majestic Trading Company, staffed by diplomats with whom the Foreign Office maintains a working relationship while denying it does so.

This diplomatic version of musical chairs has not affected Taiwan's position as the biggest beneficiary of the US Generalised System of Preferences, which in 1984 allowed Taipei to export to America $3,200,000,000 worth of duty-free goods. Nor has it affected Taiwan's popular status as the most active counterfeiting country in Asia. In 1984 its tape piracy was authoritatively valued at $25,100,000, with an extra $2,700,000 from ripped-off LPs and records. Aware it could lose its favoured GSP status – and frightened also of much needed foreign financial investment not being attracted to such a notorious copying nation – by 1985 Taiwan was prepared to make some public gesture against counterfeiting. But couldn't. As a non-existent country, it was not permitted to declare itself party to either of the international agreements that would have empowered it to put its house in order: they are the International Union for the protection of Literary and Artistic Works, signed in Bern in 1886, and the Universal Copyright Convention, determined in Geneva in 1952. So in June 1985 Taiwan passed its own copyright act. Predictably – almost inevitably – there was a catch. To be protected, foreign works have to be registered in Taiwan and the country reserves the right to deny such registration or recognition. As a further indication of goodwill, Taiwan has established a National Anti-Counterfeiting Committee of Industry and Commerce whose function is to respond to and resolve complaints of infringements.

That International Intellectual Property Alliance report – as was only sensible given the contradictions – questioned whether the Copyright Act and the Anti-Counterfeiting Committee 'are not more in the nature of a public relations effort than a serious attempt to deal substantively with what is a very pervasive problem'. The answer – to a rather thickly worded question – is undoubtedly 'Yes – it is public relations and nothing more.'

I have frequently heard that word pervasive used to describe the stealing initiated in Indonesia, where the multi-millionaire counterfeiter Joseph Gondobintoro has influential friends within the government which – by the most conservative of estimates – has received $300,000 in tax from the bootlegged Live Aid tape. Another estimate, again conservative, is that in 1984 the value of pirated tapes emanating from the country was $70,000,000. Those American investigators into GSP allocations had to admit in their 1985 report that it was unclear to them whether Indonesia offered any specific protection to sound recordings under a 1982 domestic copyright act which only protects foreign works if they are published or produced first in Indonesia. The country withdrew from the Bern Convention in 1952, ostensibly because they did not want to go through the 'delays and burdens' of getting translation or adaptation rights from the copyright owners. What the GSP investigators did discover was that pirated tapes and records were of a very high quality, excellently packaged and sold at less than $2. Indonesia's entire domestic market consists of pirated tapes; every year 25,000,000 are produced. In addition, 30,000,000 are turned out for export. The international music industry says that means a total yearly loss of $180,000,000.

In an attempt to comply with the 1982 Copyright Act – and plug the loss – the International Federation of Phonogram and Videogram Producers employed lawyers to explore the possibility of international recording companies establishing local companies to which master copies of a recording could be licensed, enabling records and tapes to be produced 'first' in Indonesia. The legal opinion was that local investment laws made it impossible. Local laws also prevented an international company from entering into a joint publishing venture with an Indonesian company.

South Korea is the second largest beneficiary – after Taiwan – of the American GSP programme: in 1984 it sold $1,500,000,000 worth of goods duty-free in the United States, with which it has a

$3,500,000,000 trade surplus. The other distinction it shares with Taiwan is that of being one of the major centres of piracy in the world. Pirated tapes account for sixty per cent of domestic sales, which is worth $40,000,000 a year. There is a Phonogram and Motion Picture Law, passed in 1967 and amended in 1984, which should protect sound recordings but it does not. The fines imposed on the few pirates brought to court average between $230 and $345 and the workings of the law actually encourage rather than discourage piracy. For the purpose of the legislation is to control the importation into South Korea of foreign record masters. Thus it works as a non-tariff barrier, greatly delaying imports, with the result that pirates move in to fill the gap created by the law.

There exists in the Philippines a copyright act which, again theoretically, should protect sound recordings; but like the comparable legislation in other Asian countries, in practice it does not. One investigatory report to which I have had access openly refers to the 'lackadaisical government attitude towards intellectual property'. And that was not the only problem: the Philippino government under former President Ferdinand Marcos was one of the most corrupt in Asia and there was extensive police bribery to avoid what minimal prosecution might be considered.

The Philippino trafficking could not, however, begin to compete with the illegal profits reaped in Malaysia which are currently put at $33,000,000. Within the country, pirate recordings account for eighty per cent of the market. All the major stores openly stock counterfeit or bootlegged recordings, selling at between $2 and $3.50 – a far higher price than in Thailand. During my research visit to that country, street hawkers at Patpong and Silom Village – two neighbouring counterfeiting districts in the capital of Bangkok – were offering tapes of Madonna, Bruce Springsteen and Elton John for as little as $1; on one occasion the price went down to 50¢. Domestic sales of pirated material are not confined to street corners. As in the Philippines, all the major department stores and music shops openly stock counterfeits. Every pop tune in the international Top Ten was available in the Bangkok branch of the vast Japanese-owned Daimaru store. Within Thailand itself, the loss through piracy to the international recording industry is put at $13,000,000 – minimal compared with the damage inflicted by Nigerian piracy.

So lucrative a business is counterfeiting in Nigeria that Joseph

Gondobintoro and Ng Chye have established local factories to meet the colossal demand. In 1982 – the year Chye set up his operation in Lagos – no legitimate music cassettes were manufactured or sold in the country, but sales of $22,000,000 were recorded. By 1984 a minimum of 35,000,000 tapes had been sold and quite openly, through retail stores in the major cities, at an estimated profit of $120,000,000. It has been suggested to me that the income was nearer $125,000,000. Sales of 'Band Aid', 'USA for Africa' and 'Live Aid' throughout 1985 and 1986 are expected to increase that figure by at least half.

Bode Akinyemi is the managing director for EMI in Lagos and the local president of the International Federation of Phonogram and Videogram Producers. He told me: 'The problem is an immense one. The vast size of my country – with borders virtually impossible to police or seal – is matched by the huge demand for music, be it on tape or record. Everybody – and I mean *everybody* – listens to music and wants the latest hit, as soon as it becomes a hit. And they don't care where it comes from, as long as they have it.' The current government, insisted Mr Akinyemi, was doing its best to stamp out the illicit business, through a programme called War Against Indiscipline. Through his own commercial outlets, Mr Akinyemi tries to monitor the creation of pirate factories or distribution centres, 'And when I discover them, I make sure the police take action. Under previous governments, any action was difficult because of the widespread corruption which existed but now that is improving.'

In Lagos an ad hoc organisation has been formed composed of all the industries in the country affected by piracy, calling itself the Nigerian Anti-Piracy Action Committee. They have submitted to the government suggested legislation under which a pirate convicted on a first offence would be liable to five years' imprisonment and a fine of approximately $1300. Under existing laws, even second time offenders only risk either two months in jail or a fine of 65¢. The international music industry is hopeful that the reform will be enacted under the present régime, headed by Chief of Staff Brigadier Idiagbon.

While an obvious improvement over existing legislation and maybe a deterrent to local copiers, it will not, however, affect the Singapore pirates who continue exporting as actively as ever. Just how actively was illustrated at the end of 1984 when customs in the

Benin port of Cotonou seized 190,000 pirate cassettes. They had been manufactured in Singapore on a GMI label and featured recordings by Bob Marley, Michael Jackson, Dolly Parton, Marvin Gaye, Smokie, Evelyn King, Boney M and Abba. Investigators believe the shipment was intended for smuggling into Nigeria and the Benin authorities promised action under a newly passed copyright act. Mr Saibou, head of the Benin Copyright Office, said that his government would 'use the full force of the law to protect the Beninois musical culture from attempts by the pirates of Southeast Asia to destroy it'.

Elsewhere throughout the world, legislation is being formulated to help protect the international music industry and prove wrong Nesuhi Ertegun's dismal forecast that in ten years' time there will not be any recorded music left to tape. In autumn 1984 the California State Legislature passed a bill against bootlegging. Under the new statute, the penalty for making or manufacturing bootlegged tapes or records is one year's imprisonment or a $25,000 fine, or both. And in October of the same year the US Congress passed the federally effective Record Rental Bill, prohibiting the rental of records without the permission of the copyright owners, so stopping the sort of home copying so prevalent in Japan. In India, a new copyright amendment law came into force in September 1984. The intention was to initiate an all-out attack on the vast local pirate industry which feeds ninety per cent of the home market and is estimated to be worth $67,000,000 a year. Referring to the increased criminal penalties and the powers conferred on police to seize counterfeit copies and the equipment on which they were duplicated, the Indian phonographic industry hailed the new law, as 'a landmark in the conscious anti-piracy legislative effort in our country'.

Following the Harare seminar on 'Copyright and Neighbouring Rights', held in February 1985, the international bodies of the music industry are hopeful that laws will be passed in Zimbabwe to prevent it developing like Nigeria. There is hope, too, that similar legislation will be introduced into Communist China which, in April 1985, had its first live exposure to Western pop with the visit of Wham! Sales of single and EP records average out at 115,000,000 a year, making China the third largest record market in the world – although tape sales are only 10,000,000 a year. Currently, piracy is in name controlled by what is known as

Regulation 154, enforced by the Office of Audiogram and Videogram Products of the Ministry of Broadcasting. The size of the country and the office's inexperience of copying has resulted in the development of a substantial pirate industry in Beijing and other major cities.

In February 1985 the British government published a consultative Green Paper called 'The Recording and Rental of Audio and Video Copyright Material' with the announcement that they were 'inclined to the view that a levy should be introduced to remunerate copyright owners for unauthorised copying of their material'. Among the recommendations then welcomed as offering major improvements was the imposition of a royalty on blank tapes, in return for which people in their homes would have the legal right to make audio and video recordings for their personal use. The Green Paper suggested a royalty – to be negotiated between the copyright holders and the blank tape industry – of ten per cent on the retail price for an audio tape and five per cent for a video tape. The feeling within the industry is that these royalty levels are too low, to which the government's answer is that at such a level there will be no damage caused to the blank tape market and that, estimated on 1984 prices, the percentages will mean an increase in income for the music and video industries in the order of £5,000,000 each per year.

In May 1985 the West German Bundestag passed a copyright bill incorporating the sort of blank tape royalty which Britain was considering at the time. Currently at 6¢ for a ninety minute audio cassette and 17¢ for a three hour video tape, the royalty figures will be reviewed every three years. The new bill joins existing legislation which imposes a levy on recording hardware – 80¢ for audio equipment and $6 for video recorders – putting Germany in the forefront of the European attempt to repair the worst ravages of piracy. The first European country to introduce the blank tape royalty, it was followed within months by France. In Britain, second, politically motivated thoughts were supervening.

European tape and record sales are cosmic, representing the second largest market in the world. In 1983, for example, the legitimate sales in the then ten member states of the Common Market amounted to $2,776,600,000, against those of the world leader – the United States – which total $3,800,000,000. The industry estimates that every year record pirates earn $100,000,000 on the backs of European companies. Behind Spain and Italy in the league table comes the United Kingdom, whose share of the counterfeit market stands at $12,000,000, with Greece close behind. Pirates earn $10,600,000 a year out of Germany and $8,400,000 from France. And the effect is not seen alone in the falling legitimate revenue of the producers. Lost sales – sales in Europe peaked at $3,600,000,000 in 1978 but have been declining ever since – mean contraction within the industry and large unemployment figures. In 1980 6975 new pop record albums were produced in France. By 1982 the figure had dropped to 6154. Over the same period in Germany the drop was from 1367 to 1140.

Although the Netherland's percentage of pirate production – $1,400,000 in 1984 – is minimal compared with some of its European neighbours, it is regarded by investigators as the main conduit through which the massive suppliers of counterfeit tapes and records pass. Of all the European countries, the Netherlands has the weakest anti-counterfeiting laws, making it the safest doorway through which to enter.

Within the Common Market, there are two pieces of legislation additional to the Bern Convention of 1886 and the Geneva Convention of 1952 through which the recording industry can protect its legitimate output. They are the Convention for the Protection of Performers, Producers of Phonogram and Broadcasting Organisations, signed in Rome in 1961, and the Convention for the Protection of Producers of Phonograms Against Unauthorised Duplication of their Phonograms, concluded in Geneva in 1971. The International Federation of Producers consistently urges its members, through the lobbying of their respective governments, to get those governments to ratify the additional conventions so as to enable European-wide action against the counterfeiters. The Federation – and Britain – is also pressing at the time of writing for a concerted anti-counterfeiting agreement throughout the EEC beyond those covered by the international conventions. Further, Britain is arguing for such agreements to be extended through the General Agreement on Tariff and Trade, an international trading code to which the elusive Indonesia is a signatory.

Jeremy Hanley is a British Conservative MP – for the constituency of Richmond and Barnes – and an eloquent advocate for an international tightening of counterfeiting laws. When we met, he said: 'International piracy and theft of copyrighted works is a disease of massive proportions. It must be attacked.' Pop star Paul Young unwittingly – and, had he known of the abuse of his copyright, most certainly unwillingly – expressed the same imperative in a song bootlegged on the 'Do They Know It's Christmas?' tape created for the Singapore Supreme label by pirate John Aw. The track was 'Everything Must Change'.

The problem is that everything is not changing, despite international pressure and even despite American threats of withdrawing favoured trading national status – not for multi-billion-dollar sound recordings nor for any of the other multi-billion-dollar products from which the untouched and untroubled counterfeiters successfully make their own billions.

CHAPTER TWELVE

The Rotten Apple

The logo of the Apple personal computer, that garage-born revolution in home-based communication, is a juicy piece of the fruit with a bite taken out. It seemed cute and appropriate when Silicon Valley founders Steven Jobs and Stephen Wozniak evolved it in 1976; five years later they were to learn just how appropriate. As I pointed out in Chapter Six, no other hi-tech company in the world has had more bites taken out of it than Apple and Taiwan is the counterfeiting country which has found it most toothsome – despite its anti-counterfeiting organisation and Taipei government assurances that it intends ridding the country of its counterfeiting stigma by swingeing legal crackdowns and the establishment of its own innovative technological industries.

Creation of those industries is centred at a science-based industrial park at Hsinchu, fifty miles south of the Taiwanese capital, where the government is nurturing a number of local hi-tech firms by ploughing back into the park forty-nine per cent of the equity. Starting in 1980, Taiwan approached leading technological firms throughout the world and invited them to establish their own factories at Hsinchu. Apple was one of those approached. Already in operation at the science park is a government-backed Taiwanese firm named Multitec. It makes computers known as Microprocessor II, III and IV. All are one hundred per cent counterfeits of Apple designs.

Recalling the company's rejection of such an amazingly cynical offer, Apple's Vice-President, Secretary and General Counsel Albert Eisenstat says: 'I asked the question: is it getting too hard for you to find the units to copy? We will make it a little easier for you. They didn't appreciate that humour, that attempted humour.' Not that Eisenstat considers there is anything amusing in the thirty different Asian counterfeiter companies – investigators believe there are probably more – copying Apple products. He said, 'I use the characterisation of we feel a little bit like the Dutch boy sticking his finger in the dyke. We plug up one and he takes his inventory apart that wasn't seized – and that is probably most of it – and he opens up twenty feet away under a new name and perhaps with new corporate officers.' Eisenstat finds it difficult to assess the amount of money Apple has spent plugging holes in dikes, but talks of 'several million dollars'.

Guan Haur Industrial Co. Ltd, in Jin Jou Street, Taipei, was one Taiwanese company against which Apple successfully took legal action. It was producing a computer called Golden 11 and sending out an operating manual identical word for word to that written by Wozniak, except that Apple had been changed for Golden throughout. Another was the Sunrise Computer Service Co. Ltd of Hsing 1 Road, which named its rip-off Apolo while openly referring to Apple in Chinese advertisements. Ideal Computer Engineering Co. of Sung Chiang Road is another counterfeiter. So is the Apollo Computer Company, which operates out of Chung Hsiao E. Road. Space Electronic Enterprise Co. Ltd, which also operates out of Chung Hsiao E. Road, offers a complete range of computing equipment, including the most successful Apple II. GGM, with Taipei Box No. 53, actually boast their counterfeit computer's suitability for all Apple software. Jardine Strauss International Ltd, another company headquartered in the Chung Hsiao E. Road hotbed, enthusiastically advertised: 'Here Comes a perfect micro computer to improve your dady (sic) life. Has the function and appearance as perfect as Apple II.'

Jardine Strauss's advertisement also points out the advantage of buying a Taiwan counterfeit as against the genuine article. The Taiwan rip-off price is $599. Apple computers sell for $1449. And Jardine Strauss are always willing to fudge the documentation to deal with such minor irritations as customs or tax requirements. Doris Hoffman, who lives at E. 17th St in the New York district of Brooklyn, bought a Strauss copy in September 1982. Acknowledging her order, which subsequently arrived piecemeal, Jardine Strauss President Karl Len wrote – and I quote verbatim: 'Your micro-computer just fresh finish and shall send you by air mail, so you shall save freight fee meantime we shall invoice under value so maybe you can save tax or import duty if any.' As good as his promise, Mr Len's invoice described the computer as a sample of no commercial value and marked it down to $100.

The Taiwanese entrepreneurs have even created American outlets. The Taiwan Machinery Trading Co. set up backroom headquarters in Belfield Avenue, Philadelphia. They called themselves Machine World Inc and in 1982 announced at a Chicago computer trade fair that they had copies of Apple II for sale. An Apple attorney, Gary Hecker, who was to be a very busy man, telephoned Belfield Avenue on the pretence of buying one and having it shipped across the country to California. Alberto Chua took the call and was tape-recorded as saying, 'Well, what we're doing is not exactly legal. We do it just for people we know.'

Chua was Vice-President of the Taiwan Machinery Trading Co. In March 1983 Customs at Oakland, California, seized a package being sent through the United States mail. It was addressed to Chua at his home in Saratoga Road, King of Prussia, Philadelphia. The return address was listed as Keh Manufacturing Ind. Co. The letterhead of Taiwan Machinery Trading Co. also carried the name Keh Manufacturing Ind. Co. Alphonso Keh is listed as another vice-president of TMTC.

Even drug dealers branched out into the lucrative Apple scam. Drugs were, in fact, what Philadelphia undercover narcotics policeman Charles Scanzello expected to find when he went in March 1983 to the apartment at 2491 N 50th St, belonging to a dealer named Joel Isadore. There were drugs – Dilaudid pills – but there were far more computer components, carefully arranged on shelves factory-fashion. There were manuals and brochures, too, and all for Apple II. While Scanzello was in the apartment, ostensibly just another drug addict, more computer parts were delivered. One of the gang was in a side room assembling the shelved components and another was on the telephone in the kitchen, discussing prices with interested customers. The sign on the doorbell of Isadore's apartment read, 'National Merchandising, Inc.'

As a result of what Scanzello saw on that mission, undercover Customs investigator Joseph Heath telephoned Isadore on 17 March 1983. The conversation was recorded. Isadore answered the telephone with the word 'National' and when Heath asked about products, Isadore said, 'What we have is an exact duplicate of the Apple II Plus.' They then set up a meeting at an apartment in Society Hill Towers, on the appropriately named Locust Street. It was the home of Daniel Ryan, who was present at the meeting; so were Scanzello, Joel Isadore and a relation, Martin Isadore. Joseph Heath was bodywired with a Nagra sound system. It worked well.

Joel Isadore is heard to say that what he was offering from Taiwan were 'the finest electronic components'. He made a suggestion for a sales pitch – 'The best way to describe it is to say it's an Apple.' Apple II but not actually made by Apple, suggested Heath. Joel Isadore replied, 'Exactly. Exactly, that's what it is.' Then the recording has him say, 'We copied it down to the finest detail . . . I mean we got all the software you ever want, by the way . . . we have it made in Taiwan . . . the disks, the manuals . . . total copyright infringement.'

There was a lot more discussion, during which Heath and Scanzello came to believe the method of smuggling from Taiwan involved shipping the fake Apples in pieces spread about boxes containing machinery. Determined to obtain convicting evidence for the subsequently successful prosecutions, Heath said to Martin Isadore: 'Joel was saying they're coming in in machinery?'

Martin Isadore replied: 'Did Joel tell you that?'

'Yeah,' is the response from Heath.

Martin Isadore: 'It's a real spy story . . . it's a real spy story.'

The counterfeit Apples did not only arrive mixed up with machinery. In some cases they were quite openly shipped to prestigious institutions – something which was only discovered when they were by mistake intercepted in the United States. One such end-user turned out to be the Royal Bank of Canada at the Alberta International Centre on 8th Av. SW, Calgary. Joseph Leung, who operated from 96th Av., Edmonton, Alberta, was the importer. His supplier was the Sunya Corp., whose address is Alley 20 Lane, Wu Hsing St, Taipei; his product, the Golden II computers made by Guan Haur Industrial Co. Ltd. The order comprised ten Golden IIs which would have been processing bank details in Calgary today but for the mistake of Sea-Land Services Inc., the shippers. The company unloaded them from the freighter *Freedom* not at the consigned Canadian port of Vancouver, but dangerously further south at Seattle in America's Washington State.

Apart from spending its millions in litigation, Apple has also taken the precaution of filing its copyright with US Customs, which enables it legally to seize and impound any counterfeits it uncovers – as it did the Royal Bank of Canada's consignment. The bank protested. On 22 April 1983 one of its officials, John Williamson, wrote a letter to Robert Hardy, District Director of US Customs in Seattle. In this letter, to which I have access, Mr Williamson pointed it out that delivery had been made to the wrong place, reminded Mr Hardy that unloading should properly have taken place at Vancouver and concluded in his last paragraph: 'We therefore petition your indulgence in releasing the goods and have Sea-Land Service perform the necessary shipment to Vancouver, BC'. US Customs did not do that. But through an incredible loophole that at the time existed in the copyright law, it did the next best thing: it returned the counterfeit Apples to Sunya. Investigators believe they arrived intact and were re-exported – within days – to Europe.

It was not an isolated occurrence. Also seized in Seattle through an off-loading mistake were 108 Golden II computers, this time shipped from Berlin International Inc., Manking Easy Rd, Section 2, Taipei – their destination, Spirale Computers Ltd, of Rue Peel, Montreal, Canada. The president of Spirale Computers was Mr A. Chen. Once more US Customs determined that Mr Chen did not realise he was trading in counterfeit products and allowed the return of the 108 fakes to Taiwan.

Those investigators advising the American government on its GSP programme estimated that from fake software alone Taiwan makes $34,000,000 a year. Judging from the discussions I had – both officially and unofficially – during my research period in Taipei, I understand the additional hardware loss to bona fide manufacturers to be in the region of $50,000,000. Less than one hour after leaving the offices of Government Prosecutor Derek Cheng, who assured me that the counterfeiting of Apple and other computers was effectively being halted, I wandered the three-tiered market in Chung Hwa Rd and its tributaries of Layong St, Kaifeng St, Hankow St, Wuchang St, Hengang Rd and Chengtu Rd. I counted twenty Apple II Plus machines and fifteen IBM personal computers, and then gave up because it seemed pointless arithmetic.

Smarting under the US International Trade Commission finding that in 1984 Taiwan was responsible overall for sixty per cent of the counterfeit goods in international trade, the Taiwan National Federation of Industries and the General Chamber of Commerce – not the government – created the National Anti-Counterfeiting Committee discussed so contemptuously by the GSP report.

The Committee, headquartered at Chungking South Rd, Section 1, proclaims its purpose is to 'assist in carrying out the clearly stated government policy against counterfeiting in the Republic of China, by promoting self-discipline in the business community and by publicising and promoting the internationally accepted concepts of industrial property rights'. There was an expensive and attractively packaged advertising campaign. The Committee printed thousands of glossy posters featuring a parrot saying – enigmatically and somewhat contradictorily, 'The parrot speaks but knows not what he says.' Less ambiguous was the slogan, 'Don't be penny wise, pound foolish.' The message was carried on the 2300 buses serving the capital and displayed in hotels, department stores, supermarkets and bus and train stations.

Committee Chairman Henry Hsu declared: 'To stop counterfeiting, not only should the manufacturers give up producing counterfeit products but consumers themselves should boycott counterfeit goods.' Executive Secretary Terry Chen told me, 'Our government has the determination to crack down on counterfeiting.' That determination, he said, went as far as their sending representatives abroad to see the extent and effect of counterfeiting – it annually costs 130,000 jobs in America alone. Further, foreign businessmen are invited to lecture Taiwanese industrialists on the harm being caused.

The American dream had soured a little for Apple by 1985. Stephen Wozniak left the company to return to academe and Steven Jobs also parted from it, in some acrimony over suggestions that he was doing that most common of things in Silicon Valley – forming a new company by hiring former Apple employees. In his letter of resignation as Chairman, Jobs said: 'The company appears to be adopting a hostile posture towards me and the new venture. Some company representatives have said they fear I will use proprietary Apple technology in my new venture. There is no basis for any such concern.' Vice-chairman Michael Marrkkula responded that Apple were considering what 'possible action should be taken to assure protection of Apple's technology and assets'.

By 1985 bitter experience, beginning in 1981, had made the company expert at fending off such threats. By that time Apple had grown out of its garage and into a company able to invest $100,000,000 in research and rightly regarded itself as the leader in home computers. A large factory geared to supply the Common Market was built on the Holly Hill Industrial Estate, at Cork, in Ireland. The printed circuit boards – both for America and Europe – were manufactured in another factory at the Ang Mo Kio Industrial Park in Singapore. These were the official factories. Unofficially, dozens of backstreet counterfeiters were in business, too. Later their locations were described as garage shops. Eisenstat recognises the irony and says ruefully, 'We shouldn't knock that because the roots of Apple go back to the same source.'

Initially – a fact partly responsible for Apple's slow recognition of the scam and consequently delayed reactions – the counterfeit computers sold in Asia without intruding on to the American or European markets. The Ideal Engineering Co., in Taipei's Sung Chiang Rd, created a profitable outlet with the MicroGram Computer Co. of Castle Peak Rd, Kowloon, in Hong Kong. They quoted a purchase price of $230 for a complete unit but insisted on a minimum order of twenty computers. The Reliant (Engineering) Co. traded Taiwan-supplied fake Apples from a box number – 33610 – at Hong Kong's Sheung Wan Post Office. Their price for a fully tested computer was $600 although, like MicroGram Computers, they bought at source for $230, awarding themselves a respectable mark-up. Reliant's literature openly acknowledged the Apple trademark as belonging to the American company.

The counterfeiters cynically retained the generic naming principle proper to Silicon Valley products. One Apple rip-off was named 'Orange'; another, 'Lemon'; yet another, 'Pineapple'. Guan Haur Industrial Co. really tried with their Golden II, plucked from the variety of apple called Golden Delicious.

Eisenstat had the scale of the counterfeiting problem visually brought home to him in 1983, by which time the company had initiated a series of lawsuits, forty at least, to put a stop to the bites being taken out of the apple. He remembered:

I visited the famed Sham Shui Po shopping centre in Hong

Kong. This is a loft building of perhaps four floors with perhaps two hundred stalls in them. The stalls are perhaps a hundred square feet. You could have bought in over a hundred different stalls imitation Apple computers, all essentially the same, but not necessarily from the same manufacturer ... I could easily purchase one of these counterfeit Apples for anywhere between a fourth to a third to half the price of a real Apple. For an additional ten dollars I learned I could purchase an Apple nameplate to make the unit look like a real Apple. With the counterfeit computer business booming, large firms have now moved into the computer copying business and have geared up to produce and distribute infringing computers in the United States by the thousands.

Apple give March 1982 as the month when the counterfeit influx began, from Taiwan into the United States. The copies of the boom-selling Apple II were identical to the prototype in every detail – the same circuit board, software and lookalike case. And there was always the ten-dollar fake nameplate to complete the fraud.

By now Apple had awakened to the dangers it was facing. With fake Apple computers dominating the Far East market, outselling the genuine article by an estimated four to one, it was time to take legal action and a Harvard-educated lawyer named C. V. Chen was retained in Taiwan to fight the counterfeiters at source. His understanding of local conditions was to prove useful: 'Most Chinese don't have a concept of intellectual property – patents, copyrights, trademarks and such – because they are just too intangible for the Chinese mind. The piracy and counterfeiting is really shameful, just like stealing, but people don't see it as such.'

As well as filing lawsuits, Apple carried war into the enemy camp by creating a test disk for the use of customs authorities all over the world. Inserted into a computer, it identified the programme contained in the machine, isolating immediately whether it was copyrighted. But the profit from fake Apples was too vast for the pirates to be deterred either by court cases or discovery disks. They began building into their fakes a mini-computer system that scrambled the fake Apple programme against customs checks; after delivery had been made, the scrambling device was removed and the computer became fully operational. A large number of the computers that escaped detection at the point of entry were later detected by Apple investigators. When tested it was found that out of about 12,000 lines of genuine Apple computer code, generally fewer than 25 lines had been changed. And those changes were simply to alter the name of the computer thrown up on the visual display unit and some of the immediate introductory words on that unit.

The energetic Guan Haur Industrial Co. Ltd, their Hong Kong outlets established and already working well through the Sham Shui Po shopping centre, moved into America. One of their outlet companies was Collins International Trading Corps, based at Encino, California; it handled the Orange computer. On the East Coast Guan Haur had North American Research at Alexandria, Virginia, which sold the adroitly named Golden II computer and another, departing from Silicon Valley tradition, entitled Mind II. It was a copy of Apple, like all the rest. The new recruits were forceful salespeople. Before Apple discovered the trail, North American representatives had put on sales displays for the NASA Space Centre and the Westinghouse Corporation.

For all its enterprise in countering the predators, Apple are fighting against heavy odds. The scale of the problem is enormous: the company have entered into lawsuits in Australia, New Zealand, South Africa, Italy, France, Germany, Holland and Britain. And even when Apple wins, as it did against Guan Haur and Sunrise, the penalty is no deterrent. The Taiwanese trial ended in an injunction forbidding either company to continue the manufacture of Apple counterfeits and a $25,000 fine – but no jail sentences. Apple's unawarded costs in bringing the case were $150,000. In the same context in which he talks of spending 'several million dollars' trying to defeat the pirates, Eisenstat says: 'Our legal costs, to say the least, are astronomical and you are tilting at windmills, at least with a very illusory defence. You stop one but you are really not stopping the problem.'

Apple continue their legal fight against infringement. It may cost millions but at least – at the time of writing – it has never cost a life. The Chinese Triads, however, who control the organised crime throughout much of the Asian counterfeiting countries, are quite prepared to kill. They have even organised fund-raising rallies to procure the contract money.

CHAPTER THIRTEEN

The Killer Pirates

The Chinese name is Huk Sai Wui. The English translation is the Black Association. It is more generally known as the Triad. Originally formed in the late seventeenth century as a political resistance movement to the Manchu dynasty, the Huk Sai Wui splintered after Mao Tse-tung's 1949 victory over Chiang Kai-shek and established themselves in every type of organised crime throughout the world. The most influential Triad is K-14, formed by Chiang Kai-shek's government and taking its name from 14 Po Wah Rd, Canton, the house at which it was formed in 1945. Today its main activity – not just in the Far East but in London, New York and Amsterdam, where there are well-organised cells – is drug trafficking, mainly in the variety of heroin that can be smoked.

In Taiwan, the Triads are referred to as Hei Ser Hui which translates not as the Black Association but as the Black Market. Most prominent is the Chuk Lung-bong, or Bamboo Gang. They are killers.

In October 1984, two of the Bamboo Gang's assassins, the then leader Chen Chi-li and a henchman, Wu Tun, flew from Taipei on a killing mission. Their target was Henry Lui, a Chinese-American journalist who was someone I knew well during a period in the early 1970s when I worked in Vietnam and he was employed by various American magazines in Asia. He was a courteous, knowledgeable man who, until the 'opening up' of Communist China by the visit of President Nixon, was regarded as one of the region's foremost 'China-watchers' and there were unconfirmed reports that he was a contract employee for the CIA. By 1984, aged fifty-two, he was working on the Chinese-language *San Francisco Journal*. He wrote critically of the Taiwan government:

part of that criticism concerned Taipei's apparent inability – or unwillingness – to control its burgeoning counterfeiting trade. The Bamboo Gang killers trapped Lui in the garage of his home in Daly City, killing him instantly in a crossline of gunfire.

Lui's wife, Helen, claimed the assassination – for which Chen Chi-li and Wu Tun were later jailed for life – was politically motivated. The Taiwanese government issued a formal denial of any involvement. It was a denial upon which at least three enforcement officials, who must remain nameless, cast doubt.

Nor was it the first time that the Chuk Lung-bong had been found prepared to kill to preserve its counterfeit empire.

The highly successful Hong Kong-based investigatory agency Commercial Trademark Service Ltd has an office in Taipei from which in 1981 agent Geoffrey Harris was probing the extent of the country's involvement in the worldwide counterfeiting of automobile parts. He was doing too good a job. Through underworld informants, CTS heard that the Chuk Lung-bong were putting out a $25,000 contract on Harris's life and actually convening a meeting of auto-part counterfeiters to raise the money. It was held in a southern district of Taipei and CTS daringly infiltrated the meeting with an agent informer. The man, a brilliant operative, remained undetected and emerged from the gathering able to identify not only the ringleaders of the murder plot but those counterfeiters willing to finance it. Evidence of the conspiracy to murder was presented to the Taiwanese police who took no official action. Instead, they visited the killers and their financiers and warned that if any harm befell Harris, they would be the first to be arrested. On that occasion, the gang took the warning seriously. Harris survived to be threatened once more – again by auto-part fakers – after accompanying police on the raid of a counterfeit factory and then going back with the case officers to a police station. Harris emerged to grab a late dinner at around eleven o'clock in the evening. His car was about a hundred yards from the police station. The moment he tried to start the vehicle, he realised it had been tampered with, to make it impossible to drive. He managed to lock the doors seconds before a gang of four men surrounded the car, leaning continuously against the horn in the hope of summoning help as they hammered on the glass. It was lucky for Harris that his car was parked so close to the station; his attackers fled when police came out to discover what all the noise was about. They were never arrested.

119

Violence is not confined to those cells of the Chuk Lung-bong specialising in fake auto-parts. It exists in that most flourishing of Taiwanese counterfeiting activities, book piracy.

The financial loss to Western publishers from books pirated in Taiwan has been put at a minimum of $110,000,000 a year. A more realistic figure is $250,000,000, which accounts for a sizeable proportion of the loss incurred worldwide – $1,000,000,000, as assessed by the International Publishers Association, although another expert assessment put it as high as $6,000,000,000. Investigators in Taiwan discovered that the government sent a trade mission to Nigeria for the express purpose of taking Nigerian orders for pirated books. One Taiwan publisher supplied a list of 155 copyrighted books available in pirated editions to the students and faculty of the University of New South Wales in Australia. Vast quantities of pirated books are exported to Singapore where pirates counterfeit the counterfeit – but on better quality paper this time – before distributing them in container loads throughout Africa, the Middle East and Asia.

A complete domestic industry has arisen adjacent to the University of Taiwan, concentrated around Hsinsben South Rd, Section 3, and Hsinhai Rd, Sections 1 and 2. The area – costing technical publishers $8,000,000 a year – is a grey and white sprawl of tiny alleys ribboning off a market street selling every other sort of counterfeit article in addition to books. In two days, highly detailed and technical textbooks normally priced at £20 are photocopied, bound and put on the streets for £4. Some Taiwanese schools have their own photocopy machines manned by students whose task is to duplicate entire books and journals in sufficient numbers to service whole classes. The paper has a high acid content, which results in a rapid deterioration. But its useful life is long enough for whatever courses the students are taking and when the books become unusable the prototype is always available for recopying.

Despite protestations of innocence, the Taiwan government is quite as aware of what is going on – if not quite as actively involved – as it was in the case of Harris and the auto-part manufacturers. It must be, considering how prominently the piracy is displayed. I found a stack of counterfeit copies of my own *KGB* book prominently for sale at Caves Books Ltd at 103 Chung Shan North Rd, Section 2, Taipei. An international bookstore open seven days a week, Caves proclaim themselves to be the sellers of 'New English titles, textbooks for all subjects, imported and local magazines, records and cassette tapes, greeting cards and brass placques, tickets for cultural events.'

Caves Books Ltd appear to have set themselves the goal of stocking every major Western author, whether 'serious' or popular, in pirated editions. In fifteen minutes I counted pirated books by Norman Mailer, Philip Roth, Arthur Miller, Anthony Burgess, Graham Greene, Jackie Collins, Jeffrey Archer, Jack Higgins, Boris Pasternak, John Barron, Shakespeare, Leslie Thomas and Len Deighton. There were many more, but I gave up counting. Len Deighton is a friend, so I bought a copy of his *Berlin Game* as well as my own *KGB* as souvenirs. Both had been stolen by Chen Ming Hwei, whose company was listed as the Huang Chia Book Store. For *KGB* they had even taken out an official Taiwanese government licensing number – 1197 – assigning themselves the ownership.

Visitors departing Taiwan are subject to an extensive baggage check and though I complied, the books – in my wife's shoulder bag – were missed by the customs which makes them pretty well unique. For the purpose of the minutely thorough customs sweep is to discover examples of counterfeiting being taken out of the country. Had the two stolen books been found, customs would have razor-slit the proof of Chen Ming Hwei's theft from the bound copies, leaving me with no legal evidence of it ever having taken place. On arrival in Hong Kong, I learned from copyright and trademark lawyers that I had been luckier than I had originally imagined in getting the intact books out of the country. Had I bought more than one copy of each book – and originally it had occurred to me to purchase six of *KGB* and three of *Berlin Game* – I would have become liable for criminal prosecution under the same statute as governs the exportation from Taiwan of excess currency and valuable gems. Had I been detected, I would almost inevitably have been jailed at least during the initial enquiries – for buying in 'bulk' pirated copies of my own book!

As fates go, though, that might still have been preferable to incurring the displeasure of Chuck Lung-bong. Derek Cheng's firm of Lee and Li have done that. Lee and Li represents companies like Apple and IBM, as well as handling prosecutions for both the US government and the Taiwan administration.

Cheng insists – and both governments agree – there is no conflict of interests. Rather, both benefit from his local knowledge of counterfeiting. Lee and Li's caseload, Cheng explains, has involved a number of investigations into the counterfeit book business and in pursuing them, the firm received numerous threats – all by phone: 'Colleagues have received calls from people who say "Gentlemen. I suggest you do not take such action. It's very dangerous to you."' There have been occasions when Lee and Li, heeding those warnings, have passed on the assembly of evidence to other firms of prosecuting attorneys in hopes of bringing the case to court. Cheng assured me there had been no harm done to or attack on anyone in his firm connected with counterfeit investigations; fully aware of the organised crime involvement in the piracy of books and every other successful commodity, however, Lee and Li regarded the transfer of responsibility a worthwhile precaution.

Two investigators with experience throughout Asia – but particularly in Taiwan – believe that the Triads have followed the lead of the Mafia in America and Italy and created extensive legitimate businesses behind which to run their counterfeiting empires. Certainly, for a country that does not officially exist Taiwan has achieved some impressive business successes. By 1985 it ranked as the thirteenth largest trading nation in the world, while its official foreign exchange reserves are in the region of $16,000,000,000, as against $8,000,000,000 in foreign debts. Unemployment in a population of 18,500,000 averages two per cent and a typical inflation figure is that of 1983, just one per cent. The foreign trade surplus for 1984 was $6,000,000,000. Counterfeiting permeates every strata of that success.

During our conversations Mr Cheng, an expert in the counterfeiting activities of his country, assured me firstly that the 1984 allegation accusing Taiwan of responsibility for sixty per cent of the international trade in fake goods was an exaggeration and secondly that the government efforts to rid Taiwan of the stigma had anyway greatly reduced whatever the real figure had been. He did not think it could be higher than twenty per cent now, not after the number of anti-counterfeiting moves since 1980. In addition to the formation of the National Anti-Counterfeiting Committee, the Yuan (Taiwan's parliament) had promulgated in 1981 the Regulation to Prevent Trademark Infringement and False Marking of

Place of Origin of Products. In 1984 punishment for trademark infringement was increased under the Trademark Law and in June 1985, the new copyright law was enacted, replacing copyright legislation passed in 1970. By 1986 a Fair Trade Law is expected on the statute books which will make illegal a common method of counterfeiting known as 'passing off'. It refers to the slavishly accurate recreation of the packaging and logo of a product which enable the copy to be 'passed off' as the original. The proposed Fair Trade Law will supersede the existing Commodity Labelling Law. Under the amendments proposed in 1985 to the Trademark Law, a victim of counterfeiting can claim up to 1500 times the value of the stolen product. Further, there is now an article entitling a foreign company without legal presence in the country to take a Taiwan trademark infringer to court, something which until that time was not permitted. And in response to the criticism that Taiwan courts are inefficient in dealing with issues of 'intellectual' property theft, a special court for trademark cases is proposed. A new patent law is also being considered and a Patent Centre established at the Industrial Technology Research Institute, close to the Hsinchu Park. Political Vice-Minister at the Ministry of Economic Affairs, Li Mou was appointed in 1985 to coordinate the activities of the Anti-Counterfeiting Committee with the Ministry of Interior and the police. In the same year the Ministry of Education was authorised to establish a committee to create a countrywide programme to educate the Taiwanese against counterfeiting. Such a programme, Mr Cheng explained to me, was very necessary in a country whose population genuinely did not think as the Western mind did that copying was necessarily wrong – a stumbling block to reform which the Apple lawyer in Taiwan, C.V. Chen, had pointed out to his new employers when first taken on by the US firm.

International lawyers with whom I have discussed the Taiwan legislation agree on its impressive appearance but, together with the International Intellectual Property Alliance, doubt its effectiveness. The new Copyright Act was again the one singled out for criticism. They regard Article 17 of the Act, which requires foreign nationals to register their works in Taiwan as a condition of protection, as violating basic international copyright principles. Further, they see it as a thoroughly cynical attempt to obtain the trade secrets necessarily revealed in the process of registration.

Overall, they believe the Act to be worded ambiguously, frequently leaving itself open to varying interpretations.

The plight of film makers – who lose at least $25,000,000 a year from piracy in Taiwan – typifies that of foreign producers trying to protect their works. For a film to be registered in Taiwan, it must first pass the country's censorship regulations. And to satisfy the censor, the motion picture company has to provide:

(a) a certificate of distribution rights
(b) a synopsis of the film
(c) a certificate of duty payment

Registration itself requires the producer or distributor to file a power of attorney, a certificate of nationality or incorporation of the copyright owner and a video tape of the film. That video tape has to show:

(a) the author
(b) the copyright owner
(c) the publisher
(d) the publishing office
(e) the selling price
(f) the first date of publication
(g) the foreign copyright certificate
(h) the screenplay translated into Chinese
(i) the screening certificate from the Taiwanese government

It is hardly surprising that although foreign film companies are extensively and expensively robbed by Taiwan copiers, few bother to pick their way through the labyrinthine requirements to protect their films. Government prosecutor Cheng rejects the criticism. He told me: 'I think Taiwan has the counterfeiting problem under control. The government was slow to act but now it has. The country's determination to beat counterfeiting is a sincere one and not something done to impress countries in the West.'

It will take a great deal to impress countries – and companies – in the West that the Taiwan efforts are genuine. One company which was impressed – as much by the effectiveness of the investigation as by the quick Taiwan response – was the world's largest wall covering manufacturer, Crown Wallpaper, headquartered at Darwen in the English county of Lancashire. In 1981 they discovered identical copies of their best-selling papers being widely sold throughout Saudi Arabia and Australia and went for help in pursuing their investigations to the Essex-based Counterfeiting Intelligence Bureau. Jack Heslop was assigned to the case. 'What I found was astonishing,' he told me.

The counterfeiters turned out to be the Crown Wallpaper Industrial Co. Ltd of Lane 113, Section 1, Ho Pin East Rd, Taipei, and their copying was complete in all but one small detail – the failure to include some written instructions on the inside of the paper roll wrapper. For the rest, the Crown logo had been perfectly duplicated and the words 'Made in England' together with the Royal warrant – attesting that they were suppliers to the Queen of England – reproduced exactly where they would have been found on the genuine article. The counterfeit was complete even down to the codes that the original Crown company use on their products to identify the United Kingdom factory. The pattern book and the hanging instructions were copied verbatim and the company even registered the Crown trademark in Taiwan, although a bona fide company, Yuen Foong Ya Paper Manufacturing Co. Ltd, already had a crown trademark recorded. Armed with these findings, Heslop decided against recourse to lengthy and expensive court proceedings but went instead direct to the Taiwan Ministry of Economic Affairs. Confronted with samples of genuine Crown products side by side with examples of the counterfeits Heslop had bought two days earlier in Taipei, Ministry officials summoned to the offices officials of the Taiwan Crown Wallpaper company and ordered them immediately to stop manufacturing the wallpaper and dispose of any remaining stocks.

This satisfactory ending to the story is, according to my enquiries, unique in a case of Taiwan counterfeiting. Less satisfactory but more typical was the experience of a French company which illustrates how easy it is for a counterfeiter to operate now in Taiwan, despite the supposed restrictive legislation and government determination to lose its copying image. It is illustrative, too, of 'passing off'.

Perflux is the trademark of Precision Mechanic Labinal, whose offices are in Paris. The company manufactures motor vehicle oil filters for worldwide distribution. The Perflux trademark was registered in Taiwan – until 1985, that is, when the company discovered that without any reference to Paris the Taipei

Trademark Office had removed the word Perflux from its register. It discovered something else, too. A Taipei firm making oil filters had registered the trademark Perhux. At the time of writing – and officials of an international motor trading association tell me that this is likely to be so for 'some years yet' – Precision Mechanic Labinal can take no legal action whatsoever against Taiwanese they know are counterfeiting their oil filters. For since Perflux is no longer a registered trademark, technically there is no infringement.

Protests have, of course, been lodged in Taipei, most forcibly by the French trade organisation Comité de Liaison de la Construction d'Équipments de Pièces d'Automobiles. I understand that the explanation from Taiwan is that the officially registered Perflux trademark was removed because the Trademark Office did not think it was being properly utilised – particularly in advertising terms – and therefore had become dispensable from being 'dormant' It is a somewhat convoluted explanation very properly dismissed by the French, who believe that the removal of Perflux was achieved by the Taiwanese counterfeiters in an eminently practical fashion – via bribery of the registration officials in the Trademark Office. 'The place is full of corruption,' I was told. 'The Taiwanese counterfeiters use the Trademark Office as a positive aid to their stealing – searching to discover the potential of a trademark and then adopting a product to fit it – rather than it acing as it should do as a deterrent.'

In the opinion of automobile and auto-parts manufacturers in the five countries I visited Taiwan is the counterfeit auto-parts capital of the world. The British Society of Motor Traders and Manufacturers – who monitor takings in Taiwan through the CTS – calculate the financial loss to its members at $100,000,000 a year, which is minuscule compared to the damage done to their American counterparts. Linda Hoffman, a director of the American Automotive Parts and Accessories Association Inc., calculates auto pirates cost them $12,000,000,000 a year in lost sales overseas and $3,000,000,000 in lost sales within the United States. Nor is that the end of it: over 200,000 jobs a year go because of counterfeiters flooding the market.

Three Taiwanese firms known to have copied the products of American companies are Kendeem Industrial Co. Ltd, Frame Ltd and Jenn Feng Industrial Co. Ltd.

Taiwanese counterfeiters create distribution links through Nigerian pirates. The British engineering group Turner and Newell found within months of opening a new £13,000,000 factory near Lagos that sales of £250,000 a month for their Ferodo range of car accessories dwindled to £1500. It cost £100,000 and jobs in Nigeria and Britain before Turner and Newell were able to close down the Taiwan-Nigerian ring and recover their share of the market.

Counterfeiting extends beyond automobile accessories, of course. Games – and particularly video games – are a popular target. American manufacturers estimate that the pirates make $7,000,000,000 a year from their copying. The Golden Shine Corp. which proudly states 'Your Game, My Game', woos its sought-after customers with a prospectus promising 'Newest Games will be available upon Request'. So many Taiwan counterfeiters copied the video-switching system perfected and marketed by the Video Commander Inc. of Santa Ana, California, that President Thomas Battenberg philosophically adopted the principle of 'if you can't beat them, join them' and did just that, transferring his manufacturing operation from America's West Coast to Taipei.

Known Taiwan counterfeiters identified to me include Actic Electronics Co. Ltd; Asia Fu Products Corp.; B.P. Allies Co.; Buffy Manufacturing Co.; Chi E. Enterprises Co. Ltd; Chilong Game Corp.; Chuan Chun Co. Ltd; Copam Electronics Corp; Dionysus Enterprises Co.; Early Spring Inc.; Friend Spring Industrial Co.; Galaga Enterprise Co. Ltd; Great Lion Co.; Grede Manufacturing Co.; Joni Enterprise Co.; Matahari International Corp.; Morrison Enterprises Corp.; Pacific Edward Co.; Sigma World Co. and Sunyard Corp.

Asia Fu Products operates from a box number address at Pei-Tou, Taiwan. Their prospectus tells of 'untiring efforts to upgrade quality' and boasts of their products' beauty, durability, simplicity and easy servicing. It continues: 'We offer previously unheard-of low costs and yet with excellent quality to an industry-high standard which you can rely on.' Their quotation lists forty-eight computer games stolen from Western manufacturers. Golden Shine, which operates from An Kung Rd, Taipei, only offers forty-four. Their literature claims: 'We have enjoyed sound reputation on filling the orders accurately and promptly due to our strict quality control, dependable after-service and attractive price levels ... we are proud to pursue our development in a most expeditious and efficient way.' Friend Spring Industrial Co., whose factory is in Son San Rd, Taipei, claims to be the leading manufacturer and exporter of coin-operated TV machine games in the country and lavishly illustrates their brochures with details of their Pac-Man game.

A common finding of Western company investigators is that Taiwan fakers of video games move easily between their manufacture and the technology necessary to copy computers. One of those investigators told me that should a company be closed down by court action, it is not unusual for it start up again with a different type of product – exchanging counterfeit games for computers, counterfeit computers for games – as well as a different company name, the better to confuse the authorities.

The Taiwanese are, in fact, adept at every kind of counterfeiting. Another area in which they excel is that of the garment industry: inside opinion has it, though the view is not unanimous, that they are the leading counterfeiters of designer-labelled clothes. Throughout Europe and America, I was told that the trade was worth at least $300,000,000 a year to Taiwanese pirates. The cost to the American garment industry alone calculated on lost exports as well as home sales, is estimated to be $2,500,000,000. Ironically the United States of America provides these pirates with their largest market. When the counter measures began to take effect – Customs ran an intercept programme called Tripwire and also ensured that Taiwan did not overstep its export quota – the Taipei entrepreneurs tried to retain their market. They did so by switching from direct exporting to transhipment through Third World countries – mainly Indonesia and the Philippines.

An American source, who helped me on an unattributable basis, said: 'In most sorts of counterfeiting cases, we can make an intelligent guess of the scale of the crime: estimate what's getting through and what we're stopping. In the case of apparel, we haven't got a clue. All we know is that it is vast.' So concerned was Washington that it pressured Taipei into a system under which Taiwan makes daily satellite transmissions to American Customs, providing complete manifest and shipping details of all official exports so that counter checks can be run when those listed shipments arrive at an American port. Nevertheless, another investigator assured me that the cooperation received from Taiwan in the battle to put a stop to the illegal trade was 'minimal'.

The Mafia of Italy – hub of the counterfeit clothing industry in Europe – and their Mafia links in America are more heavily involved with their Taiwanese counterparts in this form of piracy than in any other. In 1983 Philip Lombardo, the seventy-seven year-old semi-retired boss of New York's Genovese Family, was named by investigators as being involved in the smuggling into America of designer jeans and the Izod company's Lacoste-labelled shirts. Named along with Lombardo, whose aliases include Cockeye Phil, Benny the Squint, Ben Purpin, Ben Grosso and Benny Demaoi, was Matthew (Matty the Horse) Ianiello, a contender for the leadership of the Genovese Family. Ianiello, quite separately, was involved in financing a British-organised perfume counterfeiting ring that at one time threatened the existence of the Chanel company.

Ralph Lauren and Jordache are two of the most commonly faked labels. In 1984 US Customs intercepted $17,000,000 worth of shorts-and-shirt sets being smuggled into American organised crime outlets for relabelling.

Taiwan does not confine its designer-product thefts solely to clothes. The criterion – not just in Taiwan but throughout the copying countries of the world – is whether or not the product sells: the next best seller, whatever it may be, is the next candidate for counterfeiting. Porsche sunglasses are an example. They are manufactured in Austria – under a licensing agreement with the makers of Porsche cars – for the Optyl Eyewear Fashion International Corp. whose headquarters are at Norwood, New Jersey. The trademark is Carrera. Six years after the 1977 creation of the Carrera trademark the volume of business had reached the $30,000,000 mark. That made it fair game by the counterfeiter's code – which acknowledges one caveat only, according to Optyl's Chicago attorney David Crossman and that is 'Don't get caught.' At the time of writing Optyl is losing $10,000,000 a year – not enough for the pirates, who are working on ways of beating the US Customs. What they have come up with so far is hardly of the same order as the scrambling device they used to baulk detection of the phony Apple computers, but it is the same idea. American law requires that sunglasses should bear the name of the country of manufacture. The counterfeits enter America with a sticker on the temple piece saying 'Made in Taiwan'. Once in, however, the sticker is peeled away, to disclose the engraving beneath which claims 'Made in Austria'. Mr Crossman says:

> The lenses in some of the substitutes are of such a poor quality that they shatter very easily. We are shuddering and waiting for the first wave of such accidents in the United States to start coming up in product liability situations where people have bought these counterfeit products believing in the reputation of our client for quality and finding that cheap, non-acceptable types of lenses are being used in these products.

Mr Crossman was anticipating a tragedy. Taiwan counterfeiters have already caused one and on a scale so massive it threatened for a time the stability of the Kenyan economy. It occurred in the 1979- 80 coffee growing season. The government purchased a fungicide it believed to have been manufactured by the American firm Chevron. It had not. It had been made in Taiwan, was heavily diluted with chalk and virtually useless. The majority of the coffee crop, a major source of Kenya's income, was destroyed.

Taiwan officials persist in declaring that the government is aware of and tackling the problem. Benjamin Lu, Director of the Economics Division of the Council for North American Affairs in Taiwan told the International Anti-Counterfeiting Coalition in February 1983:

> I want all of you to be fully aware that my government deeply regrets the conduct of counterfeiters in my country. While most of the manufacturers are law-abiding citizens, a handful of counterfeiters are hurting everybody. As a country which has and will rely upon international trade for foreign technology for the development of its economy, we cannot afford to tolerate counterfeiters.

Three years later counterfeiters were still being tolerated. And among the many officials I encountered during my time in the country, I detected the attitude that if Taiwan stopped, the gap would be filled at once by those of its neighbours already active in the counterfeiting trade. The British colony of Hong Kong was one frequently mentioned by name.

CHAPTER FOURTEEN

A Feeling Less Than Ecstasy

Britain's Rolls-Royce guards its products and its trademarks with the justifiable jealousy of the world's leading automobile manufacturer. Just as jealously, the fakers try to steal them. The most unusual and bizarre attempt ever occurred in February 1984, on the mainland Kowloon side of Hong Kong.

A Rolls-Royce is a status symbol in Hong Kong, as it is anywhere else in the world: the famous Peninsula Hotel – also on the Kowloon side – send one as a luxurious gesture to collect guests arriving at Kai Tak airport. Rolls became curious by a spate of newspaper advertisements proposing transportation in one of their vehicles to a newly opened nightclub. Alerted by its own observations – the company maintains vigilant watch over its interests from headquarters at Crewe in Cheshire – Rolls-Royce sent legal representative Lewis Gaze to the colony to investigate.

Not even Mr Gaze, accustomed to attempted infringements, anticipated what he discovered. The club is in the newly developed eastern section of Kowloon, near the trade centre – an ideal location for a business whose prices, among the highest anywhere in the colony, are tailored for businessmen on credit card expense accounts. The original idea had been to ferry customers, accompanied by a hostess, the fifty yards from the bottom of a long walkway along a covered gallery to the club in appropriate style. But once the razzamatazz of the official opening was over, the idea was quickly dropped when it was discovered that the exhaust produced by the Silver Shadow filled the gallery. There were so many complaints that the management was failing to provide an advertised service that in the end the engines were removed and the car modified to make the short journey under electric power. It was not the modification which caused the chief offence to Rolls,

131

however. Their trademark had been infringed before ever the car was reached. For all along the handrail of the walkway, at frequent regular intervals, copies of the famous flying lady bonnet motif – officially, the Spirit of Ecstasy – provided the decoration. And the hurt went beyond the legal infractions: the name of the club is Volvo – set out in the distinctive white and blue lettering of the Swedish car manufacturer, as well!

Rolls have enforced the removal of its decorative Spirit of Ecstasy and at the time of writing the Swedish company are considering legal action too. The episode is indicative of the sophistication of Hong Kong counterfeiters. Another example was that of the Black and Decker Dustbuster – a tool for loosening the dirt on walls and siphoning it away, which was extensively advertised by the British company in 1983. That same year it was purchased and stripped down for reverse engineering by Continental Engineering Products Co. Ltd of Hong Kong. They produced a copy called the Turbo Duster. The counterfeit was uncovered by the CTS and there began a protracted exchange of legal correspondence in which Continental Engineering agreed to change its design to avoid infringing copyright. Further, Black and Decker engineers were to have the right to approve the new design. Twice the alterations were rejected as insufficient; the third attempt was accepted.

Every year the Governor's Award for Hong Kong Design Competition is held, an occasion organised by the colony's Industrial Design Council of the Federation of Hong Kong Industries. In February 1984 Governor Sir Edward Youde presented at Government House a certificate of merit in the electrical products category to Continental Engineering Products Co. Ltd and designer Gabriel Tong Yui Lung for the Turbo Duster!

There are on the statute books in Hong Kong laws that are more rigorously enforced by a more determined government to combat counterfeiting than are to be found in any other Asian country involved in product theft. I believe, too, that the volume of copying and infringement has been greatly reduced since the 1970s when Hong Kong was unquestionably the world leader in piracy. But counterfeiting remains a huge industry in the colony and from my meetings with officials I gather that the trend is upwards once more because of the peculiarity –and uncertainty – of Hong Kong's political situation.

Under an agreement concluded with Britain in 1983, Hong Kong will in 1997 revert to Chinese sovereignty. The agreement has been carefully worded so as to reassure residents of Hong Kong that its special status will be respected and maintained by the mainland Chinese. It is an assurance accepted by very few Hong Kong Chinese or colony residents, some of whom are Indians or Eurasians who came to Hong Kong in the service of Britain. There is particular anger that the British National Overseas passports entitle the holders to consular protection only while denying right of residence in England. When I was there – a full twelve years before Beijing takes over control – the exodus had already begun. Canada is a country sympathetic to Hong Kong emigrants and a common arrangement is for the breadwinner to remain in the colony but for his or her dependents to leave and try to establish a new life there.

A Chinese lawyer – and an expert in counterfeiting – told me bitterly during a lengthy meeting:

> Despite all the rounded words and the supposed promises, the undeniable fact is that Hong Kong has been abandoned by Britain. Abandoned in more than one way, in fact. London is scuttling out and agreeing to Beijing's every demand. And denying the right of entry into Britain to any native of Hong Kong who might want to leave rather than live under Beijing's control. And that's the majority of people on the island. Long before 1997, all the British expatriates who have lived here for years, enjoyed a colonial lifestyle and grown rich on the back of the colony's enterprise will follow London's example and scuttle out, too. Leaving the rest of us betrayed. The last few years leading up to 1997 will be a panic, for a lot of people. The main consideration will be to get out, in any way possible. Already there are indications of forgery shops setting up, to produce passports and travel documentation: anything to get out and into another country. Equal to that consideration will be the money to finance it. And that money will come from the activity which Hong Kong knows best. Counterfeiting.

The evidence is that the product pirates of Hong Kong know that business very well indeed.

The Vincent Computer Centre 2nd Floor, 10 Observatory Rd, Tsimshatsui, Kowloon, counterfeits computers. Chief customers for Harvard Computer International of Flat 10a, Causeway Tower, Causeway Rd, Causeway Bay, Hong Kong Island, are Europe – particularly France and Italy – and the United States. Chi Luen Warehouse and Trading/Transport Co. in the K.K. Industrial Building on Mok Cheong St are electronic copiers linked to Asian organised crime and with outlets in the United States. One of the most prominent Hong Kong counterfeiters is EACA Computer Ltd of the Eaca Industrial Building, Chong Yip Street, Kwun Tong, Kowloon. The Manager-Director is Albert Chu, who has links with counterfeiters in Taiwan. United Progressive Trading Co. supplies from its premises at Causeway Tower on Causeway Bay counterfeit computers to the smaller retailers, usually located in Kowloon on the mainland side. ERE Data Systems Ltd, located in the Wing Yue Commercial Building in Des Voeux Rd West, Hong Kong, counterfeit Tandy and Northstar computers. The Apple lookalike 'Pineapple', named as well as modelled after its prototype, is made by Pineapple Computer Products (HK) Ltd at Peninsula Centre, Mody Rd, Tsim Sha Tsui East, Kowloon. Run by Managing Director Gary Cheng, the premises back directly on to cargo docks. Hunter Trading Co. (also known as Hunter Trading Systems) operates from the Sino Centre at Nathan Rd, Kowloon. They do, in fact, legally represent NEC, Tandy Corp., Texas Instruments and Commodore Computers. They also supply counterfeit Apple and Tandy computers. Video Technology Ltd of the Freder Centre on Sung Wong Taoi Rd, Tokwawan, Kowloon, are games manufacturers supplying Hong Kong and Taiwanese outlets with games copied from American or Japanese originals. Armed guards are posted at the doorway of Comx World Operation Ltd at Wo Kee Hong Building, Castle Peak Rd, Tsuen Wan, in the Kowloon part of Hong Kong. The President is Edward Yu. The sole product of Comx World Operation is counterfeit computer products. Komtek Technology is a world-spanning counterfeiting company, headquartered at Kings Rd, North Point, Hong Kong, with a secondary outlet at Tai Yip St, Kwun Tong, Kowloon. The Manager is David Ho. President, Chief Engineer and Managing Director is Heili Lee. They specialise in counterfeiting the Osborne computer. Funding and design for the Osborne lookalike is provided by Paul Chin, President of Chenin Technologies Inc. of 2782, Third Place, Baldwin, New York. There is a further box number – 1325 – for

2 River Rd, Highland Park, New Jersey. The name of the Komtek rip-off is Nuborne 1. Cheng Tsa Wah is the President of the Zirius computer counterfeiting company at Kimberley Rd, Tsim Sha Tsui Section, Kowloon. Gamma Electronic and Computer System Co. proudly located at the First Class Shopping Centre, Tok Wa Wan Rd, Kowloon, is a considerable counterfeiter of Tandy, Apple, IBM and NEC computers.

James Tunnell is a computer expert and a consultant who went to Hong Kong specifically to discover the extent of the piracy of Osborne computers. Confirming the Chinese lawyer just quoted who bitterly forecast a resurgence in the counterfeiting industry, Tunnell told a committee of American politicians of his conclusions:

> I discussed the Apple, IBM, PC and Osborne counterfeiting problems with two senior US Customs agents in Hong Kong familiar with the quantity and export of computer products. They said that rather than the situation getting better – because of legal action towards the offenders by legitimate manufacturers – the problem and expanded sale of such hardware and software appeared to be getting worse.

Following in the footsteps of Albert Eisenstat, general counsel to Apple, Tunnell toured the counterfeit computer emporium at Sham Shui Po. He also went to Apliu Street, so crowded with phony Apple machines that even the taxi drivers know it better as Apple Street. In the course of his peregrinations, Tunnell actually bought a fake Apple. It came with two programmes. The first was the scramble designed to fox US Customs; once loaded, this produced the figure of a tiny dwarf complete with wand who announced 'Hi, I am a fairy computer.' Tunnell's supplier advised him to return to America with the fairy programme and that the Apple copy should not be inserted until he was safely beyond any official checks.

Tunnell described what he saw while making his purchase.

> The computers, plus the copies of the game tapes and business diskettes and documentation are sold with as little fuss as the cabbages or the frogs down the street. And the proud customers can be seen strutting out of the market, their

135

computers banging against their legs in unmarked, flimsy cardboard cartons, tied sloppily with pink nylon string.

The vendors are unashamed that most of the computers and other hardware are rip-offs of established brands.

Some vendors operate simply from street pitches, arriving to trade with a computer balanced at either end of a shoulder pole, squatting patiently for customers. I personally saw three such street pitches in Osborne Road, while I was in Hong Kong. The prices of course, are a fraction of what the prototypes are retailed at, $300 as opposed to $1300. Some were as low as $230.

Before he left Hong Kong Tunnell managed to meet several leading counterfeiters, including Lin Hsiaochi, Manager of Sunrise Computer Services. It was an encounter of special interest since Sunrise was the company successfully sued by Apple:

> We met in a small Hong Kong computer shop. He believed I was an American tourist – nothing more. He spoke excellent English and readily admitted that his firm's computer was a direct copy of the Apple II and he clearly feels no shame, either over the piracy or being caught.
>
> 'When you are starting out, you have to copy something,' he said. 'That is the way you gain knowledge and experience. Later you can create, innovate.'

Cheng Tsi Wah concurred. He is the owner and operator of Zirius of Kowloon and told Tunnell: 'We have learned everything we can from Apple II and basically we have made what we can. It is time to move up the ladder, maybe making Apple III's but maybe tackling a more difficult product.'

Cheng's colleagues have already been applying their considerable wits to the challenge of duplicating circuit boards capable of military application. For at Sham Shui Po, Tunnell found readily available a 188B interface mandatory for use by the offices and agencies of the United States Department of Defence. Appalled, he hurriedly warned the American authorities. Tunnell says such circuit boards were offered to him on four occasions when he enquired about 'any special control chips or boards'.

Nor were these the only offers made to him. No one buys in Asia without bargaining and computers are no exception – even though the average asking price for a counterfeit is already only a fifth of what the prototype would fetch in the West. Tunnell said he was offered a five per cent reduction; a year and a half after his visit I got a matching rate in Apple Street. Given these rock bottom prices there has been a certain amount of speculation as to the quality of the Hong Kong component construction. But computer experts have found that the colony's manufacturers lead the counterfeit market, ahead of Singapore, rated second, and Taiwan, rated third. With staggering cynicism, the traders of Sham Shui Po and Apple Street actually use legitimate Apple products to beat customs detection! From the official Apple factory supplying the European Common Market in Cork they obtain genuine spares kits, which they install into phony cases and with phony keyboards with sufficient expertise to make them appear genuine European Apples to border examiners. Another innovation in both shopping areas is that any trader will make an on-the-spot electrical current conversion between the European 220 and the North American 110 voltages.

Not everything in the Hong Kong-made computers is phony, of course. The chips that make the machines work are usually stolen from Silicon Valley. Easily smuggled out because of their minuscule size, they are brought to Hong Kong for fitting into counterfeits which are re-exported throughout the world. One wheeler-dealer who grew fat on the proceeds was Barry Ching-bor Poon. He ran an efficient family business with widespread connections and himself as the pivot in San Francisco, where he headed a company called Microware Exceltek. The business was a front for the purchase of stolen chips and it was a sting operation set up by private detective Richard Camps that led to Poon's arrest. When police seized him, Poon had at his house about $300,000 worth of chips belonging to National Semiconductor Corp. and Signetics Corp. which had been sold to him by Camps in the course of setting him up during the undercover operation. Camps later testified that Poon, a Hong Kong-born Chinese, had told him one of his brothers lived in Hong Kong and another in Canada. A team of couriers carried the stolen chips from California to Hong Kong, for fitting into computers manufactured there. Once in their new settings, they were shipped out again – mainly to the third Poon brother in Canada, who made good use of that country's conveniently wide-open border with the United States.

Computers are not the only sector of the counterfeit market in which Hong Kong competes with Taiwan for the lion's share. There is also the garment industry. The piracy of designer labels has been described to me as practically the colony's most traditional form of copying. Stanley is the main outlet. Located on the south side of the island, across a spectacularly sharp mountain ridge known as Victoria Peak, Stanley is a one-business hamlet. Known to all enforcement agencies in the colony, this is the selling of counterfeit clothes, which it does quite openly. The concierges of every hotel direct tourists to it, cab drivers need only to hear the one word 'Stanley' and tour guides talk about it as one of the major attractions of the island. It seems invulnerable: no legal action seems able to affect its sales.

The chief shopping highways are Main Street and New Street. Halfway down Main Street there is a building boasting the Stanley Maifong Welfare and Advancement Association, an unnecessary organisation considering how ably the counterfeiters advance their own welfare. In a fifteen minute stroll along both streets, I saw clothes labelled Jordache, Fila, Levi, Gloria Vanderbilt, Valentino, Ralph Lauren, Nieman Marcus, Dior, Gucci, Calvin Klein, Lacoste, Oscar le la Renta and Yves Saint-Laurent. The Ming Fai Native Products Ltd emporium displays a sign by which it makes itself out to be an authorised Jordache dealer. The Artshouse Fashion Co. claims the right to deal in Nieman Marcus and Ralph Lauren products.

During my time in the colony, the Deacons firm of solicitors served some traders with formal 'cease and desist' letters instructing them to stop selling certain brand names. In Stanley market, those warned simply cut the labels and the packaging in such a way that while the name was no longer easily visible, it could still be understood. Prospective customers, myself included, were then told that the obvious signs of interference were proof that the articles were genuine – obtained illegally, it had been necessary to deface the labels in order to prevent police prosecution!

Specifically, Deacons had served warning notices on traders to stop sales of a lightweight, jerkin-type jacket sold under the label 'Members Only'. Manufactured in America by a firm called Europe Craft Imports Inc., it is the most popular type of sports jacket sold in the United States, with a worldwide sale of

$100,000,000. The firm's American lawyer, Stanley Yavner of Wolder, Gross and Yavner, 42nd St, New York, estimates Europe Craft Imports loses $5,000,000 a year through fakes and publicly names Hong Kong and the Stanley market as among the top counterfeiters. Yavner also acts for Calvin Klein, who at one time was losing $20,000,000 a year. Again, Hong Kong is one of the major producers of the fakes; Israel is a leading customer nation.

The Calvin Klein fashion empire was created by Klein and a partner, Barry Schwartz. Its yearly sales are in the region of $250,000,000. Yavner says: 'What Messrs Klein and Schwartz have achieved, through trademark infringement and counterfeiting was and is being taken away from them in the same sense that one might take their wallets or property by theft.'

It is not necessary to cross the Peak to buy counterfeit clothes, although the spectacular drive through the Riviera-style Repulse Bay, with its orange-roofed villas, make it a pleasant outing. I bought Lacoste shirts from a stall on Mody Street in Kowloon with another trader vying for my custom with a faked Cartier watch, quickly changing for a Longines when I showed lack of interest.

Communist China is the leading supplier of the materials from which Hong Kong counterfeiters fake their designer-labelled clothing. It is also a manufacturer itself, using Hong Kong as its trading outlet. A second outlet, and another manufacturer, is the Portuguese pinhead colony of Macao, a ferry ride into the mouth of the Pearl River from Hong Kong. Like Hong Kong, it is about to be returned to Chinese control and there is widespread disquiet at the prospect. Unlike Hong Kong, it is unfettered by any legal restrictions on counterfeiting. Investigators assured me that counterfeiters can buy from Macao government officials whatever documentation they want to ease their way – a facility that has proved awkward for the mainland Chinese.

For Communist China is one of the largest producers of legitimate clothing and the fourth largest supplier to the United States. A CIA report of June 1982 stated that in addition to its American quotas China exported $771,500,000 worth of clothing to Hong Kong. There the government admitted that at least $447,000,000 worth was reshipped out to Europe and to America. Since that time Beijing has attempted to centralise export licensing procedure to control the traffic. At the time of writing, the campaign has only had limited success. I was also told by an intelligence operative in the colony that official Beijing licenses had been found on some Hong Kong counterfeiters, together with visas covering the importation of Chinese materials which could only have come from bribed government officials. I found fake designer-labelled garments made from Chinese imports everywhere I went in Macao and was assured by a Western customs official, who was trying to monitor the trade, that the materials cross the border quite openly at Gongbei. Street stalls along the route to the impressive frontal façade of St Paul's church – nothing else remains of the building apart from that frontage – offered Fred Perry sportswear and Lacoste and Members Only jackets at prices cheaper than the Stanley market I visited the previous day. That same customs official described Macao as 'a haven for counterfeiters. And one that will remain so until Beijing takes over: and maybe even after then.' In anticipation of that 1997 takeover, Beijing has already established a patents office in Hong Kong and lawyers with whom I discussed counterfeiting said that the Communist officials manning it were sympathetic to complaints from Western manufacturers.

Other things are happening in anticipation of 1997. One is the remanning of the police force which plans to complete the switch to Chinese officers and men by the time of the takeover. The Hong Kong police have a checkered reputation. In 1977 there were widespread allegations – some of which were proven – of corruption among high-ranking officers. The scandal ended in the consignment to the colony of a contingent of British officers to form an anti-corruption squad. An official closely involved with that squad told me:

There's been some cleaning up but it's little more than a cosmetic gesture: bribery is endemic. It always has been and always will be. We know that some newly promoted Chinese officers actually held a meeting in the second week of June 1985, carving up the colony between them. Each was accorded his pay-off area and no one will poach: it will be their way of getting money in advance of the Beijing rule. Everyone will have to pay protection money: we know of one man running eleven heroin 'stalls' – they're called stalls, not dens – who is paying off at the rate of £8,000 a week. Every counterfeiter in the colony is paying off, too.

One of the biggest pay-offs of which my informant was aware involved the Prince Philip Dental Hospital in Hospital Rd, Hong Kong. It was equipped with £15,750,000 worth of counterfeited equipment with which surgeons refused to operate. Everything had to be replaced. A hospital official involved in the counterfeiting was never charged although his identity was known to investigating officers.

Collection and distribution of the bribes is well-organised throughout the police force. One of the premises at which the protection money is distributed is the Seven Dragons Club.

Counterfeiters do not only have to pay off the police. The Triads also have to be paid, for protection. They can also be paid to kill. One of the most experienced detectives in the colony estimated that a murder contract could be taken out for as little as $50. As my inside informant from the anti-corruption squad told me:

> No one is stupid enough not to pay off, both to the police and the Triads. It's the understood system: the way the colony operates. The way this part of Asia operates, in fact. And there's another fact: so much money is made from counterfeiting that there's enough for everybody. And despite all the efforts to stop it, that's the way it's going to be. Always.

That's the way it is in other Asian countries, too. Thailand, for example.

CHAPTER FIFTEEN

The Unsweet Smell of Success

The Durian fruit stinks. The flesh is sweet, however, so the trick is to eat it while trying not to breath in. As well as its taste and smell being curiously at odds, it is an unusual-looking fruit – rather like a prickly coconut. And its foliage looks just like the leaves of a cherry tree. It is a great favourite throughout Thailand and is sold on street corners in every city and town, particularly in the capital, Bangkok. So great is the demand that plantations are cultivated throughout the country. Some of those plantations produce another cash crop – one which sells at a far higher profit.

The Durian grows on tall trees, offering ample cover for anything. On one such plantation, counterfeiters of Johnnie Walker whisky – both Black and Red label – run unhindered and uninterrupted a factory supplying Bangkok. Its location, about five miles outside the capital in the direction of Samut Songkhram, was pinpointed for me before I arrived in the country by an official of the investigating agency which first uncovered it.

After only half a day in Bangkok, I had not only confirmed the factory's existence but discovered for myself that it is run with the efficiency of a military operation – and the metaphor is an appropriate one considering the number of weapons in evidence on the plantation. Another analogy is Chicago in the bootlegging days of Al Capone. For Bangkok bars, restaurants and even the city's leading hotels are persuaded to take on the fake Johnnie Walker through a combination of threats and bribery. And those threats and bribes extend to the police and the enforcement agencies, allowing the counterfeiters to operate without any fears of official reprisals.

My taxi driver refused to take me any closer than a mile of the area I sought. I covered the remaining distance on foot and from the description given to me was able to identify three lorries leaving on delivery trips and one returning. There were armed men in the cabs and clearly visible through rear awnings. There were more armed Thais at the plantation entrance, from which I kept a safe distance having been forewarned. They will kill you, European or not, I had been told by my informant, whose identity I am not disclosing because he still operates in the area. I believed the warning. The Thai authorities appear to be wary, as well. When the information on these illicit activities was taken both to the police and the army, with the request that the distillery be closed down, neither would act on the grounds that it was too dangerous. It was unclear to the agency registering the official complaint which was the greater deterrent – fear of an open shoot-out or the size of the bribes. The agency refused to allow any of its own people to attempt an entry unprotected by government officials. So the distillery continues to operate.

In Bangkok, it is easier to procure a contract killer at the knockdown price of $50 than anywhere else in the counterfeiting countries of Asia, so I was assured. These bargain basement rates are accompanied by a certain theatricality. An American who annoyed the mob by making too many protests at the counterfeiting of his company's clothes received an unwritten warning: a silver bullet. He took it seriously and left the country.

Johnnie Walker is one of the British Distiller Group's best-selling labels and its government-condoned counterfeiting is not confined to Thailand. In 1984 Communist Bulgaria was discovered to be officially involved in establishing a factory turning out fake bottles of both Black and Red label. The Sofia government of peasant-born President Todor Zhivkov put £80,000 into setting up the Bulgarian premises which manufactured the whisky which, when opened, had a perfumed smell. It was created from chemical alcohol and whisky essence by a French chemist named Pierre Galibert. A company named Studie Industries SA was also created – with offices in Zurich – to market the product to South Africa. The delivery route was a circuitous one, with fake whisky going first to the Greek port of Piraeus and then by ferry to Patras in Italy. From there it went to a further Italian port, Ancona, for final shipment to Durban in South Africa. Its noticeable smell made it unsuitable for the white South African population, but it found a ready market amongst the poor blacks.

There is no such easily identifiable smell to the Thai product, the counterfeit of which the government refuses to act against. Recognition of that refusal was contained in the investigators' report examining whether or not to continue the annual $192,000,000 worth of aid to Thailand under the GSP scheme.

> As in other territories, copyright protection particularly of foreign works, has a very low priority with the police. In order to secure their cooperation, close personal rapport with the officers concerned has to be established in addition to the provision of necessary 'incentives'. The situation is complicated further by the arrangement of overlapping jurisdiction and powers of particular forces. Furthermore, 'disincentives' from the opposition are always on offer.

The counterfeiters and their outlets know all about incentives and disincentives. Everywhere on the Bangkok streets stallholders push their counterfeit goods, from Johnnie Walker through to fake designer-labelled fashions, luggage and the leather goods of Louis Vuitton, Dior and Gucci and the jewellery and watches of Cartier and Longines. Most favoured locations are Silom village, and the area round Silom Road, Patpong Road and the Surawong Road near the Montien Hotel. This is also a district of clip-joint sex shows and brothels.

At the time of my visit to the Thai capital, the going pay-off rate for policemen on the beat was between $10 and $20 a day per stallholder. That represented a rough average of $600 per day per policeman. The beat policemen, of course, then had to pay off their superiors. Besides this 'hush money', protection has to be bought from the gang suppliers. For rivalry for the stallholders' custom is fierce, sometimes fatal, with each Triad trying to take over outlets from the next one. When a tape pirate named Prasong got caught between warring factions in July 1984, to secure his operations – and his life – he had to transfer to the barracks of a Thai army brigade in the capital.

It was suggested to me that the pay-off rates were higher at the tourist-thronged floating markets along the oil-black canals or *klongs* and at places like the Thonburi snake farm because their greater popularity meant they could afford to hand over larger amounts to the Triads. At the floating market and at the snake farm I not only saw counterfeited every article produced by people like Louis Vuitton and Dior but some things the companies do not even make, like Louis Vuitton belts, for instance.

There is upon the Thai statute book a copyright act, passed in 1978, but one investigator experienced at working in the country told me: 'The only time anyone ever gets prosecuted under it is if they haven't paid the right sort of protection to the right sort of people.'

There is a further difficulty hampering prosecution. In July 1931 Thailand became a signatory to the founding international agreement on copyright, the Bern Convention of 1886 which has since been revised at an international conference in Berlin in 1908 and in Paris in 1971. All straightforward enough; the complications arose when in February 1985 the law within Thailand as covered by the Bern agreement was changed with a number of amendments by Royal decree. 'The simple fact,' one international lawyer told me wearily in Bangkok, 'is that no one really knows what the hell the law is. Nor can they work it out. Maybe they don't want to work it out. There's more money to be made for everyone the way things are. A fortune, in fact.'

Film-copying is another way in which pirates make fortunes, in Latin America as well as Asia. In view of the violence of the Thai counterfeiters, it was rather appropriate that the hottest-selling stolen film in Bangkok should have been *A View to a Kill*.

CHAPTER SIXTEEN

There's No Business like Show Business

Appropriately, *A View to a Kill* made a killing – for the film and video pirates, that is – just like all the James Bond films. And *The Godfather*, I and II. And *The Deer Hunter* and *ET* and *Close Encounters of the Third Kind* and *Airport* and *Chariots of Fire* and *The Killing Fields*. Every major successful international film, in fact. Accountants for the Western motion picture industry – predominantly from the American Film Marketing Association and the Motion Picture Association of America – put the pirates' yearly income from stolen films at $1,000,000,000 worldwide. One American official employed solely to monitor the extent of the rip-off told me in Hollywood: 'That figure is a gross underestimate: a more realistic assessment is twice that amount.'

Pirates wiped out the ethnic Indian cinemas in England. Pirates – and not legitimate distributors – dominate viewing in *every* Asian country and in at least four Latin American countries. In India – the country with the largest film industry in the world – they control fifty per cent of the market. The official quoted above said further: 'And it's likely to get far worse, as more and more people throughout the world either get their own video recorders or access to a replay system.'

American investigators looking into the privileges allocated under the GSP accuse the governments of some Asian countries of operating a 'deliberate national policy' whereby copying and pirating is permitted and in a report to US politicians insisted: 'These countries must be advised that further delays and excuses in taking immediate corrective action will no longer be tolerated.'

One of the most flagrant offenders is Singapore, whose premier, Lee Kuan Yew, publicly declared in 1968 that his country would not pay television performance royalties – his excuse, the need to preserve foreign reserves. Singapore was identified to me both in Hollywood and Hong Kong as the major film pirating nation in East Asia. Its well-organised gangs, which exploit the film industry as just one of many protection rackets, have forged operating links with gangs in Singapore's near neighbour just across the causeway, Malaysia. Through Malaysia, outlets have been created in Pakistan which is the route through which the illicit market in India is fed.

It was in Singapore that *A View to a Kill* was copied and distributed throughout Asia, where it was available even *before* its London premiere. During my time in Bangkok I found ten copies openly for sale in the Japanese-owned Daimaru department store which also stocked the tape Top Ten. Frank Knight, Regional Director of the East Asia Film Security Office of the Motion Picture Association of America told me: 'Of course the directors and the buyers of the store know that it's a pirate version. They couldn't care less. It's pointless protesting; they just shrug and go on buying and selling.'

The industry officially estimate its sales loss within the island country through video cassette piracy at $11,000,000, a figure which does not take into account the additional loss sustained through the unauthorised showing of pirated films in hotels, bars and restaurants. Nor does it take into account Singapore's huge export market. Three people closely involved in the piracy – and efforts to stop it – gauged that export trade to be worth between $35,000,000 and $50,000,000 a year.

Until 1986, Singapore supposedly observed a locally amended version of the Imperial British Copyright Act of 1911, the wording of which is archaic and non-applicable to modern video cassettes. And Singapore law was a jungle of absurdities benefiting only the pirates whose activities were virtually sanctioned by the authorities: under the country's censorship legislation, video dealers had to be licensed by a government fully aware that what the retailers were selling were stolen copies of Western films. In March 1986, however, a new copyright bill received its first reading and there were undertakings for it to become law by the end of the year. There were further assurances of Singapore acceding to the Universal Copyright Convention.

The regulations governing the registration of foreign films pointed up the absurdities of the existing Singapore laws, which

THE STEAL

some investigators to whom I spoke described as intentional
absurdities, maintained to make the pirates' lives easier. Under the
1911 act, films had to be registered to prevent illegal importation.
The agency responsible for regulating this was the Register of
Imports and Exports which the government of Lee Kuan Yew
abolished without naming a successor – not until June 1984, that is,
when the Registry of Trademarks and Patents was appointed. That
designation was withdrawn almost immediately on the grounds that
the appointment was illegal without parliamentary consideration.
In the meantime – November 1984 – Twentieth Century Fox
brought a civil infringement suit against some local video dealers
and found itself in the ridiculous position of having to plead to the
Singapore court to excuse its failure to register with a non-existent
agency. Despite the necessity of a legal approach more befitting the
trial scene in *Alice in Wonderland* than a sober law court, the
company succeeded in obtaining the injunction it sought.

What legal redress is available to Western motion picture
companies existed under the censorship laws and those are used
more to the advantage of the licensed Singapore retailers selling
pirated films than to the benefit of the genuine producers. There are
fifty dealers licensed on the island. And 150 unlicensed. And it is
more often the licensed dealers informing on the unlicensed for
muscling in on the multi-million dollar industry that provokes
action from the censorship board than complaints from Western
film makers.

Film investigators who helped me with my own investigations on
a non-attributable basis dismiss as 'cosmetic and meaningless'
government statements promising action against the copiers who
steal their films and as 'publicity-seeking nonsense' government-
sponsored anti-piracy announcements and meetings. Said one: 'It's
an empty effort to convince the West that something positive is
being done. One or two will be hit to make it seem to be effective
but the action will be motivated more because the guy hasn't paid
off the right people than because he's a movie counterfeiter.'

Those same investigators also warned that, as Lee Kuan Yew
pointed out, in 1985 Singapore encountered its worst economic
crisis since independence and that it was likely to continue until
1988. They said:

That's bad news for the people of Singapore, who had twenty

148

years of uninterrupted growth, high wages and substantial – if government enforced – savings. But it's worse news for the victims of property theft. It'll mean more people coming into the rip-off market and going after the big money available. The bigger the recession in legitimate industry, the greater will be the growth of the illegitimate businesses, no matter what statements are made to the contrary by the government.

At the time of writing, the penalty in Singapore for criminal infringement of copyright is that set in 1911: a $23 fine for each copy, but not exceeding $450. A repeat offender risks imprisonment not exceeding two months.

Frank Knight attempts to stem the piracy trade in Singapore through the censorship laws but complains that progress is slow. From my meetings in Asia and Hollywood I know that despite the difficulties, Western film companies intend to continue seeking injunctions, minimal though penalties may be. I also understand that they have agreed among themselves to make a rule of applying for an Anton Pillar order whenever a pirate is identified. This enables the wronged company to search the premises where it suspects its products are being duplicated and to carry away the counterfeits. Besides these measures, American film companies are making a bid to defend their own interests in particular as the chief victims of the Singapore pirates. All the major US studios are pressing the government of President Reagan, a former film actor himself, to apply the only really effective sanction that exists and that is the threat of withdrawal of Singapore's favoured status under the GSP scheme. Early in 1986 diplomatic sources let it be known to Singapore that their existing concession, which enabled the country to import more than $600,000,000 worth of goods into the United States free of duty, was under intensive review by both houses of Congress.

A common Asian defence is to claim that since in more than fifty per cent of the cases concerned the master video or film copy is supplied from within the Western film industry itself, the latter should put its own house in order and deal with the problem at source. It is a claim whose justice the industry is ruefully forced to acknowledge, though it does point out that the copying of a television original – which only requires a simple VDR unit – is usually done by an Asian accomplice and not somebody within the industry itself. However, copies of films made for the cinema are necessarily supplied from the inside. Methods include fraudulent copying by a studio technician before release and taping during a pre-release showing – either at one held officially in order to gauge audience reaction before the first night itself, or at a strictly unofficial showing where the film is run purely to enable a duplicate to be made on a VDR. 'Two or three thousand dollars is pretty good pay for a couple of hours of practically undetectable larceny,' an official told me in America.

Frank Knight talks of reproducing 'factories' where the masters are put to work as soon as they reach their Asian destinations. The set-up is simple enough: a battery of copying VDRs – known in the business as 'slaves' – which monitor the master tape, a conveniently large room and not more than one or two operators to ensure there are no breakdowns. The factories never stop duplicating, day or night, with the changeover between regulating operators as the only interruption. Explains Knight:

> In a week a simple factory can turn out thousands of copies for a ready and waiting market. The pirates don't think it's wrong and the governments condone it and the profits are immense. We don't even scratch the surface in obtaining the seizures that we do: someone we close down one day will open up the next in a different location. Detection is little more than a temporary inconvenience.

Detection is anyway very difficult since the equipment is so basic that it can be installed literally almost anywhere. In a seizure in Malaysia a factory was discovered completely concealed beneath the premises, reached through a hidden door behind a cupboard.

That seizure was so rare as to be almost an isolated occurrence. For as is the case in Singapore and throughout Asia, Malaysian law is an inextricable tangle whose intricacies shelter the pirates. And the country's 3800 video dealers, all of whom trade in pirated films, have banded together in a number of trade associations whose considerable political influence is concentrated against any change in the existing legislation likely to rebound to their disadvantage.

The current copyright legislation is modelled on the United Kingdom Copyright Act of 1956. Enacted in Malaysia in 1969 and amended ten years later, it requires that for a film to be protected it must be shown within thirty days of its first viewing anywhere else in the world. But to be publicly shown, films have first to get censorship clearance and that takes longer than thirty days. The result is that to be covered under the Copyright Act, film makers and distributors have knowingly to break the Censorship Act by showing their films without clearance. One investigator who talked of piracy in Malaysia being 'rampant' told me in disgust: 'It means that to beat the crooks, we've got to break the law ourselves – to get protection from the law!'

The government of Malaysia has announced its intention to increase to either sixty or ninety days the period within which a film has to be shown to be protected. But film industry lawyers do not think this would make a significant improvement because the censorship requirements remain stringent and clearance can frequently take longer than three months.

The loss to Western film companies from sales of pirated films within Malaysia is estimated to be $13,000,000 a year. Additionally, pirate exports are put at $30,000,000.

Lawyers and investigators complain at there being no specialised enforcement body within the country concentrating on film piracy and say that the existing police force give the lowest priority to stamping it out. The well-organised gangs and dealers have created within police and government 'significant infrastructure corruption', as one American agency report described it. That same report said: 'Because simultaneous raids are rare, pirates quickly get news of a raid after the first pirate's goods are seized and thus are able to close shop or hide their pirated goods.'

Bribery is also a way of life in Indonesia, where legal recourse is even scarcer for film makers. The domestic copyright law passed in Jakarta in 1982 appears to insist that to get protection, films must be shown in Indonesia *before* being displayed anywhere else in the world. An international lawyer said: 'If that is the case, it's unique to any other country I've ever encountered. And there's no legal precedent or guidance coming out of Jakarta to make the position clear. Requests for clarification have been ignored. We're guessing.'

Also on the statute books in Indonesia is the ubiquitous censorship legislation. Under pressure from religious groups within the country, Jakarta limits importation and distribution of video cassettes to just five companies, which have formed the Association of Video Recording Importers. The five can only import films from a legitimate source that have been properly censored and the licensing documents must be approved by the Attorney General. It means that censorship in Indonesia is more rigidly enforced than in any other country in the region, but that only heightens the demand for the pirated versions from all those too impatient to wait for the release date. Naturally, the pirates capitalise on a situation which brings in a yearly income of $17,000,000. The value of the pirate export is estimated to be a further $25,000,000.

The difficulties confronting Western film makers in South Korea are, according to some studio and enforcement officials to whom I have spoken, even greater. Its population of 42,000,000 possesses more than 1,000,000 TV sets and 300,000 VCRs. There exists in the country a Motion Picture Law, amended as recently as December 1984 in order to increase the penalty for the importation or duplication of unlicensed films from $2300 to $5700. The experience of Western film lawyers is that while appearing good on paper, the legislation is largely meaningless because it is not enforced. In June 1984 the South Korean Ministry of Culture and Information proposed amendments to the country's Copyright Act, but the suggested improvements were withdrawn within weeks. The official reason given was that the proposed improvements were inadequate. But I was told in confidence by three different sources that the real reason was that copiers, who make $16,000,000 a year from home-sales and the same again from exports, 'paid off the right people to make sure things remained as they were'.

As it stands, unamended, the 1957 Copyright Act only covers foreign films if they are shown in Korea ahead of any other premiere. What that means, in effect, is that there is no legal recourse for any Western film company anxious to guard its property. Also, foreign films from legitimate sources must run the gauntlet of quota requirements, taxes and import delays, all of which benefit the pirate market. At the beginning of 1986 there were indications from Seoul that South Korea intend by 1988 to become a signatory to the Bern Convention. If that is so, Western film makers will at last obtain a measure of real protection. But an expert who has made film larceny in South Korea his study told me: 'I – and the rest of the film industry – will believe it when we see it. At the moment it's open house for pirating in South Korea and the amount of money being generated makes it highly unlikely that there is going to be any dramatic, overnight change.'

So concerned at this state of affairs were the enquiry team reporting to the American government on the GSP programme that its 1985 report recommended that the duty-free benefits – worth $1,500,000,000 a year – should be completely withdrawn or at least curtailed until such time as a new copyright law were enacted to protect foreign works.

Widespread police corruption in the Philippines makes possible another 'open house' country, resulting in an annual loss to the foreign film industry of $20,000,000 in the Philippino home market, with a further loss of $20,000,000 on pirate movies shipped abroad. An American intelligence agency probing the extent of that corruption provided the following, euphemistically worded affidavit: 'Although a number of agencies carry out piracy raids, it is reported that they demand "mobilisation fees" before they act and are, to varying degrees, reportedly also susceptible to the offer of "demobilisation fees".'

That same affidavit suggested there were 650,000 VCRs in the country, supplied with pirated movies from 5000 video shops in the capital, Manila, with a further 1000 outlets in outlying towns and cities. In four years, beginning in 1980, the loss of legitimate income to cinema and theatre owners reached $50,000,000, as a result of which over 400 cinemas were forced out of business. American researchers claim evidence of over 3000 Hollywood films being copied and put at $19,000,000 the yearly loss to the industry. Lost exports brings that up to $30,000,000.

Under pressure from the West, in April 1984 the Marcos régime had the Philippine Board of Review for Motion Picture and Television order anyone engaged in the film, video or television business to obtain a certificate from the Censor's Office. Legal action was promised against anyone trading without such a licence. Besides this edict, there is a Philippines Copyright Act which came into being in December 1972 by Presidential decree. Equally, of course, there are several loopholes through which the pirates can escape prosecution. Article 10 (2) of the Act contains a private-use exemption permitting film or television reproduction if the work has lawfully been made available to the public. Section 53 permits the recording of broadcasts for teaching and scientific use, as well as for private use. Lawyers interpreted a further section of the Act – 51 – to mean that it was unnecessary to obtain infringement protection for the two copies of a film to be deposited with the National Library, and learned that the law was ambiguously worded when an American action was dismissed on the grounds that the film in question had not been 'registered' with the library. 'There's always a way out,' one US film attorney told me with an air of resignation.

Due to the labyrinthine censorship and registration requirements for film protection in Taiwan, which I set out in all their restrictive detail in Chapter Thirteen, Western films remain largely unprotected and the Taipei pirates capitalise on the weakness, as they do on every lucrative loophole in the law. The importation from Singapore of films like *A View to a Kill* and *The Deer Hunter*, *Chariots of Fire* and *The Godfather* I and II makes the racketeers $25,000,000 a year from internal distribution. And that is without taking into account the losses from the unauthorised use of video cassettes in video parlours, hotels and bars, all of which abound throughout the country and bring the figure up to a minimum of $40,000,000 annually. Western film lawyers are only too familiar with the fact that the Taiwanese home market for video cassettes is almost entirely a pirate preserve. There are in the country 3300 retail video stores, all knowingly selling stolen films, and since their license to trade is government issue, the authorities are necessarily implicated in the fraud. In 1985, the last year for which I could find statistics, there were 850,000 VCRs in use on the island. But the prediction of those experts monitoring the situation was that by 1987 sixty per cent of all Taiwanese households would own a VCR, which would bring the figure up to 2,550,000. 'And would mean,' an investigating officer told me, 'that the loss to the film industry would be practically incalculable unless some effective, enforceable legislation is introduced.'

Certainly, none exists at the moment. Nor, when a Western film company bothers with the intricacies of censorship and registration, are those laws that do exist impartially imposed. Under the 1970 Copyright Act, a convicted pirate was able to commute a term of imprisonment into a negligible fine, rarely in excess of $500 – a blatant miscarriage of justice which even Government Prosecutor Derek Cheng could hardly ignore. During our meetings, however, he prudently limited himself to conceding that the legislation 'contained certain anomalies'. Just how gross those anomalies can be was vividly illustrated in October 1984 when a Taipei film maker, Hung Chien Audio- Visual Co., was convicted by the Taiwanese High Court of pirating eight local Mandarin- language films. The penalty imposed was a staggering $4,300,000.

Under the new Taiwan Copyright Law of June 1985, penalties have supposedly been increased. Convicted pirates are liable to imprisonment for not less than six months or more than three years with a discretionary additional – but not alternative fine – of approximately $1660. Sellers of pirated works are subject to two years in jail, with no minimum term specified, plus a discretionary maximum fine of $1110. Penalties for piracy conducted 'as a profession' carry jail sentences from six months to five years, with a maximum fine of $2775. Of course, these reforms do nothing towards imposing an impartial interpretation of the letter of the law. An American lawyer called 'lamentable' the disparity between sentencing for foreign and local film pirating, though he did concede a faint hope within the Western industry that the 1985 act would be more fairly and stringently interpreted by Taiwanese courts than its predecessor had been.

The law is still less effective in Thailand, where there are 400,000 VCRs in use and where – as in Taiwan – pirates have captured close on one hundred per cent of the local market, a loss which costs Western companies an expensive $12,000,000 a year. Peculiar to the country – and beneficial to the pirates – are a number of legal exemptions which one embittered lawyer described to me as 'practically making the ripping off of films a legitimate activity, without even the need to bribe the law to keep your ass off the burner'. The exemptions are, in fact, the least convoluted aspect of a highly convoluted act.

Section 34 (1) of the 1984 Copyright Act permits 'unauthorised public performance of a work in restaurants, hotels, resorts, transportation stations and vehicles if not done for the purposes of making a direct profit from such a performance, i.e., charging admission'.

Section 34 (2) provides a blanket performing rights exemption for 'associations, foundations or other organisations having charitable, educational, religious or social welfare purposes'.

Section 30 (2) allows reproduction of copyrighted material 'for one's own benefit or use for one's own benefits and for the benefits of members of his family or relatives and friends'.

In the unlikely and rare event of a pirate being brought to court, under existing legislation he faces a minimum fine of $182, rising to the maximum of $1820. There is no provision for imprisonment unless the activity is proved to be conducted for commercial purposes, when the term is not more than six months. An infringement repeated within five years carries a sentence of two years' jail and double the original fine. A group of examining American lawyers said in a report in 1985: 'These low fines are easily absorbed as a cost of doing business by wealthy pirates who are reported to be able to afford the most effective protection and from whatever source.' Investigators have established the existence of a clearly defined distribution network channelling the products of the Asian counterfeiters through Malaysia and Pakistan into the Indian subcontinent. In the most heavily populated democracy in the world, the demand for films is enormous. Enormous, too, is the indigenous pirate business, preying on what is the world's largest legitimate film industry. Mohad Katre, Director of India's Central Bureau of Investigation, told me in New Delhi: 'It has been calculated that the illicit income from film copying runs into millions of dollars, possibly representing the country's single largest industry.'

Seemingly effective legislation exists to combat the trade, under India's Copyright Act, Counterfeiting Act and a 1984 Certification Act, covering cassette manufacture and distribution. But the reality is that the Indian enforcement authorities only initiate prosecution if prima facie evidence is provided by independent, private investigators. 'We do not have the manpower to operate in any other way,' apologised Katre, who conceded that counterfeiting and piracy of all kinds permeate every level of Indian life.

The pirate film industry has gauged its home market well, showing recopied Asian imports in thousands of video parlours which charge only pennies for admission: 'Pennies become pounds, millions of pounds, in a society of 900,000,000,' explained Katre. 'And these illegal video parlours allow our people, who are consumed by films and television, access to entertainment they would otherwise be denied. Poor as the country is, people can usually find a few pennies for their favourite relaxation. Millions cannot afford the $700 for a TV set or the additional $1000 for a VCR.'

Nor is it the internal market alone that amasses an illegal fortune.

India possesses a pirating export infrastructure every bit as sophisticated as that of Singapore or Malaysia or Indonesia. The recopied imports are re-exported throughout the Middle East, the United Kingdom and Africa, in each of which there are large immigrant audiences ready-made for the Asian product – as there are for India's own films, which are relentlessly counterfeited and copied, for the export market. So concerned at this was the Indian Videogram Association that at the end of 1984 it sought membership of the English organisation formed to combat film piracy, the Federation Against Copyright Theft Ltd (FACT) – too late, however, to save their legitimate outlets in Britain. By 1980 every ethnic Indian cinema in the country had closed, unable to withstand the competition. Robert Birch – formerly Solicitor to the Metropolitan Police, but at the time of our meeting, Director General of FACT – told me: 'They were being pirated like fury. When the Indian Association joined us, piracy of the Indian videograms was up to 85%–90%.'

Given the history of the subcontinent, it was understandable that the Indians should look to an English protection organisation. FACT, though, had its hands full dealing with the problems on its own doorstep. As Birch told me: 'when we started, at the end of '82, the headquarters of video piracy was London. We were exporting pirated cassettes throughout the world.' He was echoing the remarks made at the time of FACT's formation by Jack Valenti, President of the Motion Picture Association of America. He described London as 'the most virulent nesting ground for piracy in the world' and went on to warn: 'It is going to destroy our business. We are not dealing in hyperbole. We are dealing in plain fact. We are in deep trouble unless we can take these hoodlums and gangsters out of the business.'

FACT was created to do just that. It is funded by every major film maker and distributor in the world. In America, that means Columbia Pictures Industries Ltd, Embassy Communications, MGM/UA Entertainment Co., Motion Picture Association of America, Orion Pictures Corp., Paramount Pictures Corp., Twentieth-Century Fox, Universal City Studios, Walt Disney Productions and Warner Bros. English supporters of FACT include Associated Communications Corp., BBC Enterprises Ltd, British Videogram Association Ltd, the Society of Film Distributors, the Rank Organisation and Thorn/EMI Video Ltd.

THE STEAL

In 1982, when the Federation was formed, those companies estimated the pirates' turnover to be in the region of £100,000,000 and discerned three distinct practices. The first was piracy pure and simple, the making and selling of a cassette copy of a motion picture not yet released on to the market. The second method was counterfeiting proper – that is, the copying of a legitimate tape down to aping the packaging. The third way was what is known as 'back to back' copying, where a legitimate video is duplicated but sold without any attempt being made to pass it off as original – minus any form of packaging and identified by the title alone which is either handwritten or typed on a plain label.

By 1985 Birch was confident that his Federation had smashed the English pirates, even if it was only to see their mantle assumed by the Asian suppliers. But within three months of our meeting, Britain's biggest-ever prosecution – it cost £1,000,000 – ended in London's High Court with injunctions awarded to thirty-five international film companies against thirty-four-year-old video dealer Christopher Robinson, naming one hundred of their films which he was specifically banned from copying. Among the films pirated by Robinson, who lived at Enderby Road, Luton, Bedfordshire, were *Jaws*, *Star Wars* and *The Godfather*. The court found that eighty per cent of Robinson's stock was pirated. During the hearing it was disclosed that, although a pirate, Robinson also acted as an informer for copyright investigators and had even allowed one investigator to operate from his premises. Although finding for the film companies, Mr Justice Scott awarded Robinson and his company, Luton Video Services, £10,000 damages for the 'flagrant disregard' of his rights displayed by the lawyers armed with Anton Pillar 'search and seize' court orders who had raided his premises.

Robinson, however, was only recording films for the English market. Pirates operating in 1982 were supplying the world: FACT's first successful prosecution was of a Plumstead counterfeiter with three floors and a copying machine which alone was valued at £72,000. In the first two years of its operation FACT saved the British video industry £17,000,000. The three pieces of legislation under which the Federation had achieved its coup were the Copyright Act of 1956, the Copyright Act 1956 (Amendment) Act, 1982, and the Copyright (Amendment) Act, 1983. Birch told me his organisation considered the 1983 statute to be their 'bible'

158

because it increased the penalty for piracy to a maximum fine of £2000. It also allowed for trial at a higher, Crown Court, if necessary, where a prison sentence could be imposed.

Although the world centre for film piracy had switched by 1986 to Asia, there is also considerable evidence of substantial copying in Latin America. Brazil was actively involved, as was Panama which made the most of its close proximity to the United States and the possibilities that allowed for – including the interception of satellite transmission. This is a particular ploy of Rexsa, a notorious pirate company operating a cable television network in Panama City which shows – and sells throughout Latin America – US films hijacked from the ether. Rexsa exemplifies within itself the parodoxes and absurdities that go with piracy in Asia. It is almost exclusively the US film industry that the company rips off, yet the majority of the American embassy personnel in Panama City are among Rexsa's 20,000 subscribers. Rexsa has negotiated a $1,000,000 loan from the Bank of America. The company also mirrors Asian corruption at the highest levels, with two former Panamanian presidents among its more substantial shareholders – and a number of politically influential businessmen, some of them actively connected with the city's legitimate television stations. Another substantial shareholder is General Manual Antonio Noriega, the country's military strongman.

So serious a matter does President Reagan consider film piracy to be that the administration's so-called Caribbean Basin Initiative – which is to all intents and purposes another Generalised System of Preferences – provides that Latin American countries may be deprived of their duty-free export quotas unless they move to counteract the scam. Secretary of State George Shultz testified before Congress in favour of the provision being included in the Initiative and in the early months of 1985 US Ambassador Everett Briggs named Rexsa in a protest to the Panamanian government, describing Rexsa's proven piracy as an 'incongruency' and reminding the administration of its obligations. The American Department of State has assured Hollywood that it will continue to press the issue, although some diplomats with whom I discussed the matter were sceptical that the government would go so far as to remove trade concessions from a country controlling a strategic asset like the Panama Canal just because of film piracy. 'Banging a loud drum to try to frighten off the bad guys without a fight,' was one way the protests were described to me.

A leading Panamanian pirate is sixty-three-year-old Isaac Zafrani, a flamboyant man who openly admits to having made $10,000,000 as a film copier and runs an empire that includes three duplicating plants and the concession at the country's international airport from which he sells his copies of Western films for as little as $12. Zafrani drives a gold-coloured Cadillac and has admitted to investigators that he bribes government officials to stay in business. His philosophy: 'Everything is for sale in Panama. Everything is for sale everywhere. Only here, it's cheaper.'

Rexsa officials fighting off attempts to put them out of business claim that the Motion Picture Association of America has an undisclosed interest in a proposed rival cable TV system that would pay American studios for the films that Rexsa currently hijacks. This is strenuously denied although three members of the Association – MCA, Paramount and MGM/UA – are negotiating to convert licence payments into a minority equity interest in the new company. Rexsa further claims that two partners in the rival cable company are cousins of the Panamanian president, Nicolas Ardito Barletta.

The cost of the Panamanian piracy is estimated to be $10,000,000 a year.

In Brazil, the stakes are even higher with, according to the calculations of Western film executives, an estimated 1,000,000 pirated video cassettes on the market in 1984. In addition, in Brazil as in India, the practice of showing pirated cassettes on a communal video for a few cruzeiros is widespread in outlying villages and hamlets. Film accountants say the cost to the industry overall is a minimum of $13,000,000.

Brazil is a signatory to a number of international agreements – including the Bern Convention and the Universal Copyright Convention – which in theory should provide adequate protection for Western film makers and the Brazilian National Cinema Council has established a pirate-monitoring organisation known as Concine to work with the police in enforcing the regulations. The Brazilian government and courts have recognised Concine as an official body and agree its authority to pursue video pirates. At the end of 1984 Concine reached an understanding with video dealers

THERE'S NO BUSINESS LIKE SHOW BUSINESS

in the country – called the Protocol of Intentions – that in return for immunity from prosecution, the dealers would freeze pirate stocks at whatever their level by the end of that year. The agreement was that the residue would gradually be discarded as legitimate imports became available. There nonetheless were some prosecutions, however, including one for copyright infringement and failure to display an official government stamp on videos. The company arraigned, the Video Club do Brazil, was identified to me by film industry officials as handling a chain of pirate video outlets which extends throughout all Latin America and is the biggest in the area. Within the country itself, it controls thirty per cent of the video market.

Despite the propaganda put about by Concine, American officials doubt that the video dealers are holding to their side of the bargain. One official estimated compliance at 'about fifty per cent – if we're lucky'. Washington made it clear in 1985 that Brazil's status as the fourth largest GSP beneficiary in 1984 was under review. Whether or not it retains its export concession, worth some $1,200,000,000 in duty-free goods, is dependent on the kind of action taken by government and police.

Film piracy is not confined to the West, Asian or Third World countries; there is a flourishing market – and pirates serving that market – behind the Iron Curtain. Hungary leads the Communist film piracy league, which includes practitioners within the Soviet Union itself. In February 1985 *Kommunist*, the regional Communist Party newspaper in the Soviet republic of Armenia, reported that three pirate dealers had been convicted of 'speculation, dealing in pornography and fictions which demean the régime' and were sentenced to between five and seven and a half years in jail. In Hungary, the government is aware of what is going on even if it is not officially recognised. In 1984 the newspaper *Magyar Hirlap* reported the lack of legal tapes available and said of the pirates: 'They didn't create the market. The demand created these undertakings.'

Helpless Western studios have reports that widely and freely available in Budapest are illicit copies of *The Texas Chain Saw Massacre*, *Gorky Park*, *Flashdance*, *The Great Muppet Caper*, *The Deer Hunter* and *The Sound of Music*. *From Russia with Love*, portraying the Soviets as villains, enjoyed great popularity. So did all the other James Bond films. Not all the stolen films are commercial blockbusters; Western pornography also has an avid market in Hungary. The country has an estimated 30,000 VCRs, which are widely and freely available for sale in all major cities, owing to Hungary's unique status within the Communist bloc as a country able to encourage free enterprise and individual profit. I have seen estimates suggesting that entrepreneurial dealers can earn as much as $1400 a month, fourteen times the average wage. To achieve that income, a dealer would have to stock a repertoire of at least eight hundred cassettes. The three legal rental outlets in the country average a stock of ten to fifteen copies of films already shown on television.

Masters of Western films are made in the West and smuggled into Budapest. The most common route is through Austria. Once inside the country, the recopying is carried out on those Western and Japanese VCR machines which are freely available for purchase in Hungarian shops. The reproduction cost to the pirate, including buying the blank tape, is about $28. The VCR costs about $1500. I heard reports in Hollywood of factories in Budapest with up to six VCR 'slaves', all making simultaneous copies of smuggled Western hits.

The Hungarian pirates have devised a variation on the group viewing common in India and Brazil. With a VCR and a selection of Western films, the pirate tours his country neighbourhood by car or van, setting up showings by word of mouth. Clubs in State-run factories or even those organised by the official Young Communist organisations are favoured and frequent venues. There is minimal effort made to avoid detection. Admittedly the film is advertised as being one approved for viewing by the authorities, but when the switch comes at the commencement of the programme no one is taken by surprise. The price per programme averages about $10, with each member contributing a few *forints*; an active pirate can expect to make a profit of $600 a month.

Videos are not covered by any copyright legislation that exists in Hungary and film pirating is only rated a misdemeanour.

Although Western film makers spend hundreds of thousands of dollars funding watchdog organisations and even more money in retaining lawyers to prosecute and issue injunctions when possible, there is widespread awareness that the problem will never be eradicated. Officials in every studio I interviewed pointed to the vast profits the pirates stand to gain and were little comforted by American threats of sanctions under its Generalised System of Preferences.

A partial answer lies with what created the video and the cassette in the first place: technology. All video producers now package their films distinctively – usually in colours chosen for ease of identification– and some indelibly inscribe the cases with a security marking, enabling enforcement authorities to separate the legal from the pirated product at a glance. Research continues in America for a device to make illegal recordings technically impossible, whether from the screen or satellite transmissions. Allen Cooper, Vice-President of the Motion Picture Association, said in 1985: 'If a system is developed that works and we can implement I think it would be broadly used. We need to protect our copyright. Without our copyright, we own nothing.'

The Massachusetts Institute of Technology is one centre at which such research is being conducted. There, scientist Andrew Lippman is trying to perfect a system in which signals are received at slightly varying intervals by television sets which are, throughout the West, sufficiently sophisticated to compensate for the variations and show the picture with no discernible distortion. VCRs – which are mechanical rather than electrical – cannot compensate. The effect of the variable signal when shown on a VCR is to lose colour or distort the picture – the technical term is 'breathing' – so that it expands and contracts.

While it is hopeful such technological protection will be developed, the film industry is sufficiently realistic to expect that mega-rich pirates will commission their own technical experts to come up with the electrical devices to counter the counter-measures. 'It's a race,' I was told in one Hollywood studio. 'And one the industry can't afford to lose. The pirates don't think they can afford to lose, either.'

But at least the film industry *has* technology to assist. Book publishers throughout the world do not even have that.

CHAPTER SEVENTEEN

They Lard their Lean Books with the Fat of Others' Work

Democritus

Ex-President Richard Nixon, to whom illegality was not unknown, personally complained to Pakistan's President General Zia when he discovered copies of his book *Leaders* being pirated in Karachi and Lahore and Islamabad. So did Nixon's foreign policy advisor, Henry Kissinger, when his memoirs were copied there as well. Zia then found himself in a paradoxical situation since his administration itself pirates textbooks on the grounds that the cost of buying them legally is prohibitive. His eventual response was a Janus-like feat of diplomacy: the addition of the 1969 West Pakistan Publication of Books Ordnance to the country's Federal Investigation Act. This empowered the government to jail the Nixon and Kissinger copiers and allowed it to present itself as a country determined to combat book piracy.

It is not – no more than China, Singapore, Taiwan, South Korea, Hong Kong, Malaysia, Indonesia, Egypt, India, the Dominican Republic or Nigeria. All are book pirate nations which each year cost British publishers £80,000,000. Alexander Burke, Executive Vice-President of McGraw-Hill and Chairman of the Association of American Publishers' International Copyright Protection Committee, estimated the worldwide cost of book piracy in April 1985 at more than $6,000,000,000. There was a further estimate that over $1,000,000,000 of that cosmic figure was represented by Communist China. One survey to which I have had access asserts: 'Mainland China is without question the largest book pirate nation in the world.'

Burke recounts an anecdote to support that assertion. A group of American publishers visited a Beijing printing works where one noticed a book being set in Chinese but with the English word 'Schaum' on the cover. Schaum is the McGraw-Hill imprint for its

164

worldwide best-selling series of college books. When asked how many were being produced, the printer replied: 'One million copies.'

China is a member of no international copyright convention and currently Western publishers are powerless to recover any royalties. Theoretically, they are not so powerless in other Asian countries. As I said in Chapter Thirteen, Taiwan vies as league leader, possibly producing $250,000,000 worth of copied books a year. The country's 1985 Copyright Act should provide Western publishers with redress but as is frequently the case with local legislation, there is a catch-22. Only books first published in countries providing reciprocal protection for Taiwanese copyright works can be registered and thus protected.

Singapore remains a major offender with the government's determination to implement its new 1986 Copyright Act as yet untried. According to Western publishers, it earns $100,000,000 in book exports which are shipped in bulk – Nigeria is again a favoured market, as it is for pirated tapes – and a further $7,000,000 for those sold within the country. There is also a massive illegal industry involving the photocopying of books.

English publishers are strongly critical of what they regard as a weak-willed British government reaction to Singapore copying, contrasting it with the freely vented complaints – and demands for change – that US Secretary of State, George Shultz made during a visit to the island state in July 1984. During his meetings with government officials in Singapore, Shultz directly referred to the Generalised System of Preferences and warned ministers that in October 1984 the US Congress were to revise the law, making it possible to deny trade benefits to countries which do not protect intellectual property rights.

The American attitude was markedly different from that adopted by the then British Minister for Trade Paul Channon when he paid an official visit in June 1985. Despite evidence of the extent of Singapore piracy, Channon categorically ruled out the option of imposing trade pressures. He said: 'There is no question of retaliatory action. We have been assured that Singapore will deal with the problem of piracy. We have been told that the government intends to introduce new copyright laws and we are confident the problem is being taken seriously.'

British publishers are not as sanguine as Channon. From what is known in advance of publication about the provisions contained in the new bill, only domestic copyright works or foreign works simultaneously published in Singapore will be covered. Neither does the draft bill involve Singapore becoming a signatory either to the Bern Convention or the Universal Copyright Convention. The 'Anti-Piracy News', newsletter of the British Campaign Against Book Piracy, commented in April 1985:

> Why a modern state, intent on developing its own copyright industry and attracting investment from the international communications industry, should adopt this parochial attitude is hard to understand. Nor is it easy to avoid the suspicion that such a policy, if adopted, would be any more than a device intended to defer, indefinitely perhaps, introduction of effective protection for foreign works and so perpetuate the organised, systematic infringement that now occurs in Singapore.

On Channon's return from Singapore, MP Leo Abse tabled six written questions in the House of Commons in an effort to discover what anti-piracy action had been urged by the Minister of Trade during his visit and with what success. The Minister said in reply:

> The government takes every available opportunity to impress upon countries whose copyright law and enforcement procedures fail to protect United Kingdom copyright owners the inequity of permitting unauthorised exploitation of foreign copyright material. Such countries are urged to join the international copyright conventions and to enact effective copyright law. The government continue to be concerned at the inadequacy of copyright protection for foreign works in Singapore and at the extent of piracy there of United Kingdom copyright materials, including printed works. The scale of such piracy cannot be accurately estimated, but it is known to be considerable. The High Commission maintains contact with the Singapore authorities on this issue, which I raised during my recent visit to Singapore. I was informed by the acting Minister for Trade and Minister for Finance that the authorities recognised the need for revision of existing law. New legislation was under consideration, although no

timetable could be given. Singapore copyright law is at present based on the United Kingdom Copyright Act, 1911. The Singapore High Court recently confirmed that this law is applicable to works first published in the United Kingdom. However, the available penalties and enforcement procedures are inappropriate to modern conditions.

With commendable restraint, considering the scale of the loss incurred by British publishers, the Campaign Against Book Piracy described the Minister's reply as 'disappointing but not entirely unexpected'. Privately, the word used by more than one publisher was 'pusillanimous'.

Under current legislation, the maximum fine that can be imposed on a pirate in Singapore is $26 for each infringed copy, rising to a limit of $503. This is derided by the Campaign Against Book Piracy – a body composed of all the English publishers – as so pathetic that it 'would not deter a street hawker, let alone a wealthy businessman making substantial profits'.

In the Katong Shopping Centre, on Singapore's East Coast Road, there exist six photocopying centres that openly advertise bookbinding and photocopy a textbook at about 2¢ a page. The price is halved, to less than 1¢, if the book can be reproduced in two page spreads. Until 1984, when Pitman raided the premises armed with Anton Pillar orders, posters were displayed at Singapore Polytechnic reading 'Get *Applied Mechanics*, price S$9.50 (official price, S$17.60)', followed by the room number on campus where copies could be obtained. The pirated books were ordered by the students' Mechanical and Production Engineering Club; receipts for purchase were recovered during raids on the home of the club's president.

All major international best sellers are copied in Singapore. Jeffrey Archer's *First Among Equals* was copied there. So were books by Sidney Sheldon, Robert Ludlam, Frederick Forsyth, Norman Mailer and Graham Greene. There have even been occasions when pirates have put the name of a best-selling author and a fictitious title on books written by other, less well-known writers.

British authors *do* have copyright protection, as Minister for Trade Channon told the House of Commons, but it is uncertain for how long. The albeit temporary protection comes from a reserved judgment given out in the Singapore High Court in February 1985. The ruling culminated in a long delayed action – it took seven years to come to court – brought against bookseller Ng Swee Nam by five British publishers. Butterworth, Longman, Stevens and Sons, Sweet and Maxwell and Lloyd Luke jointly claimed that Ng Swee Nam sold or offered for sale numerous, mainly academic, titles which had been produced without copyright licence. The hearing was limited solely to the preliminary issue of whether Singapore law offered protection, under the 1911 Copyright Act, to works published in the United Kingdom. Mr Justice Thean held that it did. The initial euphoria of British publishers – and also of the music industry which saw the ruling as offering protection against tape piracy – was tempered within months by an appeal lodged against the ruling by Ng Swee Nam. There is no date yet fixed for the hearing of that appeal; if the bookseller is successful, even such limited protection as exists will be lost.

Whatever happens at the hearing, American books will be left exposed to the pirates, for the ruling does not cover them. A major target for the Singapore counterfeiters, they are urgently in need of protection and Secretary of State Shultz pressed for the swift passage through parliament of a modern copyright bill to take in all the countries threatened by piracy – not just the UK. He also urged that Singapore join the internationally binding Bern and Universal Copyright Conventions.

In London, I was independently told by several people within the publishing industry that too often the industry itself – despite that £80,000,000-a-year figure – does not consider piracy sufficiently seriously. The Campaign Against Book Piracy only came into existence in 1983 when three container loads of pirated books destined for Nigeria were seized in the Taiwanese port of Keelung. I was further told that the Department of Trade and Industry certainly does not recognise book piracy for the problem it is, a failure of perception which was reflected in the remarks made by its minister after his visit to Singapore.

A concern of Western publishers is that if, under trade pressure from America, Taiwan and Singapore do tighten their piracy restrictions, other countries will step in to continue the business. South Korea, where at least $16,000,000 worth of pirated books are sold every year, was frequently identified to me as one of the likelier contenders. The US International Intellectual Property

Alliance estimates that in 1984 South Korean copiers produced and sold worldwide $70,000,000 worth of books, predominantly scientific, technical and medical journals. It claims that one Korean book catalogue listed over 5000 pirated titles. Ian Taylor, coordinator of the British anti-piracy group, assured me there were available in Korea 10,000 stolen titles. In Seoul two huge bookshops – Kyobo and Chongo – stock nothing but copied books. An American study claims that 90% of the English language textbooks assigned to colleges are pirated and continues: 'There is also extensive photocopying of entire textbooks within the university system.'

The current Korean Copyright Act, that of 1957, only offers protection to foreign authors if their work was first published in Korea – a restriction unaffected by the proposals for amendment put forward in June 1984. Nor did these proposals interfere with a completely arbitrary permit allowing reproduction for educational purposes where 'deemed necessary', which leaves any compensation for such copying entirely at the discretion of the copiers. Hardly an effective deterrent – indeed, American investigators estimate that university and college stealing made up the bulk of that $70,000,000 loss sustained by the industry in 1984.

I understand that some American publishers are considering bringing a deterring action against some pirates under the Korean 'Unfair Competition' law. As the maximum penalty is only $575, it is scarcely likely either to impress or worry. The litigation is anyway being delayed while international lawyers decide whether any American company is entitled to bring such an action directly. The International Intellectual Property Alliance warns that technical book piracy is likely to 'increase rapidly' as Korea expands technologically. In its 1985 report, the Alliance warns: 'Immediate action is necessary to prevent the further growth of commercial and consumer forces in Korea that depend on, and profit from, piracy.'

Some British publishers are similarly concerned. The view of the Publishers' Association is that the proposed new copyright bill is 'insubstantial and completely inadequate'. They add that the bill is anyway not in itself intended as law but as the enabling legislation from which law can subsequently be promulgated under presidential decree. They further believe, with objective cynicism, that the withdrawal of that enabling legislation from the country's parliament in 1984 resulted from the opposition to it from Korean book pirates.

The Philippines is regarded by the American publishing industry to be among the top four Asian pirating countries – the others are Singapore, Taiwan and South Korea – which between them steal at least $427,000,000 worth of titles every year. Manila is calculated to be responsible for $70,000,000 of that. And there actually exists a law to make it all legal!

Presidential Decree 1203, issued by ex-President Marcos on 27 September 1977, provides for the automatic right to reprint any textbook or reference book selling for more than $2 – which covers every publication – and which has been 'duly prescribed by the curriculum' and certified by the registrar of a school, university or college'. The legalised piracy is not limited to educational institutions. The same decree permits the reprint of any reference book 'intended exclusively for government use' and certified as such by the head of any government agency. Some reprinting is done blatantly in the universities or government departments themselves, but the bulk is carried out by pirate printers. A futile gesture is made towards giving this decree an appearance of international legality by including a clause compelling the pirates to pay copyright holders a 2% royalty fee, less a 35% government tax. One American publisher received a cheque for $53 for reprinted books valued at $5768.

The Philippines is a beneficiary of the American trade preferences scheme and US publishers are lobbying Washington to use the scheme to get the legalised piracy clauses removed from the statute book. Because of those clauses, the majority of American publishers have ceased trying to market at all in the Philippines.

Manila is a signatory to the Bern Copyright Convention and there also exists within the country a copyright law, contained in another Presidential Decree, numbered 49. Widespread bribery throughout the supposed investigating agencies virtually nullifies it, just as it does the 1982 domestic copyright law in Indonesia where the annual $17,000,000 turnover in pirated books is mainly made up of sales of technical publications and textbooks.

Indonesian publishers appear to be concerned about the illegal trade. Dr Soetoyo Gondo, Chairman of IKAPI, the Indonesian Publishers' Association, estimates that between 1982 and 1984 a thousand titles were ripped off by Indonesian pirates committing a crime 'that could endanger the life of publishers and may also paralyse the book world'. Balai Pustuka, the state publishing agency, have publicly demanded that Jakarta courts should imprison rather than fine convicted pirates. Under the existing law, a maximum term of three years' imprisonment is possible. Lawyers who carried out a survey for American politicians considering renewal at the Generalised System of Preferences commented in their report: 'While it appears that there is growing concern over piracy of foreign works ... it is unclear whether this concern will be translated into revisions of the copyright law necessary to provide adequate and effective protection of foreign works.' The problem confronting Western publishers is that to obtain protection under the 1982 Act, just as under the 1957 Korean Act, books have first to be published in Indonesia. And, as in the Philippines, the government has given itself the right to copy where it considers it to be in the 'national interest' providing a 'reasonable compensation' is paid.

The American lawyers surveying the situation declared that in their opinion Indonesia could emerge as one of the takeover countries if anti-piracy action were successful in Singapore.

Despite the fact that Malaysian copyright law theoretically provides greater protection – and higher infringement penalties – than any other developing nation in Asia, book piracy is still extensive. An American estimate put its yearly value to pirates at $15,000,000 – a figure ridiculed by an English publishing authority, who told me the true figure was nearer $25,000,000.

Current copyright legislation is modelled on the United Kingdom law of 1956. Malaysia's was enacted in 1969, amended in 1979, and there are proposals to tighten it still further with a new bill. The Dewan Bahasa, the state publishing authority, is urging the government to go beyond implementing the new law and to accede either to the Universal Copyright Convention or the Bern Convention. There is no indication of Malaysia doing either. The country's Supreme Court ruled in May 1985 that to be covered under the existing Malaysian law a book must be published in the country within thirty days of its being brought out anywhere else in the world. A convicted pirate faces a fine of approximately $4200 for each infringed copy, with a ceiling of $42,000, and a maximum term of imprisonment – which can be imposed as well as a fine – of five years. However, according to a report produced by a group of

American lawyers: 'While these amounts are facially substantial, fines are rarely more than minimal and imprisonment is rare. This fact ... results in little deterrent effect upon the pirates.'

Extensive links exist between Singapore and Malaysian pirates for channelling books – as well as films – through to Pakistan and India. In a worldwide survey conducted by the British Campaign Against Book Piracy, Pakistan was one of two countries – the other was Peru – identified as being dominated by book pirates whose major outlet there is the Urdur Bazaar in Karachi. It was in the Urdur Bazaar that a number of arrests were made after Richard Nixon had used his influence as a former president to bring pressure to bear on President Zia. The adding of the 1969 ordinance to the Federal Investigation Act, which made those arrests possible, is protested by publishers within the country. Salam Aktar, Chairman of the Pakistan Publishers and Booksellers Association, actually placed proclamations in the press calling on Zia to withdraw the Act. What Aktar and his colleagues want is for it to be replaced with the new copyright act which has already been promised to them.

Salman Rushdie was a victim of Pakistan piracy, with his Booker-prizewinning novel, *Midnight's Children*. As he later recounted in *The Times* in November 1984, it was impossible to ascertain how many copies of the pirated edition had been sold, but it must have been considerable because – adding insult to injury – the pirates sent him a greetings card of thanks on the festival of Eid ul-Fitr. They were not so lucky with another Rushdie novel, *Shame*. Although no banning order was issued against the book by Pakistani authorities, the author was warned that distributors in the country would be put at risk. When the pirated editions appeared in bookshops in Karachi and Lahore police raided them – not because they were stocking counterfeits but because of the contents of the original. *Shame* was regarded as unacceptable. Police made no seizures, because the edition had sold out in advance of the raids. But the raids themselves were sufficient to deter the pirates from reissuing that particular book.

Rushdie's *Midnight's Children* was also pirated in India. He actually had a pirated copy presented to him in a Delhi bookshop by a woman who argued with him for refusing to autograph it. Jeffrey Archer was another victim of the Indian pirates. Counterfeit copies of *First Among Equals* were found freely available in

Bombay, despite the specially low-cost Indian edition licensed by English publishers Coronet specifically to prevent illegal reproductions.

In August 1984 the Indian parliament passed a Copyright (Amendment) Bill praised by Western publishers for its toughness. Its provisions include setting the minimum sentence for infringement at six months, rising to a maximum of three years, and the minimum fine at $5032 with a ceiling of $20,128. For a repeated offence, the minimum rises to one year in jail and a $10,064 fine. The Bill empowers police to seize, without a warrant, all copies of a stolen book and the plates used to print them. Copyright infringement is identified as an economic offence, so there is no period of limitations under the Code of Criminal Practice.

It has been estimated that between four to five hundred Western titles are stolen every year in India. The hope now is that with the swingeing legislation available, that number will be considerably reduced – although one American publisher with whom I discussed Indian piracy doubted there would be any appreciable drop until some pirates were heavily fined and jailed, as public proof that the law had teeth. 'We're still waiting,' he said, with resigned weariness.

Expensive technical trade manuals and textbooks are among the main targets of the pirates, as they are elsewhere in Asia – and in the Middle East. Egypt was identified to me as the major pirate nation, supplying from the north the Middle East and Gulf nations as actively as Singapore and Malaysia from the south. American investigators calculate that 90% of all medical books and 50% of all academic books sold in Egypt are pirated. The loss to American publishers alone is put at $10,000,000 a year and Western publishers know that so rich are the pirate rewards that Lebanese entrepreneurs have moved to Cairo to set up business.

Egypt has an anti-piracy unit headed by Brigadier Halawa, which operates under the aegis of the Ministry of the Interior. In February 1985 officers of the unit raided two bookshops operating unfettered from flamboyant, Arabian Nights-style tents outside a teaching hospital at Qasr-El-Aini in Cairo. Technical and medical textbooks copied from eleven British publishers were seized. Ian Taylor was assured, when he visited Cairo in his official capacity, that as a result of the raid the pirate business outside the hospital had been stopped. So he went to the tented emporiums where he found, he recalls, 'it was business as usual'. When he complained, the unit made another swoop.

During his visit, Taylor learned from legitimate booksellers that the pirate production in Egypt dates from 1974 when President Anwar Sadat's 'open door' trading policy resulted in offset printing and photocopying machines becoming available in the country. The first organised illegal photocopying and binding of books was traced to the University of Alexandria, from where it later spread to campuses throughout the country under the active encouragement of the Islamic Students' Association. Then came the advent of the Lebanese entrepreneurs who literally moved into the business in the early 1980s. Taylor recounts visiting a pirate warehouse and finding a sign announcing that 'now in stock' was the Weatherall edition of the two volume Oxford Textbook of Medicine. At the time, the legitimate edition was not on sale in the country. Taylor estimates that between 30% to 40% of the pirated books available in Egypt are photocopied. The black plastic coverings and bindings lead him to believe that they probably come from no more than three suppliers. Also available at the time of his visit were offset-printed facsimiles, with varnished covers in colour which he thinks originated in Asia.

Egypt, whose university system runs a budget of $12,000,000 for the purchase of books, is a member of the Bern Convention. Theoretically, this should provide those member countries not separately covered by bilateral agreements with Cairo with what is called 'back door' protection, which means a work is protected if there is simultaneous publication in another member country within thirty days. From the raid on the Qasr-El-Aini tented bookshops, it does not appear that the Egyptian authorities interpret the international agreement that way. While pirated English editions were seized by the police, pirated American and German books were not. American publishers are campaigning for Washington to apply pressure on Cairo to clarify its interpretation.

British publishers do not consider the current fines for infringe-ment – a minimum of $13 and a maximum of $135 – any sort of deterrent against copying.

Another discovery Taylor made during his visit was that pirates have virtually taken over the market supplying English academic textbooks to first year medical and engineering students. The technical publishers Churchill Livingstone estimate their loss to be E£750,000 a year. McGraw-Hill – some of whose books were found but ignored during the Qasr-El-Aini raid – calculates to lose a turnover of $1,000,000 because of pirated academic works. Following the Qasr-El-Aini swoop, Cairo's book wholesalers, Dar El Maaref, recorded a noticeable increase in demand but the Campaign Against Book Piracy warned British and other Western publishers that a way had to be found to get legitimate but, lower priced first year texts into Egypt. Taylor commented: 'Students cannot afford unsubsidised, full-price textbooks and the zeal of the Egyptian authorities may be hard to sustain in the face of the sort of student unrest that could well result from the disappearance of the pirates.'

Pirates operate throughout the world. International surveys carried out from Britain claim photocopying endangers academic and university textbook publishing throughout North and South America. In addition, pirates erode other branches of publishing in Mexico, Argentina, Uruguay, Paraguay, and Bolivia. The Dominican Republic and Puerto Rico are the major pirating countries. American publishers, for example, calculate they lose at least $8,000,000 – largely through textbook sales – at the hands of pirates in Brazil. The total cost, to publishers worldwide, is at least double that. The success of the illegal industry in Brazil is due to importation and tariff restrictions which preclude legitimate copies being shipped into the country. But overall in the Americas, according to the British surveys, the problem is the one isolated by Ian Taylor in Cairo and that is that students cannot usually afford to pay up to $14 for a textbook and fail to see why they should when a $2 photocopy is readily available.

This is also the problem confronting that most ready of markets for the pirate product, Nigeria. There, too, pirated and photo-copied textbooks predominate. According to Chinke Ojiji, Chairman of the Anti-Piracy Committee set up by the Nigerian Publishers Association: 'The pirates no longer care about quality as they produce fake copies that are glaringly different from the original titles for what could be rightly termed as a "sellers market".' Ojiji criticised the slow and often obstructed progress of litigation in Nigerian courts and said: 'I have a strong belief that until we secure convictions at the courts against the pirates, it would be difficult if not impossible to find a substitute deterrent to the daredevil pirates and their illegal businesses.'

Internationally, the British Campaign Against Book Piracy and the American Publishers' International Copyright Protection Committee are trying to provide as much of a deterrent as possible. Their other function, as they see it, is to highlight the problem. At the 1985 book fair at Frankfurt – the world's top gathering of publishers – the British Publishers Association mounted an exhibition illustrating examples of counterfeited titles.

The most obvious cost of such piracy is money. There is potentially another far greater cost. As Nigeria's Chinke Ojiji pointed out, pirates don't care about the quality or accuracy of what they produce. This means that it is possible for medical students – particularly in underdeveloped African or Third World countries – to study dangerously inaccurate medical textbooks – just as it is possible for them, once qualified, to prescribe in good faith medication that can damage or kill.

Pharmaceutical counterfeiting is another thriving and deadly business.

CHAPTER EIGHTEEN

The Bitter Pill

There have been deaths impossible to calculate, and permanent injuries; blindness, too, sometimes permanent. All caused by the most pernicious of all counterfeiting activities, the faking of medicines and drugs – and not just supposedly legal drugs. One group of American counterfeiters trying by artificial means to produce a drug of abuse went grotesquely wrong, creating a substance that induced Parkinson's Disease in those who took it. In California, another group – not thought to comprise more than three or four chemists – has synthesised an artificial heroin a thousand times stronger than the real drug which kills the unknowing on the first injection. Incredibly, it is increasingly becoming the drug of choice for addicts who *do* know. Perhaps even more incredibly, the counterfeiting chemists are breaking no American law.

The Philippines have been identified to me as a medicine and drug counterfeiting country by one of the few pharmaceutical investigators prepared to discuss the trade, even unattributably. So has Indonesia, although I am aware of one counterfeiting ring – dealing in antibiotics – which spread its manufacture throughout Europe to evade breaking the law of any one single country and *supplied* Indonesia. Within months of American scientist Jonas Salk feeling able to announce his polio vaccine in the United States in 1955, crooked chemists were counterfeiting what they claimed to be a polio vaccine. An unknown quantity was distributed throughout the United States. It is believed to have been more widely sold, throughout Africa and Asia. It was useless. Medical and aid agencies have no way of assessing the number of people who were crippled by it.

According to an American medical official with worldwide

experience – particularly in underdeveloped countries – who spoke with me on the strict understanding that his remarks would be left anonymous:

> Counterfeiting drugs and medicines is simply murder. In parts of Africa and Asia, medication is often prescribed by semi-trained assistants who work by packet colour coding or brand name. Frequently genuine brand names are changed simply by the omission or insertion of one letter and supplied in the belief that they will work. And all too frequently they are quite ineffective. And the obscenity compounds itself when innocent, semi- or illiterate people try to care for themselves by buying from street traders maybe one or two of the useless tablets they identify from what was the phony colour coding or passed-off brand naming in the first place. So they die. Or become permanently disabled. And that death or permanent disability is put down to the insanitary or ineffective medical conditions of the country when in fact they have been killed or maimed by counterfeiters. So no statistics are possible: not even estimates. But I believe there are thousands. Frighteningly, maybe even more than thousands.

Medical authorities and investigators in Europe believe all the pharmaceutical counterfeiting carried out there is for export, although there is known to exist within the European community what is referred to as parallel trading or parallel stocking. The expression describes the buying of a genuine product sold at a lower price in one country – Italy, for example – for repackaging in counterfeit containers or wrappings to be passed off still at slightly less than the retail price, in a country where the genuine product costs more. This is also the method used to make a profit from proprietary drugs and medicines on which the medical authorities of various countries – in England it is the Dunlop Committee of the Department of Health and Social Security – have imposed a 'shelf life'. Invariably, in Europe, the authorities err on the side of excessive caution, so that products which have overrun their sell-by date remain efficacious. Nevertheless, they should be destroyed. But I was assured by two independent investigators that repackaged proprietary drugs regularly find their way back on to the market, to be sold from street stalls and cut-price pharmacies. I was also assured that such was the bulk of the trade that it was practically impossible for the multi-nationals to be unaware of the recycling. Without exception, every major pharmaceutical manufacturing company in America and throughout Europe to which I put the question insisted it never happened. But then they also denied the existence of counterfeiting. Both exist, despite the denials.

The attitude of medical experts to whom I have spoken and who do accept the practice exists is that while it should not occur, at worst there is at least some medical value left in the parallel-stocked products and at best they are unchanged, so that the risk of death or disability is minimal. This is philosophic realism, not complacency. Of far greater concern among doctors and relief agency personnel is the out-and-out counterfeit. Sometimes the supposed medication possesses none of the generic, medically effective ingredients it purports to contain but is simply a useless placebo. More often the ingredients are there but not in the correct proportions stipulated in the approved, medically tested and patented formula – an imbalance which results in either an under- or an overdose, both of which can kill.

The British Wellcome Foundation – one of the companies which declined to be interviewed on drug counterfeiting – discovered its Septrin antibiotic being counterfeited in Thailand and warned the Bangkok government: 'A child with typhoid treated with spurious Septrin tablets is likely to die ... the possible death rate from the quantity of these spurious drugs we have seen is enormous.'

In the Hong Kong offices of the Commercial Trademark Services investigation agency of Anthony Gurka, I saw a black museum of seized fake antibiotics that could kill, eyedrops that could blind and skin ointment that could disfigure and scar for life. All looked completely genuine, complete with the formula, wrapper and packaging copied from the real manufacturer. A counterfeited Austrian protein concentrate for the victims of starvation or malnutrition contained no nourishment whatsoever – but carried instructions for the use of sterile or distilled water!

Taiwan and Malaysia were the manufacturing countries.

'Those are the ones we have seized,' said Gurka. 'The awful tragedy is that there are hundreds we haven't.'

From Taiwan, phony antibiotics have followed the familiar route to Nigeria whose 90,000,000 inhabitants make it the most heavily populated country in Africa. There, clinics run active birth control campaigns. I have been given an estimate that twenty-five per cent of the birth control pills on the Nigerian market are faked in Taiwan, and do nothing to prevent conception. This has resulted in a thriving abortion industry whose backstreet victims frequently develop infections. These are treated with those phony antibiotics. The British Beecham Group admit to introducing a special, hopefully counterfeit-proof packaging for Ampliclox, an anti-bacterial product that is extensively used in Nigeria to treat septic abortions. ICI managed to impound some shipments of Tetmosol soap – its brand name for a preparation to treat scabies – on their arrival for sale in West Africa. The counterfeiters were traced to South Korea. The company was unable to do anything to stop production of the soap there. In 1983 the US multi-national drug company Pfizer traced fifteen useless imitations of its Terramycin antibiotic on sale in Nigeria. A spokesman was quoted as saying the fake antibiotics were 'sub-potent'.

Investigators report fakers throughout West and Central Africa taking a particular and distressing advantage of the simplistic colour coding system. Gonorrhoea is widespread throughout the continent and one of the commonest treatments in hospitals and clinics is by the use of ampicillin. Copies of its easily recognisable black and red capsules are available in most town and village markets. They are utterly useless: 'which means,' a venereologist attached to a relief agency told me, 'that an already rampant complaint continues to spread unchecked throughout the continent'.

Not all the phony drugs and medicines circulating in Nigeria – and via Nigeria throughout West Africa – come from the Far East. Intelligence agencies have also located a conduit which begins in the parallel-stocking country of Italy and passes through the ever-open doorway of Bulgaria by means of a government-backed import–export firm. KINTEX has been shown by those same agencies to trade in fake whisky and narcotics which enter Europe from the Golden Crescent and the Golden Triangle producing areas of Asia. Headquartered at Anton Ivanov Boulevard, in the Bulgarian capital of Sofia, KINTEX has created a separate company – Evrotrans – which ships medicines and drugs from Europe into Africa. Italy is not the combine's only source of illegal medicaments. Evrotrans is suspected of being involved in the shipment from India into Zambia of Mandrax, one of the most widely used drugs of abuse in the African continent. Drug enforcement officials identified the Mandrax – a legitimate sleeping pill capable of creating a heroin-like soporific effect if taken in large quantities – as originating in Calcutta, the centre in India of drug counterfeiting.

India itself is both a victim and a producer of counterfeit medicines. Conjunctivitis and other eye complaints are widespread throughout the vast continent which is the principal market for the phony eye lotions and ointments manufactured in Taiwan, the Philippines and Indonesia. During the time I spent in the country there were reports of fifty people being blinded in the Nagpur region by quack doctors using quack medicines. Two gangs known to be involved in the production of the counterfeits are Hadi Mastan and Sukur Narain.

The export route for the drugs begins by arab *dhow* from around the inlets and creeks of Gujarat across the narrowest part of the Arabian Sea into the Persian Gulf. Indian merchants, particularly those based in Dubai and Abu Dhabi, vie with displaced Palestinians as the traders in the Gulf where the illicit drugs from India are redirected into Africa. Zambia's President Kaunda is an avowed opponent of narcotics and drug abuse and in November 1985 he convened a tribunal to investigate the importation of the Indian-produced Mandrax. During the enquiries, ex-Vice-President Reuben Kamanga was named as responsible for the smuggling of 300,000 tablets into the country. Also implicated were a former Foreign Minister, Vernon Mwaanga, and a onetime member of Kaunda's cabinet, Sikota Wina, and his wife, the Lozi Princess Nakatindi.

No injunctions, however, were taken out against one of the most brilliant counterfeiting rings of them all – even though the ringleader was identified. Investigators have traced the fake antibiotics from Italy – it is thought via Evrotrans – into Indonesia where they lost the trail and so are unable to establish whether the drugs were re-exported from Jakarta to Africa or Asia. The investigator who described the route – and the way a spurious legality was achieved -- did so on the understanding that I did not identify some of the technical and scientific methods of establishing the product to be a fake. I can disclose, however, that the antibiotic is manufactured by a British-based company and widely used by doctors throughout Europe. The fakes detected contained the formula ingredients but not in the proper quantities: of those analysed, the most actively useful drug was grossly under strength.

The legality was achieved by spreading the manufacture and packaging throughout Europe, originating in West Germany. It was here that the base powder was ordered. But as no manufacture was attempted, there was no contravention of any German law. The powder was legally shipped to France, where the importation manifest was changed before delivery to the pharmaceutical firm which was contracted to manufacture the pills. These were neither described nor sold as the genuine article, so again – just – there was no illegality. From France, the shipment moved to Spain where the pills were inserted into the metal-foil packaging which forms part, but not all, of the original's trademark. Again, no attempt was made to sell in the country of manufacture. The title sticker, formula details and final package were printed in Italy where the metal-foiled pills were sent for completion. Once more, no attempt was made to sell lest the legitimate manufacturer be prompted to investigate on suddenly discovering a glut of its product on the market. From Italy, via Bulgaria courtesy of Evrotrans, the dangerous antibiotics were finally routed to Jakarta.

The investigator who solved the case explained why the offended company, which at first threatened prosecution, was content to accept the ringleader's undertaking to discontinue his activities:

It was the classic and usual resolve. Drug companies are terrified of any publicity surrounding their product, particularly something like an antibiotic which in the public mind is associated with serious illness and not something like a simple cold or a cut finger. The universal attitude is that a danger greater than the counterfeit itself is the risk of their losing public confidence both in their product and in their company. They'll move heaven and earth with threats and desist letters rather than actually go to court and undergo the publicity. It's an understandable attitude commercially but a cynical one from any sort of humanitarian viewpoint. And in many instances and ways, it's self-defeating. The committed pharmaceutical counterfeiters know exactly what they're doing and the reluctant attitude of the companies they're stealing from. So they know the chances of their being prosecuted and risking any sort of court appearance, public exposure, fine or imprisonment are absolutely minimal. So the only people who really suffer are the poor bastards who take or buy the phony stuff and are either mourned by their relatives or spend a long time wondering why they're not getting any better.

The curtain was lifted slightly before an American Congressional enquiry in 1983 by James Bikoff, President of the International Anti-Counterfeiting Coalition, a group of more than 140 concerned US corporations, associations and law firms. Bikoff talked of stepping out of the South Korean Patent Office in Seoul in March of that year, when he was part of a US government group attempting to stop every sort of counterfeiting in the country, and buying a jar of fake Vaseline in the shop next door. Bikoff then produced the fake and a jar of genuine Vaseline. The only way he was able to illustrate to the investigating legislators that the Vaseline – legal manufacturer, Ponds – was counterfeit was to isolate the spelling of petroleum. On the label of the fake jar, the 't' had been left out. Bikoff also showed the enquiry a jar of fake Vick's Formula 44 and said that he understood from the Vick company that their enquiries had shown it to have been manufactured 'in the jungles of Indonesia with a lack of sanitary conditions and absolutely no quality control'.

The fake narcotics of California are, by comparison, produced in laboratory conditions and they can kill quicker than any other known counterfeit drug. Their appearance was first recorded on the streets of Los Angeles and San Francisco during 1981. Initially, the drug defied any sort of scientific analysis. It was guessed to be some sort of heroin derivative and labelled China White because of another erroneous guess which suggested Asia as its place of origin. Thirty people died from overdosing before a specially equipped investigatory laboratory on the outskirts of Washington, DC, recognised it as the methyl analog of fentanyl, an analgesic opiate.

By 1985, when it had been renamed a 'designer' drug, it was causing a nightmare for enforcement agencies and continuing to kill its unwitting users. Ninety were diagnosed by postmortem examinations to have died from overdosing. Further examination by the Washington laboratory which first isolated the true identity of the drug determined that it was a thousand times stronger than heroin. The amount needed for an effect better than heroin could produce was so small than an active dosage amounted to only 50 micrograms, so small that it would have fitted on a pinhead and was undetectable in any laboratory without the apparatus to test to parts per billion or per trillion.

And it is legal. To be illegal, it must be described and listed as such under the US Controlled Substances Act and the counterfeiting scientists remain one jump ahead of enforcement agencies by simply changing slightly the molecular structure of the fentanyl as their previous adjustments are added to the list proscribed under the Act. Three variants are already listed – the last, 3-methyl-fentanyl, in April 1985 – and the Drug Enforcement Administration has succeeded in reducing to thirty days the time it takes to get the newest mutation proscribed. One agent told me in Hollywood: 'They're still ahead. And winning. And people are still dying.'

Public warnings have been issued about the danger of the heroin counterfeit but all evidence indicates, to the bewilderment of enforcement and treatment specialists, that at least a fifth of California's addicts choose to use the fentanyl derivative because of its greater potency. A DEA official told me:

> The stupid bastards know they're killing themselves, using adulterated heroin in the first place. Consciously switching to a fentanyl derivative the strength of which they have no idea how to measure or control is like playing Russian roulette with all the bullets in the gun and an assassin standing by just in case you miss.

Chemists employed by the enforcement agency calculate that there could be as many as two hundred variations on the fentanyl base. One told me: 'It would be an incredible – although obscene irony – if American addicts' use of genuine heroin were solved by the growers in Asia being forced out of poppy production because US chemists can make a more attractive and cheaper synthetic alternative.'

So concentrated is the synthetic drug that the illegal chemists can in two weeks produce 200 grams, or sufficient for 4,000,000 doses! My DEA informant said: 'It's a man-made monster, like Frankenstein or Dr Jekyll's Mr Hyde'.

THE BITTER PILL

It is some measure of the degree of concern felt by the US authorities at the manufacture of counterfeit heroin that led in 1985 to Congress considering changing the law to provide a blanket prohibition on the manufacture of drugs that produce effects similar to heroin. The authorities have also warned Europe of the danger of heroin counterfeits. British Home Office minister David Mellor, responsible for the country's fight against drug addiction, calls 'horrendous' the possibility of fentanyl analogues adding to the abuse problem in England and he confirmed in 1985 that the government was considering the sort of complete ban debated in the American Congress.

A group of Californian chemists, separate from that which is manufacturing fake heroin, devised a drug which even better deserves the horrendous epithets of my DEA source. It occurred in 1982 when in an unknown laboratory in northern California chemists attempted to counterfeit a proprietary drug tradenamed Demerol. Manufactured by the Breon company, the real drug is composed of meperidine HCI – a highly addictive narcotic analgesic, used by the medical profession as a substitute for morphine and by addicts as a popular drug of abuse. Its pain-relieving qualities are less pronounced than those of morphine and in addition it has a sedative effect. In the manufacturing process, the counterfeiters overheated their formula and created a drug known as MPTP. They still marketed it to addicts, however, like pharmaceutical pirates everywhere, without the slightest concern at the effect upon the buyer. MPTP gave its users Parkinson's disease. Twenty people in the state have been permanently afflicted and physicians expect five hundred more of those who used the tainted batch to develop the disease during their lifetime.

The lethally strong artificial heroin or the badly made Demerol counterfeit are not the only fake drugs to have caused death or permanent disability. The American Medical Association talks of an unknown number of deaths or cases of crippling paralysis being caused by phony amphetamines and tranquillisers, and the US Food and Drug Administration have identified twelve drug abuse deaths from amphetamine counterfeiting – including that of a twelve-year-old child in New Mexico who went into a fatal coma after taking two counterfeit biphetamines. Even counterfeit birth control pills have been introduced and sold in America, products similar to those so prevalent in Africa and Asia.

185

In 1984 the American manufacturer G. D. Searle and Co. – a subsidiary of Monsanto based in Skokie, Illinois – received complaints from women of heavy bleeding and discovered that their birth control pill had been copied, but with insufficient levels of oestrogen. They immediately notified the US Food and Drug Administration and recall instructions were issued to retailers. More than a million counterfeit pills were recovered, but too late to prevent some women from becoming pregnant. The medically unsafe pills were labelled like the genuine article, Ovulen 21, and from legal proceedings initiated by one woman who unwillingly became pregnant, the indications are that they were manufactured in Panama.

That woman is Mrs Beverly Butler who lives in Augusta, Georgia. In October 1985 she and her husband began a $1,600,000 suit against the retail outlet, supplier and importer of the pills. According to statements already filed in the court, importers Interstate Drug Exchange Inc. – based in Long Island, New York – sold the Panama-made bogus pills to Richie Pharmaceuticals Co. – headquartered at Glasgow, Kentucky – which supplied them to the Southside Pharmacy in Augusta. G. D. Searle have also initiated a legal action against Interstate Drug Exchange Inc., alleging patent infringement and trademark violation.

In December 1985 Mrs Butler, who gave birth to a son – Zachary Scott – through the ineffectiveness of the counterfeit pill, told an interviewer: 'I am afraid of how common this is.' Officials of the US Food and Drug Administration already knew how common medical and pharmaceutical counterfeiting was in America. As long ago as May 1978, they had hurriedly to recall 357 intra-aortic balloon pumps in use in 266 hospitals throughout the country during open heart surgery operations. The $20,000 pumps had been fitted with an $8 false component.

Mechanical component faking is, in fact, another example of the worldwide multi-billion-dollar counterfeiting industry.

CHAPTER NINETEEN

We Are Not Amused

Queen Victoria originated the remark in 1900, and the technical advisors to her descendant were not amused either at the widespread publicity which followed the suggestion, made in 1983 during an American Congressional enquiry into counterfeiting, that the life of Queen Elizabeth was endangered because bogus parts had been fitted into a helicopter of the Queen's flight.

Specifically, the US House of Representatives Energy and Commerce Committee heard from James Bikoff that fake brakes had been installed instead of the genuine article manufactured by the Birmingham-based Dunlop company. It is unfortunate that the publicity the disclosure naturally engendered should have had the effect of obscuring from the public other examples of potentially lethal copying. Because no fake parts were ever supplied or fitted to the Queen's helicopters, the apocryphal story tended in the succeeding years to delude people into disregarding accounts of aero-parts counterfeiting as exaggerated. They are not. Deaths have been caused and catastrophes involving civil airliners packed with people narrowly avoided.

From the extensive enquiries I made in trying to establish the truth about the Queen's flight, I learned that at the Dunlop factory there exists a separate and tightly secure department through which all components and parts of the Royal aircraft fleet are channelled. And before being supplied, each item – down to individual nuts, bolts and screws – is individually examined and stress-tested before going on to the Ministry of Defence, where another equally secure department repeats every examination upon every article.

According to a Dunlop official, who spoke without any hesitation or reluctance about cases of counterfeiting of company products that *had* occurred: 'The supervision and quality control involving

187

everything about the Royal Family is absolute. And subject to constant oversight, review and revision. It is not just inconceivable for bogus parts or fittings to get through. It's impossible.'

It was this kind of vigilance that in 1977 led to another British firm, the Westland Helicopter Co. of Yeovil in Somerset, initiating enquiries in America which disclosed extensive aero-parts counterfeiting. The enquiries produced some unexpected and worrying disclosures. For as well as uncovering clear examples of inferior and lethal components, the probe found a ridiculous system in the US Department of Defence – one that still exists, despite protests – which actually assists counterfeiting! Nor was this all. In the opinion of Westland technicians, the part which had originally aroused their suspicions was in fact better than the one US Government regulations required they buy and fit.

Involved was the Model 47, a two-seater helicopter made by Bell Helicopter Textron of Fort Worth, Texas and manufactured under a licensing agreement at Yeovil by Westland, Britain's only helicopter company. By early 1977, when Westland technical experts first became suspicious at slightly different identification markings on American-supplied parts, the British firm had already built and sold three hundred of the helicopters to which they affixed the additional designation 3B1. The British RAF were the major buyers, supplementing with the 47–3B1 their Scout helicopters. The British firm Bristow was also a buyer. So was the Yemeni Air Force.

The component which particularly attracted the interest and concern of Westland was the main rotor driveshaft, one of the most vitally important parts of the machine. In its approach to Bell Helicopters, however, Westland asked that Westland's entire stock be reviewed by the parent company. The warning booklet subsequently produced by the latter's Product Assurance Department states somewhat laconically: 'The evaluation disclosed that most of their stock, which had been purchased from dealers in the United States, was, in fact, bogus.'

The enquiries following on from that evaluation found fake parts fitted into more than six hundred helicopters in use in NATO and American air forces. Apart from Britain's RAF and the Yemeni Air Force, I know the air forces of Belgium, France and West Germany were flying machines fitted with spares unapproved by Bell or authorised by the American Federal Aviation Administration. Most of those helicopters affected which were in service in Europe had come from Westland and the cost of the phony parts with which the craft had been supplied was put at $40,000,000 by some authoritative sources. Markings had been forged indicating that the parts had been manufactured by Bell. Some were also found with markings indicating that they were parts approved for Sikorsky machines, manufactured by the United Aircraft Corporation. All were shipped with misleading certificates of airworthiness.

Manufacturers of these unauthorised spares were later identified as Heliparts Inc., Schultz Enterprises Inc., National Helicopter Service and Engineering Co. and Banner International – all located in California. They were named in a $35,000,000 lawsuit filed by Bell, alleging conspiracy to manufacture and the sale of bogus parts. In a subsequent settlement, Bell was granted a permanent injunction restraining the firms involved from manufacturing, or having manufactured, or marking replacement parts for helicopters manufactured by or designed by Bell with trademarks, inspection stamps, serial numbers or any other identifying marks which duplicated or so closely resembled those used by Bell as to mislead prospective purchasers as to their manufacture. The four were also ordered by the court to surrender to Bell all stencils, marking tools, dies and stamps in their possession which duplicated or closely resembled those used by Bell. In addition, the counterfeiting companies had to pay Bell an undisclosed sum of money, described in court documents as 'substantial'.

Those listed above were not the only companies named in the action. Aviation Sales Inc. of New York was identified in the court documents as the company through which the parts reached Westland. Also identified were Aviation Helicopter Sales (UK) Ltd and Hyfore Manufacturing Corp. of California. All three were owned one hundred per cent by a man named Jack Dadourian. At the time of the settlement, Bell's chief counsel said the lawsuit would be continued 'vigorously' against Dadourian and his companies.

Dadourian did not wait for any hearing. He fled and is currently still on the run. Some people involved in the case have told me that they believe he is hiding in Brazil. A Los Angeles District Court issued a judgment of $41,100,000 against him and his companies.

Federal Judge Mariana Pfaelzer also issued permanent injunctions against Dadourian and his named companies. That injunction restrained them from using in any manner in connection with manufacture, use or sale of helicopter parts, Bell Helicopter Textron's inspection marks or marks so closely similar that confusion, mistake or deception was likely. Dadourian was also forbidden to employ in any manner the numbers used on various Bell Helicopter models, all of which were available from illustrated parts manuals, or the distinctive 'bh' trademark of Bell Helicopters or to copy or simulate that trademark or falsely to represent or certify to purchasers that helicopter parts made or sold by him or his companies were manufactured or inspected by Bell or an approved supplier. Dadourian and his companies were also ordered to surrender for destruction all dies, forgings, casting equipment, moulds, drawings, specifications, part stamps, certification stamps, part number stamps and parts or anything else in their possession or control bearing the marks or stamps of Bell Helicopters.

An official at Westland who was involved in the investigation and later lawsuits told me in Yeovil: 'One of the most astonishing things about the whole episode was that our technical people here considered the main rotor driveshaft Dadourian supplied to be better than that which was approved by the Federal Aviation Administration or complied with Bell's specifications.' Nevertheless, because the part officially held no airworthiness certificate it had to be removed from every machine throughout the world which Westland had made and supplied. But because of its considered belief that the bogus part was not inferior to the Bell driveshaft, the firm allowed what was described to me as 'certain relaxations'. These avoided the inconvenience of mass groundings by making the necessary substitutions during normal servicing or at the least inconvenient time.

By far the most astonishing discovery made during the enquiries, however, was of how easy it had been for the counterfeiters to obtain the specifications and copies of the markings they used to convince buyers that their parts had been approved by Bell. A Westland official described this to me as 'a hell of a loophole. And one that remains to this day, despite the strongest and continuing protest, by us.'

The loophole is created by the American company's tie-up with the American army, which runs what is codenamed the Breakout Programme – an attempt to keep military costs to a minimum.

Whether it succeeds is debatable. What is not is the potential civil and military danger caused by Breakout. For under this budget-conscious programme, the army takes Bell Helicopter drawings obtained under the terms of its production contracts with the company and seeks bids on the open market from any manufacturer who wishes to make the parts. The drawings are then offered, complete with specifications and markings, to those manufacturers who express an interest.

Foreign governments and civil aircraft companies are as interested – some even more so – in cost cutting as the American military. One way of achieving that economy is to buy military surplus. In a warning to potential buyers Bell, with seeming illogicality, says: 'Just because it is a military surplus part for a Bell helicopter doesn't mean it is a genuine Bell part.' The warning, contained in an official issue guidance booklet, continues:

> Parts procured under this programme may be made by companies other than Bell Helicopter and Bell Helicopter approved suppliers.
>
> These parts are not necessarily approved for commercial use by the FAA [Federal Aviation Administration]. The government also substitutes military specifications for Bell process specifications.
>
> The suppliers of these Breakout parts may not have the stringent quality controls that are maintained by Bell Helicopter Textron. For example, periodic conformity inspections and destructive tests to assure the continued quality of the product.

Bell is not the only American helicopter manufacturer with which Westland operates a licensing agreement. By 1986 a thirty-eight-year-long association with the Sikorsky company actually reached the point of a $109,520,000 American takeover bid for the financially embattled British company. Urging shareholders to agree the takeover, Westland said: 'Our partnership with Sikorsky is tried and tested.'

An official of the company told me: 'The Breakout Programme operated by the military and referred to by Bell in their warning manual to potential buyers continues to operate with Sikorsky.' The official referred particularly to the Westland-built Sea King helicopter, of which 305 had been sold worldwide at the time of the takeover negotiations. From my conversations with Westland and British Ministry of Defence officials, I know that because of Breakout – and its earlier experience with the two-seater Model 47 – Westland imposes stringent checks on all American-supplied spares.

The Westland takeover was a bitter one. There was a rival bid, which the British firm resisted, from a European consortium and Minister of Defence Michael Heseltine, who backed the European counter-offer, resigned in January 1986, protesting that Premier Margaret Thatcher's presidential style of leadership stifled proper and sufficient Cabinet discussion of alternatives. At the height of that wrangling, a Westland official was telling me that because of the Breakout system, the company on occasion obtained some spares from Europe. He said:

> The danger does not just exist from being supplied with military surplus obtained by American middlemen and passed off as that approved by the parent company: they at least attain some quality control, even if it does not comply with that required by the company or by the Federal Aviation Administration. The danger is that unscrupulous companies will obtain drawings and specifications through the programme and manufacture grossly inferior, potentially lethal parts which will get fitted into a machine.

This has frequently happened.

A fake Bell rotor driveshaft, fitted into a Model 47 helicopter during the 1977 counterfeiting scandal, failed after less than six hours of operation. The machine crashed. The pilot was killed. A clutch drum on the same model helicopter failed during takeoff over a 125 foot cliff: the pilot's back was broken. Bogus and inferior tail rotor hub assembly bolts fractured, causing three separate accidents. During the investigations of the late seventies, the Bell and Westland officials recovered Model 47 tail rotor slides, transmission cases, pillow blocks and gear sets, all of which would have failed if fitted. There was an occasion when a mechanic stopped short of installing a gear assembly because it did not fit 'quite right'. Tests showed that it had not been properly heat treated and that the gear teeth had not been carburised. It would have collapsed under operational conditions. In October 1985 – eight years after the first cases had been discovered – the crash of a

Peruvian Air Force helicopter, supplied by Bell, was traced to worn-out tail rotor blades. They had been recycled by a Miami firm.

In an effort to defeat counterfeiting, Bell maintain a bogus parts hotline (area code 817, 280 3118) on which buyers can obtain instant advice if they fear any stock they purchase may not be genuine.

Bell is not the only American aircraft manufacturer to have had its machines endangered by counterfeiters. Again in 1977, Boeing discovered fake fire detection and control units actually installed in some of their airliners. Some were in Boeing 727s, others in Boeing 737s like the British Air Tour's flight KT328 which burst into flames immediately prior to takeoff from Manchester airport in August 1985 with the subsequent loss of fifty-five lives. The cause of the Manchester disaster is still, at the time of writing, being probed by crash investigators. I have seen remarks from Boeing officials that the 1977 copies – manufactured from stolen blueprints – were of a reasonably high quality. Still, the American Federal Aviation Administration grounded thirty aircraft and insisted on the bogus parts being replaced with properly approved parts.

Aero-parts counterfeiting is not limited in America to passenger carrying aircraft. Vigilant engineers at the NASA space centre at Houston detected before fitment fake transistors intended for use in a test programme to be run on the country's trouble-plagued space shuttle and Department of Defence engineers found – again, fortunately, before fitment – bogus components for its F-4 fighter aircraft and Chaparral and Lance missile systems. Department of Defence officials with whom I talked in Washington conceded that aero-parts counterfeiting was a problem, but not that their Breakout Programme was a contributory or dangerous factor. Instead, they insisted its influence was minimal and quoted the timely discovery of the bogus components for the F-4 and missile systems as evidence that their checks and supervision provided the necessary safeguards.

The British Dunlop company, which so scrupulously protects aircraft of the Queen's flight, has, however, been victim of aero-parts piracy, too. The components were brake units which were installed in Strikemaster fighter training aircraft belonging, with some irony, to the air force of that leader among pirating countries, Singapore. The counterfeit was discovered when the brakes on one Strikemaster failed on landing during a training exercise in 1980: the plane corkscrewed the length of the airfield but fortunately stopped without crashing or injuring the pilot.

The fake parts were made by Staravia Ltd of Ascot in Berkshire. Established soon after the end of the Second World War, the company held a Category B1 classification from the Civil Aviation Authority, licensing it as an organisation 'approved for inspections overhauls, repairs, replacements and embodiment of modifications to aircraft, engines, components or items of equipment'. It was certainly not licensed to do what Dunlop's special anti-counterfeiting department discovered it to be doing on investigating the Singapore crash. The department found that the Staravia-supplied brake units, which should have been manufactured from hard steel, were made from mild, soft steel. This meant, according to a company expert who advised me in the preparation of this book, that when the aircraft brakes were applied on landing they crumpled and practically melted like cheese under a grill.

Nor was this Staravia's only counterfeiting activity. It also made phony brake equipment for the HS 748 Avro short-haul airliner. Capable of carrying up to forty people, the HS 748 is known as the Andover. There are Andovers forming part of the Queen's flight and during my enquiries into the 1983 allegations that fake parts had been fitted to royal aircraft, it was suggested to me that the apocryphal accounts arose from rumours within the British aircraft industry linking the phony brake equipment for the Andover with the royal fleet. But, as a Dunlop official told me somewhat stiffly: 'The British Royal Family do not buy second-hand goods.'

Singapore appeared quite prepared to do so. On 6 April 1979 Staravia supplied 126 brake rotors to the country's air force. The rotors were marked AFM 6546 – the Dunlop number for its own spare brake rotors – and had been ordered from Staravia the previous month, on 19 March. Dunlop could not have filled the order in under nine months: unwilling to allocate warehouse space to spares for aircraft which may soon be obsolete, the company does not stockpile but manufactures replacement parts to order. Staravia delivered in under a month. Singapore's order was marked 'AOG' which stands for 'Aircraft On Ground'. The acronym appeared on the invoice for the Staravia phonys and, according to Mr Justice Oliver speaking at a subsequent Appeal Court hearing, it underlined the urgency of the order. Made from mild steel – hard steel would have taken too long – Staravia's 126 brake rotors would have equipped the Singapore Air Force for two years – only if the aircraft had survived, that is.

After the corkscrew landing of the Strikemaster in August 1980, the Singapore government protested to Dunlop which initially treated the complaint as a warranty claim. An official of the company told me: 'At first our aviation division couldn't believe it could be a case of counterfeiting, not of brakes.' Technical examination between December 1980 and February 1981 of two samples of the Staravia-supplied brake rotors proved to the disbelieving aviation division that it was exactly that. Giving judgment in the Appeal Court hearing, Mr Justice Oliver commented: 'The continued use of rotors of this type could be extremely dangerous, if not indeed disastrous.'

It took some time for Dunlop to identify Staravia via the records of the 'primary' companies – Civil Aviation categories A1 and A2 – which had supplied it. Identification was not positive until 20 May 1981, when Staravia was about to be pinpointed as the firm that had so cynically provided the substandard parts for the Andover short-haul airliner. That equipment had been ordered sometime between May and July 1980 by another British aero-parts firm, Flight Spares Ltd, and was delivered in February 1981. But the accompanying documentation did not contain the certification required by Civil Aviation Authority regulations. Flight Spares Ltd did not, therefore, sell the parts. Instead, it took samples to a now retired but extremely alert Dunlop official based at London's Heathrow airport. Linsey Dean quickly identified them for the fakes they were and Flight Spares immediately returned them to Staravia – who almost at once redelivered the consignment, this time accompanied by the necessary certificates.

By the time Dunlop discovered what had been done with Flight Spares' original order – and the Civil Aviation Authority had issued a worldwide warning notice – the counterfeits had been supplied to airline companies in New Zealand and South Africa. In no instance, however, had they actually been fitted to an aircraft. This was possibly due to the speed with which Linsey Dean reacted when he heard of the Strikemaster counterfeiting. At once he warned Dunlop headquarters of the samples he had seen from Flight Spares Ltd. That warning coincided with the receipt by Dunlop of anonymous information from a Staravia employee at Ascot. From investigations he made through the network of secondary suppliers of parts in England, Dean independently came up with the name of Staravia.

Dunlop brought successful legal actions against Staravia, which lost an appeal against the Anton Pillar orders issued against it, and throughout the world all the copied parts were withdrawn and destroyed. A company official told me: 'Our general policy, upon the discovery that we are being counterfeited, is to squeeze the guilty company until the pips squeak, to discourage others.'

The motorcar preceded the development of the aeroplane and its aero engine. It leads, too, as one of the largest of the world's counterfeit engineering industries. And while Taiwan is a long way ahead of its nearest competitors, India holds the record as the most innovative among the countries involved.

No cost was too great to maintain the ostentation of the Indian aristocracy at the height of the British Raj and a particular aspect of that ostentation was the vying of the competing maharajahs for the largest number and biggest range of motorcars. Custom-built Rolls-Royces were the favourite. But the stables contained other models, too, like Mercedes and Hispano and Facel Vega and even Model-T Fords. All are prohibited by statute – laws enacted after India's independence in 1947 to strip the aristocracy – from being exported or sold outside the country. Whatever is forbidden – particularly if it is a forbidden luxury – feeds illegal markets. Unique among them is India's illegal vintage car market. Equally unique is the way that it is fed.

In a series of extensive meetings in Bombay and New Delhi with police officers and lawyers, details were disclosed to me of the thriving business supplying today's equivalent of the yesteryear maharajahs – wealthy Westerners determined to own, irrespective of cost, what no one else can have. It costs them more dearly than any of them suspect.

The Hadi Mastan gang, active in pharmaceutical faking, are heavily involved, through Gulf-based Indian middlemen linked with entrepreneurs predominantly in America. Centres of the business are at Faridabad and Gurgaon, near the New Delhi capital, and Ulhasnagar, conveniently situated at the top of the Bombay peninsula near the coast and the border of Pakistan. In factories at these three locations, the vintage cars – complete with logbooks detailing the history and, inevitably royal, ownership of the vehicle – are cut up to be taken out of the country. The customary smuggling route is across the border into Pakistan, either by road or by ship, hugging the coast round the gulfs of Khambhat and Kachchh. Sometimes, so the Indian authorities believe, the vehicles are reassembled in Pakistan; more usually, they are reshipped, still in conveniently packaged pieces, across the Persian Gulf to the waiting Indian traders who form the link with the Western salesmen. Abu Dhabi and Dubai were identified to me as places where the reassembly is more frequently done. There, the cars are crated for shipment to customers, who are told how the vehicles were got out of India and warned against going to the main service agents or suppliers for routine work or replacement lest they set off an investigation into how so unique a vehicle came into their possession in the first place.

'That last part, the warning about any contact with genuine dealers or mechanics, is the most important part of the whole scheme,' a senior police officer assured me in Bombay. 'It's vital the car is maintained by a small, no-questions-asked garage who brings in any parts from the outside, bona fide supplier.' Why? Because the whole thing is a counterfeit operation, reproducing from drawings and surviving examples facsimiles of genuine vintage cars. Obviously, the maharajah-naming logbooks, too, are faked. 'They are very well and expertly made,' my informant told me. 'But they would not withstand any detailed scrutiny by factory-trained mechanics.'

From evidence provided by one arrested member of the Hadi Mastan gang, the Indian authorities believe there are at least two phony Model-T Fords and a fake Rolls-Royce in Houston – and another replica Rolls in Dallas. A car copied in this manner is also thought to have been shipped to Coventry, in England, although the authorities are unsure of the supposed vintage model.

The Indian authorities are not, in fact, interested in any sort of investigation because the industry is not in breach of their criminal code. According to an official in New Delhi:

The statute covers genuine cars, not copies. The crime is fraud,

197

technically initiated in this country but perpetrated thousands
of miles away through a series of middlemen. To mount any
sort of enquiry, a complaint would initially have to be made to
the authorities of the country where the owner – who in the
first place has been warned he has bought something obtained
illegally – discovers he has been cheated and then channelled
to us. Which of course never happens. If someone discovers
what's happened, he keeps quiet either through embarrassment or through fear of having to admit to his own authorities
that he knowingly committed an offence, receiving illegally
obtained goods. It's the most perfect counterfeit operation
imaginable.

Other counterfeiting activities in India neither produce such
flawless copies nor are so invulnerable. Those same factories at
Faridabad, Gurgaon and Ulhasnagar turn out fakes for the two
models of locally produced vehicles currently in use in India – the
Ambassador, legally modelled on the old English Morris Oxford,
and the licensed copy of an Italian Fiat saloon. In Bombay, New
Delhi and Calcutta I was assured by the authorities – and had it
freely admitted by the kamikaze drivers themselves – that the
brakes on the majority of taxis were fakes, because the pads
provided by the legal manufacturers were too expensive to fit.
Swingeing import duties – in some cases up to 250% – are imposed
by the government of Premier Rajiv Gandhi on imported cars and
the spares necessary to maintain them. Counterfeits are available,
of everything for every model. Even in garages and workshops
officially approved by the manufacturer – Mercedes was quoted to
me as a case in point – a customer will be asked, quite openly,
before any work is begun whether he wants real or counterfeit
parts fitted. There is also an active trade, practised by Western
diplomats at embassies in New Delhi, in importing and selling
spares for cars of their respective countries' manufacture at a profit
but still greatly below the import tariff price. An Indian
businessman friend of mine services his Mercedes this way. He
also purchases his brand-name whisky, gin and wine through
foreign embassy channels because that way he knows it will be
genuine. Bombay and Calcutta are the counterfeiting centres for
brand-name alcohol. A high-ranking New Delhi detective talked
of a factory in Bombay solely engaged in the making of fake

Johnnie Walker bottles, to be filled with day-old 'whisky' in another, nearby factory.

The counterfeit auto-parts industry of India is entirely indigenous with no reliance on the multifarious exports of its market leader, Taiwan. The Kendeem Industrial Co., which I identified in Chapter Thirteen, copied the entire product list of car mirrors produced by the Roberk Division of the Parker Hannifin Corp. of Shelton, Connecticut. The Taiwanese-registered Frame company stole the Stanadyne Model 50 filter made by Stanadyne Diesel Systems of Hartford, Connecticut. The Jenn Feng company counterfeited the Xanteck 12-volt reading lights produced by the Xantech Corp. of North Hollywood, California. Every sort of battery which can be used to power such lights is copied in and around Taipei. I was assured in Taipei by Government Prosecutor Derek Cheng and later by the Hong Kong infringement lawyers, Deacons, that a stop had been put to the counterfeiting of the Union Carbide company's Eveready range – which had been counterfeiting on an incredible scale. In 1983 it was estimated that a total of 17,000,000 phony batteries were being manufactured and shipped out of Taiwan every year. Fan belts and the Champion spark plug are two more common targets for the Taiwan counterfeiters, one of whom made a rare misjudgement when he copied a successful line of accessories for the car interior and then tried to market it under a name only slightly changed from that of the British originator, as is common usage among pirates. The British firm was called Avus. The Taiwan pirate named his product Anus. It did not sell.

England has remained remarkably free from the dangers of fake auto parts, although in the late 1970s an alert engineer queried some brake diaphragms he was about to fit to a Hants and Dorset bus at the company's engineering centre in southern England. They were found to be Taiwan fakes, returned to England from Hong Kong as part of a supposedly surplus consignment.

Hong Kong is more a conduit for Taiwan-manufactured auto fakes than an original producer. The use to which these imports are put, however, is an original one. There exists in the colony a vehicle inspection programme, modelled on the British MOT test, designed to ensure that cars comply with a certain standard of roadworthiness. Many of those cars – particularly taxis and other vehicles put to public use – use counterfeit parts and these would certainly be discovered during such checks. So there exist on Hong

Kong island and on mainland Kowloon garages to which owners can take their vehicles just prior to inspection to have the fakes replaced by the proper brand-name parts which are rented by the hour. Once the vehicle has been passed, the driver returns to the garage where his own, counterfeit, parts are put back.

The automobile industry began in America, where counterfeiting is now so extensive that the legitimate companies are employing task forces to fight it. In the first nine months of 1984 Ford initiated proceedings against twenty-eight counterfeit distributors and manufacturers. General Motors have also formed an anti-counterfeiting division: within months of its creation, they had detected American-made fake brake shoes which marked under the pressure of a thumbnail, antifreeze that corroded engines and transmission fluid that froze solid when the temperature dropped below zero.

Linda Hoffman, of the American Automotive Parts and Accessories Association, estimates the value of spares and replacement parts to the accessories industry – she calls it the 'aftermarket' – at $54,000,000,000 a year. Within America, it provides double the employment provided by the vehicle manufacturers and their dealers. She complained to Congressmen investigating the extent of auto-parts piracy: 'Product pirates have made a multi-billion dollar business out of stealing the good name of American parts and accessories manufacturers ... in the process of idling our plant capacity, product pirates have stolen or prevented the creation of hundreds of thousands of jobs for Americans.' Ms Hoffman blamed foreign counterfeiters – particularly those in Taiwan – for seventy-five per cent of the world's supply of auto-part fakes and said:

In the battle with counterfeiters for international sales, American firms stand to lose any way you look at it. On the one hand, market share is stolen if a counterfeit works and the customer returns to buy more of the low cost fakes. But, even more commonly, when the product fails to perform, the customer blames the American firm named on the label and the sum of dissatisfied customers means sagging demand for American products. Damage to the company's hard-earned reputation is difficult to assess in terms of dollars, but it is an incredibly serious aspect of this problem.

The loss of reputation suffered by the legitimate manufacturer blamed for an inefficient or faulty counterfeit part is not confined, of course, to the auto-accessories industry. It is the danger confronting every bona fide maker who is being ripped off and sporting goods manufacturers are prominent among them.

CHAPTER TWENTY

Play up, Play Up and Play the Game

Western manufacturers of sports equipment and clothes suffer more greatly from the counterfeit catch-22 syndrome than perhaps any other legitimate industry. They get robbed twice! Brazil is the country that perfected the double rip-off. Mexico copied it and Japan modified it. Taiwan just goes on copying.

Under existing Brazilian law, a manufacturer cannot register a trademark unless it can be proved that the product is used in the country. Under another piece of legislation, sports goods – particularly American sports goods – are embargoed. Thus the first part of the catch: if a firm cannot sell, it cannot prove use and therefore it cannot protect its copyright.

The American firm of Super K Sports Corp., headquartered in Brooklyn, New York, is a prime victim. Basketball is a popular game throughout Latin America but the game's most favoured ball, made by Super K, is never that which is used – the Super K trademark is, though. This becomes possible because the trademark has been registered by a number of Brazilian copying firms, who under Brazilian law retain the right to mark their products 'Super K' irrespective of any trademark that may exist outside the country. They supply to Venezuela, Colombia and Paraguay. The loss to the Brooklyn firm is in excess of $1,000,000 a year.

Ms Maria Dennison, Washington DC Director of the American Sporting Goods Manufacturers' Association, explains the second part of the catch:

> If Brazil someday opens its markets to imported US sporting goods, not only will the cost of buying back the US trademark be prohibitive, but the counterfeit activity is so entrenched

that the US manufacturer will not be likely to penetrate the Brazilian market with any type of success.

Another American firm confronts a similar problem in Mexico. One of the most popular baseball bats worldwide is trademarked the 'Louisville Slugger'. It is made by a company named Hillerich and Bradsby, which operates from Louisville, Kentucky, and Clarksville, Indiana. The bat is not for sale, because of current trade importation law, in Mexico. But to avoid the sort of prohibitive buy-back fee it would confront if the law were ever to change in its favour, Hillerich and Bradsby spent $3000 re-registering an expiring trademark which it cannot, at the moment, use. The decision was made after bitter and expensive experience. When the company tried to sell in Spain, it discovered its trademark already registered there. To reclaim it cost $40,000 – which was slightly more expensive, but inestimably less time-consuming, than the fight for the right to sell the Louisville Slugger in Japan where baseball competes with golf as the country's most popular participant sport.

There are 61,000 teams with 1,600,000 players in Japan. It took the American sports industry four years to get a foothold in a marketplace almost exclusively served by Taiwanese counterfeiters, at a profit to themselves of many millions of dollars a year. The chief obstacle was the Tokyo government itself.

Japan operates what the US sports industry discovered to be a three-tiered certification and approval system for sporting goods which effectively closes the market to any Western manufacturer. Initially, US lawyers found imports had to be approved by private Japanese sports organisations. Even with the help of American government lawyers, it took two and a half years of patient, frustrating negotiation to discover that in addition to the resistance put up by private organisations, there was also the recalcitrant Japanese Ministry of International Trade and Industry to be dealt with. As an aluminium bat, the Louisville Slugger had to be approved by eight different divisions within the Ministry – which offered endless possibilities for the deliberate procrastination suspected by some sporting officials in both Europe and America.

It was the US Sporting Goods Manufacturers' Association which was behind this effort to break into the Japanese marketplace and it did so on behalf of all sporting goods manufacturers and their products, not just Hillerich and Bradsby and its baseball bats. During the protracted negotiations, various firms within the Association were approached by Japanese company officials – and, the Association suspects, by fronts acting for counterfeiters – with separate, advantageous importation offers. The purpose of these attempts to get individual agreements was to split the concerted US trade and government efforts to enter the Japanese market, so as to leave the field comparatively open to the counterfeiters. All those US firms approached resisted.

The result was that after a four year fight, the Japanese government revised a total of seventeen laws affecting product certification. Although the fight had been specifically fought on behalf of American sporting goods, the effect of the amendments spread to automobiles, electronics, home appliances and pharmaceuticals made all over the world. Ms Dennison says with justifiable pride: 'Not only did we win for the United States, we won it for the European Community and everyone else at the same time.'

There remain, of course, concessions that still have to be won. For Super K's basketball even to be considered for approval, the extortionate 'fee' of approximately $25,000 must be paid to the Japanese Basketball Association – which is composed of Japanese basketball manufacturers.

Taiwan is the most active sports goods counterfeiter in Asia. And despite the Taipei undertakings to apply its amended laws more stringently, Ms Dennison said: 'Our manufacturers report that no real enforcement is taking place.'

Although the incident occurred before the supposed tightening of Taiwanese trademark and infringement legislation, the US Sporting Goods Manufacturers' Association quotes as an example of weak law enforcement the experience of Super K, which discovered that phony copies of its basketballs were being produced in Taiwan and exported – sometimes in containerloads of 10,000 at a time – to Chile, Colombia, Venezuela, Greece, Indonesia and Malaysia. It cost the American company $25,000 in legal fees successfully to sue one Taiwanese counterfeiter for damages and that amount does not include the cost of locating the counterfeiter in the first place. The Taiwan court fined the man $45.

Another example quoted is the tale of the Hillerich and Bradsby golf club. With the golf-obsessed Japanese as comparatively near neighbours, the Taiwanese sports goods fakers have attempted to monopolise the golf equipment market not just in Asia but throughout the world. Hillerich and Bradsby market a club called the 'Power Bilt'. An unknown number of counterfeiters have made a fortune in passing off a replica perfect in all but one minuscule detail. The Taiwan pirates have named theirs the 'Power Bolt'. British standard trading officers have discovered Power Bolts in British shops. They were also put on sale in Australia, and in California and Texas. A set was openly displayed at the Professional Golf Association Trade show in Florida.

Hillerich and Bradsby spent $10,000 stopping the sale of the fifty Power Bolt clubs offered for sale in California. Ms Dennison told investigating American senators: 'If the cost of trying to stop the sale of fifty clubs in the US marketplace is $10,000, the cost in the international marketplace would be prohibitive for a company producing sales in the $1,000,000 to $25,000,000 range.' As it is, Hillerich and Bradsby spends an average of $150,000 a year trying to monitor the global rip-off of their products. Said Ms Dennison:

> It appears common practice that if American companies do not register their trademarks in countries around the world, even where they do not have markets, they run the risk of having their trademarks stolen and counterfeit products produced. The burden of trademark and patent protection is placed disproportionately on the back and on the pocket-books of the American manufacturer. The only real solution for protecting US intellectual property rights and slowing the growth of counterfeit activity is for the countries of the world to have in place legal mechanisms to exercise, secure and enforce protection of worldwide trademarks, patents and copyrights.

That is also the view of English sports equipment manufacturers suffering at the hands of Asian counterfeiters. Dunlop officials refuse to estimate the financial loss suffered by the firm from the counterfeiting of its sports goods but as the result of a series of meetings with a number of experts in the field, I would put the figure at hundreds of thousands of pounds. The best-selling tennis racquet range is a particular target. So is Dunlop's distinctive

Slazenger range of sportswear. I understand that Taiwan exports
the counterfeited clothing both direct and via the more round-
about route of India. It arrives in England unmarked – and
therefore not subject to import restrictions – and is transported to
the Midlands' towns of Birmingham and Coventry which have high
local Indian populations. Independently imported are millions of
Taiwan-printed decals of the distinctive leaping panther
trademark. Only when the sportswear and the markings are both
in England are they combined, in workshops throughout the
Midlands. An official of the company told me:

> We fear there is a massive trade – worth many thousands – in
> this sort of counterfeiting in England. We take action
> wherever and whenever we can, but we are not really
> succeeding in stopping it. Because it is firstly too easy and
> secondly too lucrative. The smuggling chains to the British
> Midlands from India and Taipei are well-established and
> virtually unbreakable.

Apart from maintaining its own anti-counterfeiting force, Dunlop
is also the founder of the British Anti-Counterfeiting Group, an
organisation currently composed of seventy companies all of which
contribute thousands of pounds a year to the fight against piracy –
and this on top of their involuntary contributions to the pirates'
coffers.

This matches the expenditure of the major American companies
– Nike, for example, which is one of the most successful sports
footwear corporations. Its yearly expenditure on protection is
$300,000. Its lawyers know that at least thirty-five people or
companies have registered the Nike trademark in Brazil – a further
twenty-five have submitted applications to the Brazilian trademark
office certifying themselves as Nike producers. And there is
nothing the American company can do about it. It is also well-
aware that the activities of the Brazilian counterfeiters – and
others in South Korea, Hong Kong and Taiwan – are costing it
several million dollars a year.

Some American manufacturers have found during investigations
that their sportswear copying is carried out in exactly the same way
as the faking of the Dunlop clothing in England, by adding the
identifying decal after the counterfeits have been imported into
the United States. General Mills, parent company of Izod and US

licensee for the Lacoste range, says that in its experience this is the most common form the crime takes. In 1983 General Mills probed 500 separate cases of copyright infringement within America, sued approximately 150 people and seized 150,000 phony Izod and Lacoste garments. Lawrence Buckwalter, the staff lawyer for Izod, testified before Congress: 'It is our firm belief that counterfeits and counterfeiters brought to justice represent merely the tip of the iceberg.'

Counterfeiters in America have adopted what Buckwalter described as a 'hub and spoke' principle, to avoid prosecution which could end in the shutdown of their operations: they ensure that those retailers and street sellers at risk only know the barest minimum about any counterfeiting operation, so that if they are arrested all that is lost is an outlet, leaving the network free to continue operating. One New York gang of street sellers evaded court-ordered seizure for weeks by using roller-skating lookouts who could negotiate the packed pavements of Manhattan to warn other members of the group after the first arrest quicker than the car-bound lawyers could get around the even denser-packed roads. An English lawyer commented: 'It epitomises the problem: the counterfeiters are always out there, keeping ahead of us.'

CHAPTER TWENTY-ONE

The Cloth of Gold

It was an alert Hermes official who recognised the pattern of the tie which Japan's Emperor Hirohito wore for an official, pinstripe-suited portrait in 1981. Initially pleased at the thought of the Emperor using its product, Hermes initiated discreet enquiries through imperial palace sources and the Union des Fabricants pour la Protection Internationale de la Propriété Industrielle et Artistique. And it was discovered that the tie had been purchased by a member of the emperor's personal staff in a Tokyo store which was not an authorised Hermes retailer. It was a counterfeit, complete with a fake Hermes label.

French *couturier* Pierre Cardin protested personally to the court of the Shah in pre-revolutionary Iran when he visited the capital, Teheran, and found a boutique named Pierre Cardin completely stocked with Cardin-labelled counterfeits. He was immediately assured by the palace that action would be taken. And it was. The following day Cardin was ordered out of the country. The Teheran boutique was owned and run by a member of the Shah's family. In 1978 Cardin visited the South Korean capital of Seoul and on his return to France called a press conference to protest at what he discovered. Cardin complained: 'I saw my name and initials on the most shoddy products, from T-shirts to sneakers. And on things having nothing to do with the name Cardin. It is scandalous that a government should allow this.' Eight years later, that scandalous government is still allowing it. So is Mexico, on the other side of the world.

There – predominantly in Mexico City – at least thirteen fake Cartier boutiques sell fake Cartier products, including clothes. After failing to shut them down with forty-nine successful court actions, Cartier went into direct competition, opening its own boutique precisely opposite the counterfeiter's main outlet in the Mexican capital. The faker, Fernando Pelletier, responded by publicly announcing that his after-sales service, including repairs to the fake Cartier watches he sold in addition to the falsely labelled clothes, only applied to his products and not to those bearing the name of the rival Cartier shop across the street. Cartier's philosophical resolve was to make Pelletier the exclusive local distributor for the genuine articles. This has reduced but not eradicated the counterfeiting of Cartier products throughout the country.

T-shirts produced by the USA for Africa Foundation to raise money for Ethiopian famine relief were counterfeited by American manufacturers and on sale throughout the country ahead of the official shirt. Financiers calculated the rip-off cost the Foundation – which means the African famine effort – $2,000,000. British copiers did the same thing with the T-shirts produced to coincide with Band Aid's 'Do They Know It's Christmas?' The loss to the British fund was at least £25,000.

All the above are illustrations of a rip-off industry earning the fakers an estimated $2,500,000,000 a year, at least £50,000,000 of that in Britain. A British investigator extensively involved in this particular aspect of counterfeiting explained:

> It's safe, profitable and virtually unstoppable. The day after we close one outlet down, a replacement opens next door. One of the most surprising things about fashion and clothing copying is that invariably the buyers *know* what they're getting is phony. Which while perhaps understandable from the financial viewpoint is difficult to accept when you realise that the article will split, fray or become unwearable after the first cleaning or washing. Which actually makes it expensive.

With fashion-name stealing – as is frequently the case with other types of counterfeiting – there is an ironic twist to the situation: for it was the business acumen and ability of that most copied of *couturiers*, Pierre Cardin, which enabled the birth of the illegal business.

Until 1959, *haute couture* remained the rarefied preserve of a select group of Paris fashion houses whose world-famed designers each season dictated the length of hems, the degree of display for busts and the shape – or lack of it – of the overall outline. The drawings which decided it all attained the importance of State Secrets and were guarded probably better – not that that was any deterrent. Mass producers tried to bribe workshop assistants for design copies in advance of the official showing and if that failed sneaked artists into the audience on the first day to make the sketches for approximate duplicates. But that is what they were and were recognised to be: duplicates without the essential cachet of a fashion-name label.

Pierre Cardin changed all that. In 1959 he licensed manufacturers to use his name on a range of luxury French items. The idea became a commercial phenomenon and the other French *couturiers* jumped on the bandwagon that has gathered pace ever since. Now, almost three decades later, it is estimated that this extended use of a designer name is worth $3,500,000,000 a year in legitimate sales to the international corporations and companies of the favoured few. No longer does the pirate need a stolen sketch, just a label with the right name reproduced in the right, trademarked way. An official of the Union des Fabricants assured me that '1959 was the watershed. Suddenly designer clothes and products were obtainable, on a mass market. People didn't any longer have to dream about the unobtainable. They *could* obtain it. The only problem remained the cost. The counterfeits were ready, to see that didn't remain a problem, either.'

Asia, with its miser-cheap labour force, led the designer clothes counterfeit boom, like it leads every other copying activity. But here again, the designers contributed to their own downfall. For they, too, take advantage of that cheap labour force, licensing companies throughout Asia to make for pennies the clothes that sell for hundreds of dollars on New York's Fifth Avenue, London's Bond Street or Paris's Rue Faubourg St-Honoré. Once the day's work has been done on the designer's order, the machines continue running, turning out the same garment – only at night, it is the counterfeiter's order that the manufacturer is filling. Within the trade, this is known as 'overrunning'. A garment trade official in Hong Kong told me:

> Every manufacturer in Asia denies the practice goes on and everyone knows perfectly well that it does. The only difference, usually, is that the counterfeit is not completed

with the label or the identifying trademark: a motif, for instance. That's made separately, shipped separately and added usually in the destination country, just like the decal for the sportswear.

Jeans are a particular target throughout the Asian copying countries of Taiwan, South Korea and Hong Kong. A lawyer acting for Levi Strauss, the world's major manufacturer of jeans, claims that the estimate of $750,000,000 a year lost to pirates worldwide is 'conservative'. Jordache talk of a $10,000,000-a-year loss in America alone. A common method of evading customs detection at any port of entry is, as the garment trade official said, to ship the jeans separately from their identifying trademark. In 1983 lawyers for the much copied Calvin Klein empire discovered that unmarked jeans manufactured in Taiwan were imported into Miami where they were fitted with 'Calvin Klein' buttons and studs imported from Italy, European leader in counterfeiting.

Marc Vincent, an executive of the French Saint Laurent company, conceded in 1981 that too many licences were allocated after Pierre Cardin's breakthrough into the lucrative mass market. Other officials, less prepared to be identified, talk of floodgates having been opened which are now difficult if not impossible to close. However, a number of international organisations do try to fight the trend – some of them specifically set up for the purpose – even though most of their designer members now accept they will never be able to eradicate the problem. Chief among them is the oldest anti-counterfeiting organisation in the world, the Union des Fabricants pour la Protection Internationale de la Propriété Industrielle et Artistique. Created in 1872, the Paris-based Union now has a thousand members. Another organisation is the Italian French COLC set up by Roberto Gucci who guesses that forty-five per cent of articles carrying his label are faked and acknowledged in 1983 that police and enforcement authorities seized three times more Gucci-designed clothing materials than the firm actually produced. Founded in 1984, it is pledged to fight designer-label counterfeiting worldwide and its members include Valentino, Fendi, Benetton, Dior, Vuitton, Balmain, Saint Laurent and Hermes. The French *couture* organisation, the Chambre Syndicale de la Couture Parisienne, liaises with both the Union and the COLC – and with the American International Anti-Counterfeiting

Coalition Inc. whose offices are in Montgomery Street, San Francisco. Most American designers subscribe to the Coalition, including Jordache, Diana von Furstenberg, Calvin Klein, Ralph Lauren and Sergio Valente.

Christian Dior, which records annual sales exceeding $400,000,000 worldwide, spend on average $500,000 a year protecting the 813 trademarks registered in its name. Coco Chanel was once quoted as saying, quite contentedly, that if she were copied – which she was – it meant she was famous. Designers no longer adopt such a complacent attitude. François Benhamou, an executive of the Chambre Syndicale de la Couture Parisienne, speaks angrily of entire streets of counterfeiters' shops named after World famous *couturiers*. The location is Seoul, where Pierre Cardin was so enraged to discover the wholesale abuse of his trademark. Benhamou is still angrier at the speed with which convicted counterfeiters are replaced – within days of the successful action.

A frequent device to evade customs interception and the quota systems imposed to restrict textile imports is 'transshipment'. Unfinished counterfeits are freighted through a third country in which import restrictions are not so severe or whose quotas are under-used. A whole consignment of counterfeit Diana von Furstenberg jeans, made in Communist China, had just one stitch added in Indonesia to qualify for their place among Indonesian exports – destination, America.

The oil-rich Middle East and Persian Gulf are still enthusiastic customers for luxury, designer-name counterfeits – Iran included, despite the ascetic régime of the Ayatollah Khomeini which has replaced the Shah and his counterfeiting relations. Taiwan is the major supplying nation, although Cyprus is an active, local producing country. The problem confronting Western designers in this part of the world as elsewhere is the absence of proper trademark laws. None exist in Dubai, Abu Dhabi, Sharjah, Ajman, Umm al Qaywayn, Oman, Qatar or North and South Yemen. Although legislation of varying effectiveness exists in Kuwait, Bahrain, Ra's al Khaymah, Saudi Arabia, Jordan and the Lebanon, the expense of time and money involved in enforcement is often prohibitive. Passing off is a common practice in the Middle East. Pierre Cardin becomes Pierre Cardan – as on a label found inside a traditional arab robe marked 'Made in Syria' – and Christian Dior is changed to Christian D'Or.

American Customs investigators working on Operation Trip-wire, the anti-counterfeiting programme referred to earlier, discovered in 1983 that the Kuwait National Bank had unwittingly become involved in the purchase by Middle East counterfeiters of a Taiwan-produced overrun which would have netted a $2,000,000 profit. And the Middle East was used as a transshipment country by an American counterfeiter trying to smuggle fake Sergio Valente jeans and sweaters into the United States. The man, Mike Tourbah, ran a firm registered as American International Designs in Hialeah, Florida. The $1,000,000 consignment was described on importation documentation as having originated in the Lebanon. In fact, the garment had been counterfeited in Taiwan and South Korea.

A development worrying the monitoring agencies trying to protect designer products is an apparently strengthening liaison between Taiwan and South Korea and that other leader among copying countries, Hong Kong. The dot-sized island of Saipan in the South China Sea makes a fourth. The Fraud Division of US Customs has learned that corporations are being formed by largely unidentified investors from Taiwan, South Korea and Hong Kong to create factories on Saipan capable of manufacturing the whole range of designer clothing whose counterfeiting currently costs the legitimate industry the $2,500,000,000 p.a. already quoted. The concern arises from the fact that after the Second World War Saipan became an American protectorate and as such can invoke favoured duty-free quota concessions. It 'would represent a doorway,' one official told me. 'And once that was open, God knows what would flood through into America and Europe.'

In 1984 US Customs uncovered what one investigator described to me as 'a possible pilot scheme'. That involved a Hong Kong company establishing two counterfeiting factories in the Maldives islands in the Indian Ocean. Despite suspicions that counterfeits were being both made and transshipped through the Hong Kong–Maldives link-up, no case was ever brought as none could have been proved. At the time of writing, the Maldives factories are still operating.

Saipan, like the Maldives, is a danger but not yet a serious one. At the moment Taiwan, South Korea and Hong Kong – with India and Pakistan just behind – remain the main counterfeiting problem for the makers of luxury, Western-designer goods. But, in the opinion of enforcement and monitoring officials with whom I discussed the world-wide problem, that line-up will soon change. Communist China is emerging into the world marketplace after its long isolation.

CHAPTER TWENTY-TWO

The Tiger Awakes

The late Walt Disney, whose corporation made a film from *The Jungle Book* with its conniving and manipulating character of the tiger Shere Khan, might have been wryly amused at the coincidence. It was, after all, 1986 before his organisation finally succeeded in its protests to the Beijing government and according to the Chinese calendar 1986 is the Year of the Tiger. Traditionally, the special responsibility of the tiger is to guard against thieves which were – and are – precisely what the Walt Disney corporation was seeking protection against. In mainland China, in 1986, the corporation at last succeeded in resolving one of its many trademark problems in that part of the world.

The word 'Disneyland' is a trademarked description of the amusement park in Los Angeles and licensed to cover other outlets worldwide – but not in mainland China, which is where it emerged to describe an amusement park on the outskirts of Beijing.

The only way – at the time – that Walt Disney could possibly protect its copyright was through Hong Kong. It briefed Deacons, the legal firm that handled the designer-label infringements covered in Chapter Fourteen. With its special anti-counterfeiting division, it was ideally suited to take on the case, which Deacons lawyer Paul Scholefield described for me:

> For once it was a completely unwitting and innocent infringement. When we complained we were told by Beijing that despite the fact that throughout the huge number of Chinese languages and subsidiary dialects there are more characters than in any other tongue, there is no construction for 'Amusement Park'. It's Disneyland. We said it couldn't

215

be: that they had to make a word to describe what took place in an amusement park. They said they had the word. It was Disneyland. It took a lot of persuading to convince them that Walt Disney had it first. Eventually we won. They've removed the Disneyland sign and are trying to create another word that will convey as much and as immediately to the average Chinese what Disneyland means. Some Chinese officials complain it isn't easy. We've had to make it clear to them that it never is.

The Walt Disney corporation was fortunate both in the choice of their lawyers and the unarguable strength of their case. They got an immediate – and by the standards of international counterfeiting – incredibly quick cessation agreement.

Another Hong Kong lawyer – whom I have agreed not to identify in any way – knew of the Deacons' Walt Disney case. That person told me:

The Walt Disney corporation was lucky, as lucky as hell. It was not a disputable case. To the affected companies in the West it's a one-off, which we might never know again. Really it isn't applicable, to the approaching problem. China is a country that for years, literally, has been sleeping. But not anymore. China is trying to achieve in months – or even weeks – what should really take years of slow, gradual development. Which isn't logically possible. The West have forgotten that China is a nation of clever traders. They are going to be reminded very quickly in the coming years.

There exists in the West the misunderstanding that the Communist society of mainland China is as strictly regimented as that of the KGB-controlled environment of the Soviet Union. It is not. Even in the Soviet Union non-party entrepreneurs sneer at and deride the controls that are attempted; the Chinese entrepreneurs laughingly dismiss similar attempts.

China-watchers in Hong Kong forecast a counterfeiting boom which will make the country as competitive as other areas as it already is in copied books – the world's largest manufacturer – and in copied textiles – a major distibutor.

A Hong Kong lawyer closely involved in trying to curb the stealing of Western products said:

We have a nightmare. It's the tremendous and already proven copying capacity of mainland China being linked to the people here in Hong Kong who have perfected worldwide counterfeiting, knowing precisely what the markets are and what is needed to supply them. There are already indications that not all the Hong Kong Chinese fear 1997: some counterfeiters actually see it as the possibility to expand.

Du Guozhen certainly saw the possibilities. He established links with counterfeiters in Taiwan and Hong Kong and actually borrowed $2,960,000 from the Bank of China in Fukien province – where he was known as 'The God of Fortune' because of the size of his bribes – to finance the enterprise. After his arrest – on charges of embezzling a total of $88,800,000 – the *People's Daily* said in an official report:

> A considerable number of departments and *cadres* had the impudence to serve him, follow his instructions and even collude with his tricks. Some of our party members have completely disarmed themselves ideologically, sold their honour for money, foresaken their Communist spirit and the party's goals and programmes and degenerated into sinners.

Du Guozhen was the biggest but not the only entrepreneur overresponding to the new government edict permitting personal profit. In October 1985 the *People's Daily* reported that a total of 67,000 government officials were either under arrest or investigation for involvement in 28,000 separate money-making scams. The information reaching Hong Kong was that at least half concerned some aspect of counterfeiting.

Yu Xilun was one of the people involved. Manager and Party Secretary of the Guangdong Provincial Medicinal Co., Xilun went into partnership with a Hong Kong counterfeiter to market traditional herbs and medicines much sought-after by Chinese throughout the world. About twenty-five per cent of the herbs and medicines which Xilun smuggled into Hong Kong were fakes. Xilun received some money in return but the payment from Hong Kong was usually in kind: colour televisions, refrigerators and, the customary method of transportation in the country, bicycles. These he sold throughout the province.

In December 1985 Xilun and a deputy in the company, Wang

Weicheng, were jailed for life in Canton. They were charged with taking bribes from the Hong Kong partner, who was not identified. At the time of writing, Du Guozhen is awaiting execution.

China – with its proclaimed determination to expand technologically and industrially – is regarded by Western and Asian manufacturers as one of the fastest expanding and most profitable markets in the world. In Hong Kong the view was expressed to me by several people that those legitimate products sold in mainland China were providing the master copies to feed the country's counterfeiting industry. Japan, now eagerly selling to Beijing, was quoted to me as the example that China was following – an Asian country whose present dominance in world trade was built upon a base of counterfeiting.

Anthony Gurka, founder of Commercial Trademark Services and someone with unparalleled experience of Asian copying, philosophically regards counterfeiting as an inevitable stage in the natural progression of an underdeveloped country towards industrialisation. He forecasts that Taiwan, and possibly Hong Kong, will eventually follow Japan's example, with legitimate manufacture replacing the counterfeit. He also believes that some Beijing manufacturers counterfeit unwittingly, fulfilling orders placed from Hong Kong without knowing that the designs and specifications constitute trademark material. He said:

> The problems in the People's Republic of China will undoubtedly increase as counterfeit products will not only be a new experience to the consumer public there, but also to the government, the judiciary and the legal profession. In due course, if not already, the People's Republic of China's own trademarks will be counterfeited, not only by other countries but also within its own territory. Furthermore, the laws offering protection have possibly never been used and therefore it can only be assumed there is little or no expertise available to combat these new problems.

Not all the experts concur with Gurka in the belief that the Asian countries currently heavily involved in counterfeiting will progress to respectability. Several thought the uncertainty over the 1997 change of administration – plus the new liaisons already being established with traders in mainland China – made any change for the better unlikely in Hong Kong. And Laurent Dubois, the Tokyo-based director of the Union des Fabricants pour la Protection Internationale de la Propriété Industrielle et Artistique, made the point that while counterfeiting in Japan had dropped below its 1970 high, it was still considerable – but in a manner different from any other counterfeiting country in the world.

Displaying the inbuilt nationalism that is possibly stronger in Japan than in any other country, Japanese counterfeiters *never* copy a Japanese product, only something produced abroad. Usually, today, it is a luxury item. Explained Dubois:

It enables the Japanese – both the illegal maker and the buyer – completely to justify what goes on. While the Japanese are outraged at anything they make being counterfeited – a manufacturer will press for the maximum legal recourse – they sincerely believe there is nothing wrong in their copying something somebody else produces. In the case of luxury items like Gucci or Vuitton or Dior, they can actually advance the argument that the copying is the *fault* of the genuine maker. The thesis goes like this: the manufacturer of the luxury creates the demand, by making the item in the first place. But invariably the genuine cost is too high, because of the price the maker imposes and then the high importation tax which is attached bringing it into Japan. Therefore the only way the Japanese can satisfactorily fulfil the dream of possessing the luxury is to purchase a counterfeit! The justification goes further. The Japanese – again in complete sincerity – have the greatest difficulty in understanding the objection or anger of the genuine maker: they claim that without exception the Japanese counterfeit is always better than the original and believe the maker should be pleased at being copied in such a superior way!

At the beginning of 1985, following the visit to Tokyo of an anti-counterfeiting delegation from the Common Market, the government promised an investigation into the continuing product piracy in the country. Dubois is not overly hopeful of any government crackdown. He said: 'Theoretically, infringement protection already exists but in reality the police laugh at any thought of action: to them copying is quite normal. Certainly not a crime.'

Dubois recounts a protest visit to the Ministry of Trade and Industry, one of the Japanese government bodies entrusted with the eradication of counterfeiting. There, in the basement of the Ministry buildings, he found a shop offering a fake Cartier belt for sale. When Dubois pointed this out, Ministry officials 'just laughed'.

Japanese organised crime, run by the 'Yakuza', is extensively involved in counterfeiting. The Yakuza is one of the most unusual criminal societies in the world: as a sign of honour its members have their bodies completely tattooed in formalised designs which have specific connotations. World enforcement officials consider the organisation's code of silence and obedience to be far more effectively imposed than that of the Mafia. The biggest Yakuza gang, the Kobe-based Yamaguchi-gumi, controls the majority of product stealing in southern and western Japan, through a network of ninety-two separate gang cells. There have been turf fights involving a Yakuza group headed by Hiroshi Yamamoto which in 1984 split from the Yamaguchi-gumi and named itself Ichiwa-kai. Other families active in counterfeiting are the Matsuda-gumi, the Sumiyoshi-Rengo and the Inagawar-kai. The last two control the Tokyo underworld.

Their role, so far as it is known, is that of financier – setting up and equipping at exorbitant rates of interest counterfeiting factories. Dubois talks of receiving telephone calls from Yakuza enforcers, who do not protest at his pursuit of product thieves – they recognise that as his function – but seek a postponement of any legal action or rare police raid until their debtor has repaid what they consider to be sufficient capital on the original loan.

'Because of the Japanese attitude – their ability always to see themselves as harassed victims of criticism, never perpetrators of a commercial crime – the country remains an active one in the counterfeiting world,' Dubois assured me. 'Their mental attitude makes them unique in Asia' – just as Italy, through the sheer volume of its output, is unique among the counterfeiting nations of Europe.

CHAPTER TWENTY-THREE

When in Rome ...

In one raid, police seized fifteen miles of counterfeited Louis
Vuitton material. Another occurred just before a faker had
$2,500,000 of new machinery installed, to increase his multi-
million dollar output. The Mafia finance and distribute and bribed
police are frequently disinclined to investigate. According to
Vincent Carratu, the world's foremost counterfeiting investigator,
it all goes to make Italy the undisputed faking capital of Europe.
And its supremacy extends still further: American investigators
believe links have been formed between Rome and Seoul to make
Italy the world's major quota-evading transshipment point for
mislabelled Asian wool and knitwear bound for the United States.

It was Carratu, a former Scotland Yard Fraud Squad detective,
and not the Italian police who in 1980 smashed the largest
counterfeiting operation currently recorded in the country. Seized
company records showed a $24,000,000 turnover in bogus Gucci,
Cartier, Dior, Vuitton, Saint Laurent and Valentino products and
distribution outlets in America, South Africa, Nigeria, France, the
Netherlands and West Germany. 'It was a well organised, multi-
national business,' Carratu told me.

The firm was Ferrari Chih Pierinedmer. Its huge warehouse cum
factory was at 29 Via Bramante, in the northern suburbs of Milan.
It was owned by Gianfranco Chih, a high-living playboy who out
of counterfeiting profits maintained an antique-furnished country
house, a luxury Milan penthouse and holidayed at his other
apartment at Portofino.

Carratu was in Italy working on another investigation when he
came to suspect the factory on the Via Bramante. In order to
gauge the extent of the operation, he posed as a prospective buyer
of fake designer luggage who doubted whether Chih had the

capacity to meet orders of the size he intended placing. 'The tables and benches overflowed with fake Dior and Cartier,' recalls Carratu. 'It was an Aladdin's Cave of counterfeit stuff.'

Chih made no attempt to conceal what was being manufactured. Says Carratu: 'He didn't have to. He was paying for police protection.'

Aware of that, Carratu made no approach to the Milan authorities. Instead he took his evidence to Paris and presented it to the Union des Fabricants pour la Protection Internationale de la Propriété Industrielle et Artistique. Officials of the French organisation returned to Italy and obtained a search warrant. To prevent Chih being warned by officers on his payroll, the warrant was enforced by police brought in from outside the city. It took a week to make out an inventory of the seized fakes and nine lorries to haul it away as evidence. There were 8,483 handbags, 44 suitcases, 10,500 belt buckles, 362 wallets, more than two miles of material printed in distinctive, trademarked designs and moulds and dyes for reproducing trademarks. The value of the impounded fakes was put at $1,500,000. During his interrogation, Chih said he had intended re-equipping his factory with $2,500,000 of new machinery and computerising his distribution.

Chih was jailed for nineteen months and the factory on the Via Bramante now produces legitimate merchandise.

Another raid, within days of that at the Via Bramante, disclosed a loophole through which some Italian counterfeiters escape justice. This second seizure took place in Florence in June 1980 and was carried out by officers of the Guardia di Finanza, a treasury enforcement agency. They found huge quantities of Cartier, Gucci and Yves Saint Laurent fakes, which they seized. They did not, however, impound the large quantity of imitation Vuitton they found, claiming that it is not a registered trademark in Italy.

This is refuted by Vuitton, whose lawyers have closed down more then twenty Italian copiers of their product, including the one in the lakeside town of Lecco where in March 1980 fifteen miles of bogus material was seized. According to Vuitton, its trademark has been registered in Italy since 1896. An official of the company, which budgets $1,000,000 a year to combat worldwide piracy, told me: 'It is a depressing effort, trying to beat the Italian copiers. Not only do we suffer at the hands of the counterfeiters, but we suffer this sort of difficulty from the very authorities who are supposed to be helping us.'

It is just that sort of difficulty which leads pirated companies to echo the criticism of Carratu and accuse the Italian police of extensive corruption, by counterfeiters. An official of a leading French designer company who spoke to me on condition of anonymity said: 'And it goes beyond simple bribery. The Italian authorities, more than any other in Europe, don't regard counterfeiting as the crime it is. More often than not it's dismissed with a shoulder shrug as something that just isn't important.'

To prove otherwise, the man quoted to me the estimate of French trade officials who put the cost to legitimate manufacturers in France alone at $250,000,000 a year. Designer-label counterfeiting is also estimated to have cost 20,000 French jobs in four years. The job loss throughout the EEC is calculated by the European Parliament at 100,000.

Anti-counterfeiting organisations and some European countries are pressing for stronger community legislation to defeat the copiers. But a lawyer involved in the drafting of some of the legislation told me: 'The basic difficulty is that we need strong customs control at borders. And one of the original concepts of the Community is to *ease* border traffic and crossing, between member nations. So we have what amounts to a dichotomy.'

Victim companies consider France to have the strongest anti-counterfeiting laws. But during an American Congressional investigation, the claim was made that the French Communist party finances itself by counterfeiting. The accusation was made by Art Gundersheim, Director of International Trade Affairs and an assistant to the President of the American Clothing and Textile Workers Union. He told a subcommittee hearing of the House of Representatives' Energy and Commerce Committee in February 1984, that the French party had invested in a number of clothing manufacturing companies throughout the country. These companies imported from Rumania, Hungary and Yugoslavia cheaply made men's suits into which they sewed the label 'Made in France'. The suits were then, said Gundersheim, exported throughout the world. In America, they were sold at 'very high and overpriced French prices'.

Gundersheim said that he had personally protested to customs and trade officials at the American embassy in Paris and asked them what could be done. He testified: 'They, in fact, said nothing. They didn't have the time nor the priority to look into this: their mandate was to be involved in other matters and that unless we could bring them chapter and verse, literally which company, where, when they were doing this, which shipment, there was nothing that they could do.'

Gundersheim conceded that his evidence was circumstantial and said that his union could not afford to carry out its own investigation, which would have been hampered by lack of access to official sources. He further testified that his union believed the Communist party of Italy was also involved in the trade. French and Italian officials of both parties deny the accusation.

Cartier, with $400,000,000 of annual sales, spend almost $2,000,000 a year combatting counterfeiters who they calculate make $7,000,000 a year from fakes; sometimes it is much more. One of the most successful Cartier watch designs ever produced was the Santos: Alain Perrin, President of the British owned company responsible for it – the parent company is Rothman International plc – personally decided to include the assembly screws on the watch face as part of the design. The watch is manufactured in Switzerland. So were Santos fakes. Company lawyers estimate that in 1980 a counterfeiting gang made $8,000,000 in just eight months from turning out Santos copies. They also consider, going on the arrest records of some convicted counterfeiters, that the Mafia are actively involved in the rip-off.

The Swiss watchmakers' trade association, the Fedération Horlogère Suisse, claim that over 9,000,000 fake watches are manufactured every year, at a loss to the legitimate industry of $55,000,000. Vincent Carratu talks of the difficulty executive experts from design-watch companies sometimes have in telling the difference between the genuine item and the well-crafted copy – rarely a problem with perfume, another multi-million dollar faking industry.

Carratu specialises in perfume counterfeiting: soon after establishing his detective agency, which now has offices throughout the world, Carratu approached all the French perfume companies and suggested they retain his service on a one-year trial basis. Dior was one company which accepted. So did Chanel and Estée Lauder, on whose behalf he smashed a worldspanning counterfeiting ring bankrolled for more than $1,000,000 by the Genovese Mafia Family in New York.

The Genovese channelled the money to two British counterfeiters through a numbered account in Jersey and a Jersey-based solicitor. The first factory to manufacture the fake Chanel No. 5, Chanel No. 19 eau de toilette and Estée Lauder's Aramis aftershave was established in the Mexican millionaire's playground of Acapulco. The fakers joined in with their fellow millionaires, to the later irritation of their Mafia paymasters. They also established and funded companies to keep and maintain their families in the event of arrest.

From Spain, Italy, Switzerland, Germany and Holland the two imported into their Mexican factory base essence, bottles, stoppers and packaging practically identical to the genuine products. They also employed a Spanish factory manager, who recognised the distinctive bottles and realised what was going on. He fled, to be tracked down in an American hideaway by Carratu. Once the Acapulco factory had been identified to him, Carratu employed William Callahan, President of New York City's United Intelligence Inc., to paraglide on a speedboat-hauled parachute past the counterfeiters' beachfront villa to confirm the presence there of the gang.

The Genovese Family was becoming annoyed at the slow progress of the perfume faking, pressuring the Britons for quicker and better results. So the counterfeiters fled back to London where they started manufacturing in two factories, one in the King's Cross area of London and the other in Hackney, whose products were distributed worldwide. One of Carratu's investigators bought a bottle of Chanel No. 5 duty-free on Kuwait Airlines only to discover, when he got back to England, that it was a fake.

The Chanel company estimate that before it was smashed the ring, which established distribution outlets in the Middle East through an Iraqi-fundraiser for the PLO, manufactured an estimated $10,360,000 worth of perfume.

The two Britons were brought to trial and sentenced to jail at the Crown Court at Aylesbury, Buckinghamshire, in February 1985. At the end of that year, however, the Appeal Court ruled they had been wrongly convicted and that charges against them should not have been amended alleging offences under the Trade

Descriptions Act of 1968. The prosecution decided against appealing the ruling to the House of Lords.

There is strong criticism among the majority of anti-counterfeiting organisations in Britain at what is considered the lack of satisfactory laws to combat faking and trademark infringement. The applicable laws currently on the statute books are the Copyright Act of 1956, the Patents Act of 1977, the Registered Designs Act of 1949, the Trademarks Act of 1938 and the Trade Descriptions Act. Apart from some of the provisions under the Trade Descriptions Act, all the others require prosecution in a civil, not criminal court.

According to Ms Anthea Worsdall, a feelance lawyer and secretary of the British Anti-Counterfeiting Group which is based in Buckinghamshire:

> We consider it quite unsatisfactory that at the moment the only criminal prosecution is one of conspiracy to defraud, under the Trade Descriptions Act. Counterfeiting should be made a specific criminal offence, in itself. Unfortunately, we do not think the government attaches a very high priority to the problem.

The Group, which is composed of the country's leading companies, intends lobbying for a criminal offence law to be introduced. Officials with whom I spoke at the Department of Trade and Industry considered existing legislation satisfactory. They also indicated that an economic weapon, similar to that available to America under its Generalised System of Preferences, existed for Britain, too, under the General Agreement on Tariff and Trade. It was this weapon that the British Trade Minister Paul Channon gave an undertaking not to use when he visited the pirate nation of Singapore.

The British computer industry, which loses £150,000,000 a year through piracy, achieved an effective piece of protective legislation when in 1985 the Copyright (Computer Software) Amendment Act was passed. The lobbyists were fifty computer firms – plus twelve trade associations – which had formed themselves into the Federation Against Software Theft. The Federation appointed an ex-chief superintendent of the Metropolitan Police, Bob Hay, to coordinate the police and trading standards officers throughout the country to ensure the new act is rigidly enforced. Hay told me: 'Now we've got the law we intend to see that it's properly used, to prosecute the thieves.'

Under the new law, a convicted pirate can be jailed for two years and is subject to unlimited fines.

Hay said: 'I don't think people fully realise how prevalent software theft and piracy is. Every time someone runs off a software copy for a friend, he's committing a crime.' In 1983 a study carried out by Dr Simon Elsom at Aston University found that twenty per cent of microcomputer companies in England suffered a serious loss of revenue from software stealing. A follow-up study decided fifty-five per cent of companies acknowledged software loss. Hay says the problem has become so bad in England that some companies cannot afford the necessary finance to develop new programmes. Educational disks are particularly badly affected, which creates a paradox; schools and universities are among the most guilty copiers. Hay said: 'It's a vicious and tightening circle.'

Employing technology to protect technology, Hay is confident he can create a data base of known offenders without contravening the Data Protection Act or the Rehabilitation of Offenders Act. He looks forward hopefully to the time when a 'site licence' will be available to software suppliers from purchasers, entitling the supplier to access to the premises that he may ensure his original is not being copied. The 1985 Act specifically states that the act of loading a programme into a computer without the copyright owner's consent constitutes an infringement of copyright. At the time when I spoke to him, Hay was also planning an educational campaign for 1986 to take in all British schools and universities in an effort to reduce the huge amount of illegal copying they perpetrate.

> Now that we have the legislation, the essential thing is that we use it. And are seen to use it. For too long the pirates have had everything their own way. Now we have the means to reverse that. The bringing of a prosecution will, of course, be the responsibility of an affected company, but the Federation will help in any way possible.

The Anti-Counterfeiting Group – whose members include Kodak, Dunlop, Lucas Industries, the Parker Pen Co., the Wellcome

Foundation Ltd and the Dunhill company – has prepared a draft bill which it hopes will convince the government of the need for the sort of change which the Federation Against Software Theft achieved with its 1985 Act. It is equally active for change in Common Market law.

The Group also maintains a computerised central data bank which is constantly updated with the counterfeiting experiences of members who have been ripped off, identifying – where possible – the fakers. One of the entries in that data bank names a Cyprus company – Stella – as the counterfeiter of a fly killer entitled Paff-Paff. The original spray is called Pif-Paf and is manufactured by Cooper, McDougall and Robertson, part of the Wellcome group. Stella produced their pass-off in a yellow and white can identical to the British product. Printed on the can is the same assurance as appears on the British can, that the product is safe to be used near food. Laboratory analysis of the counterfeit showed it contained the ingredient DDVP, a phosphorus-like compound which should *not* under any circumstance be used near food nor in any sort of confined space.

The Anti-Counterfeiting Group liaises with the International Chamber of Commerce which, from its Paris headquarters, has created a world-spanning network of agencies and organisations pledged to combat faking. Vincent Carratu said:

> Only the people closely involved – which means those being robbed – really appreciate the extent of the crime. It's the biggest theft in history and despite the international liaison and the occasional legislation, it's a business that is growing all the time. Counterfeiters are clever, professional criminals: as clever and as professional as the businessmen and the inventors whose products they steal.

Conclusion

The current estimate of Western anti-counterfeiting agencies is that product stealing in all its forms represents three per cent of world trade. It has been suggested to me by experienced experts in America, England and Hong Kong that such a figure is an under-estimate. The true figure is closer to five per cent – an assessment which takes no account of the loss to genuine manufacturers from technological and industrial espionage, 'the value of which', an American enforcement agent told me, 'makes counterfeiting penny ante stuff'.

This is an opinion borne out by the figure of $2,500,000,000 which IBM put on just one case of industrial espionage. The settlement eventually agreed, of $300,000,000, did not indicate any change of mind about the potential cost of the theft – the IBM board considered the restrictive clauses imposed on Hitachi by that agreement more important than the size of a financial penalty.

Such cosmic profits make it impossible completely to stop the trade: to paraphrase the common analogy of fingers in dykes, fresh sources open up as soon as existing leaks are plugged. And other professionals, besides Hong Kong's Anthony Gurka, argue that counterfeiting should be regarded – although not tolerated – as a necessary part of the industrialised maturing of underdeveloped countries. This is in no way to suggest that the efforts to plug the leaks should be abandoned. Indeed, more countries – particularly hesitant Britain – should follow America's example in exerting whatever financial and trade pressures they can to force look-the-other-way governments to introduce and then properly enforce preventative legislation. *None* of the countries where I researched *The Steal* are currently doing this. Those that do have laws hardly enforce them; those that do not prevaricate and postpone their introduction, not wishing to lose the multi-billion dollar illicit business, irrespective of the assurances and promises they publicly profer.

Taiwan is emerging into industrial maturity and needs not only continued American trade support but also foreign investment. So it can be pressured. Singapore, too, is vulnerable: after twenty-five years as one of the economic miracles of Asia, in 1985 it confronted the unthinkable – a reversal approaching six per cent in its hitherto uninterrupted economic growth rate. This setback reinforced Western insistence that resulted in Singapore introducing infringement protection. Singapore, the most active of pirating nations, also has the most stringent government control: it is precisely that control which has enabled its unrivalled progress in the region. And it is that control – coupled with the will to use it in this connection – which could subdue counterfeiting and copying in the island country more quickly and more effectively than could be done anywhere else in the region. In Japan, a uniquely puritanical work ethos and deep-seated nationalism assure that counterfeiters only copy foreign bestsellers and regard industrial espionage as acceptable, producing enormous and contested trade imbalances with the West. It is in its recognised right to resolve these imbalances that the West has found a useful bargaining counter with which to control the Japanese rip-offs.

Checking counterfeiting and pirating in these three countries would at least represent some progress – though there would still be a long way to go.

Mainland China, which has already established itself as the major book-stealing nation in the world, threatens further expansion. In 1997 it will regain control of Hong Kong, already a conduit for mainland fakes, and the pervading unease in the Colony over the pending takeover has produced a marked increase in counterfeiting. Beijing's draft five year plan for 1986 to 1990 complains of the 'extreme backwardness' of much of the country's hi-tech and industrialised development. Some experts with whom I spoke in the area believe that the legitimate, multi-billion trade deals Beijing is currently concluding with the West in order to make up that lost ground will give Western governments the means to combat the feared growth in piracy – through linked restrictions on the foreign exchange and soft loan agreements on which Beijing insists. Other experts say the scramble to obtain the orders is such that Western governments, still less Western businessmen, do not consider that a viable proposal. One man with fifteen years' experience of business – and counterfeiting – in Asia told me:

> The Chinese could make a nonsense of it if it were tried. If one country or company tried to impose restrictions, they'd simply look to another country and another company, who'd jump in, without the slightest qualm. For loan restrictions to have any effect, there would have to be a coordinated policy, with no one breaking ranks. And that would never happen. 'Business is business' would be the response.

This indicates a Western cynicism to match the Asian cynicism with which the other copying countries in the region regard efforts to halt the trade. It is typified by the Indonesian government's reaction to the worldwide outcry which followed the exposure of the Live Aid theft. There were meaningless undertakings to set up a judicial enquiry from Jakarta's Foreign Minister, Mochtar Kusamaatmandja: no action whatsoever was taken against the main pirate, Joseph Gondobintoro; a total of $30,000 was contributed to famine relief, leaving the government with a profit of $270,000 from the tax they exacted on the bootlegged tapes. As a further gesture, the tapes were withdrawn from sale within the country, which had anyway never been the major market. That was the Middle East and Nigeria, where they continue to be marketed.

There are examples of matching political cynicism in the West. The British Conservative government published a consultative Green Paper which categorically said they were 'inclined to the view that a levy should be introduced to remunerate copyright owners for unauthorised copying of their material'. It first appeared in February 1985: exactly one year later the then Home Secretary, Leon Brittan, was lobbying to reverse the recommendation of his predecessor, Norman Tebbit. It was not, however, Brittan's personal view. He was reflecting the reluctance of Prime Minister Margaret Thatcher to impose another tax, given that her government was committed to cutting taxes. Against the background of concerted demands from all the anti-piracy groups in England – the International Federation of Phonographic Industries even complained that the levy proposed by the green paper was too *low* – publication of the follow-up White Paper necessary for further parliamentary discussion was delayed pending the announcement of EEC copyright proposals. The hope was that the Community suggestions would include a tape levy, whose implementation would enable the British government to avoid the additional tax accusation by having to adopt legislation already acceptable in the Community. In June 1985 France adopted a copyright law covering blank tapes, as Germany had in May.

Intelligence and enforcement agencies forecast an increase in technological and industrial espionage from the Communist bloc. It is inevitable, they believe, considering the proclaimed determination of Soviet leader Mikhail Gorbachov to close the hi-tech gap which has been publicly admitted to exist between East and West. At the end of 1985 the Soviet Politburo endorsed a new Five Year Plan which demanded an eighty per cent increase in computer production. Other government proposals include the computerisation of the economy in every one of the union's republics and the installation of 1,000,000 microcomputers in Soviet schools and academies. Western analysts point out that, currently, the Soviet Union only possesses 30,000 mainframe and mini-computers to serve the entire vast country. They doubt Russian ability fully to utilise the claimed invention of an all-Russian computer able to input two hundred instructions every second and quote, to support that doubt, the case publicly disclosed in a November 1985 issue of *Izvestia*. The newspaper revealed the invention at the Chelyabinsk Polytechnic, in the Urals, of a revolutionary new method of rolling and drawing metals, saving both energy and raw material. It was patented and is now used in thirty-five different countries throughout the world. In the Soviet Union, it was installed in a factory in Novosibirsk. The process was invented in 1966; in 1985 – in Novosibirsk – it was still regarded as an experiment. Criticised *Izvestia*: 'As we can see, twenty years have gone by. But those who should back up the inventor and put scientific and technical progress into practice do not do so.'

In the West, Europe continues to be critical of its NATO ally, America, over what it considers to be Washington's manipulation of COCOM to benefit its manufacturers. Despite the insistence of the British Secretary of Trade and Industry, Paul Channon, that the COCOM restrictions strike a fair balance, English manufacturers with whom I discussed the American-muscled embargo list point out that in 1984 – the last full year at the time of writing for which statistics are available – Britain's trade with the Soviet Union amounted to just under £1,500,000,000, less in 1985. The corresponding American figure was the equivalent of £2,340,000,000. There was further irritation that at a time when the Pentagon's Richard Perle was urging continued restraints upon COCOM partners, the American Secretary of Commerce, Malcolm Baldridge, led to Moscow a charter-jet sales force of 450 leading American industrialists, all eager for hi- tech business.

It was even suggested to me that the much-heralded memorandum of agreement between London and Washington – under which Britain appeared to become the first European country to participate in the hi-tech developments of America's $2,700,000,000 Strategic Defence Initiative – was a meaningless political manoeuvre, to stop Europe carping at COCOM restrictions. A British defence analyst insisted that:

> The Pentagon and Richard Perle have got the ear of President Reagan. The sort of technology that is going to be employed in Star Wars is the highest state of the art there is. It is unthinkable that the Pentagon – which is distrustful of European hi-tech security – will permit anything of that magnitude being developed outside of their own country.

This seemed to be borne out by remarks made in December 1985 by Lieutenant General James Abrahamson, Director of the Star Wars programme. He publicly warned: 'It is important to point out that the fundamental basis for allied participation must be technical merit. We have made it clear to allies that there can be no guarantee of a certain level of effort.'

There was another absence of guarantee. The British Minister of Defence at the time of the memorandum of agreement, Michael Heseltine, pushed US Secretary of Defence Caspar Weinberger to commit $1,500,000,000 worth of Star Wars technology to British firms. Weinberger refused, arguing that the laws and regulations governing the awarding of American defence contracts insist that the Pentagon accept the lowest tender, 'which provides another escape,' the analyst said. 'British firms – denied by COCOM from tendering to the Eastern bloc and often mainland China – will go through the expensive charade of submitting for American

233

contracts to be told after a face-saving passage of time that they have been underbid by an American firm.'

Although West Germany and Italy are negotiating with America for participation, France – home of the COCOM trade group but not a NATO partner – has made it clear to Washington that it has no wish to be involved. So, too, have Norway and Denmark. From my encounters with US intelligence and enforcement agents and Pentagon officials, I doubt whether any Scandinavian tender would ever have been entertained after Richard Mueller's Swedish operation. His continued existence is not their only apprehension. American officials, who naturally reject the accusations of their COCOM allies, insist that other operators like Mueller remain to supply the Eastern bloc in a Europe insufficiently concerned at the haemorrhage. Judging from the amount of official, legally proven documentation made available to me, this seems likely to be true and it means that the United States will remain suspicious of Europe and that Europe will remain suspicious of the United States. Above all, it means that, although increasingly restricted, the Eastern bloc will continue to benefit from the scientific advances of both.

Sources

US CONGRESS

Hearings into transfer of technology by the Senate Permanent Subcommittee on Investigations, 2, 3, 11 and 12 April 1984

Hearings into transfer of United States high technology to the Soviet Union and Soviet bloc nations by the Senate Permanent Subcommittee on Investigations, 4, 5, 6, 11 and 12 May 1982

Hearings into unfair foreign trade practices by the Subcommittee on Oversight and Investigations of the Committee on Energy and Commerce, House of Representatives, 27 June, 27 July, 2 August, 21 and 23 September 1983, 29 February, 6 March, 24 July, 26 July, 6 August and 20 September 1984

'Transfer of Technology', report by the Senate Permanent Subcommittee on Investigations, October 1984

'Transfer of United States High Technology to the Soviet Union and Soviet Bloc Nations', report by the Committee of Governmental Affairs, United States Senate, made by the Permanent Subcommittee on Investigations, November 1982

'Unfair Foreign Trade Practices: Stealing American Intellectual Property – Imitation Is Not Flattery', report by the Subcommittee on Oversight and Investigations of the Committee on Energy and Commerce, House of Representatives, February 1984

US GOVERNMENT

'Assessing the Effect of Technology Transfer on US/Western Security', Richard Perle, Assistant Secretary of Defence for International Security Policy, February 1985

'Secrets, Spies and Citizens', FBI, May 1978

'The Technology Transfer Control Programme', report by Caspar Weinberger, Secretary of Defence, to the second session of the US 98th Congress, February 1984, and to the first session of the 99th Congress, February 1985

William Webster, speech to the Washington University School of Business, November 1983

William H. Webster, Director of the FBI, his testimony on the 1985 Appropriation Request, before the Subcommittee on Appropriations, House of Representatives, April 1984

OTHER US PUBLICATIONS

'Piracy of US Copyrighted Works in Ten Selected Countries', report by the International Intellectual Property Alliance to the US Trade Representative, August 1985

'The Suggestion Plan', 'Business Conduct Guidelines', 'Protecting IBM's Information Assets', 'Staying in Charge: an Executive Briefing for Improving Control of Your Information System', 'Security Assessment Questionnaire', 'Some Technology Landmarks', from the annual report, IBM Publications, 1984

OTHER PUBLICATIONS

'International Federation of Phonogram and Videogram Producers: the First Fifty Years', International Conventions and Copyright/Neighbouring Rights Legislation, 1985

Index

Buckwalter, Lawrence, 207
Buffy Manufacturing Corp., 127
Burke, Alexander, 164
Butler, Beverly, 186
Butterworth, 168

Cadet, Raymond, 64
Callahan, Richard, 65–9, 70
Callaghan, William, 225
Campaign Against Book Piracy, 166–7, 168, 172, 175, 176
Camps, Richard, 137
Cardin, Pierre, 208, 209–10, 211, 212
Carr, David, 84
Carratu, Vincent, 221–3, 224, 228
Carrera, 129–30
cars, 196–201
  parts, 119–20, 126, 127, 196–201
Carter, Jimmy, 84, 85
Cartier, 144, 208–9, 222, 224
Casey, William, 46, 58
Caves Books, 120–1
Chambre Syndicale de la Couture Parisienne, 211, 212
Chanel, 129, 212, 224–5
Channon, Paul, 165, 166–7, 168, 226
Chen, A., 113
Chen, C. V., 116
Chen, Terry, 114
Chen-li, Chen, 118, 119
Cheng, Derek, 113, 121–2, 154, 199
Cheng, Gary, 134
Chenin Technologies Inc., 135
Chernayev, Anatoli, 81
Chi E. Enterprises Co., 127
Chi Luen Warehouse and Trading/Transport Co., 134
Chih, Gianfranco, 221–2
Chilong Game Corp., 127
Chin, Paul, 135
China Computer Technical Service Corp, 91–2
Chipex Inc., 90–1
Chu, Albert, 134
Chua, Alberto, 111
Chuan Chun Co., 127
Chuk Lung-bong, 118–19
Churchill Livingstone, 175
Chye, Ng Teow, 97, 104
CIA, 10, 45, 48, 58, 85, 87, 118, 139
Civil Aviation Authority, 195
clothes, 128–30, 138, 208–14
COCOM, 27, 28–38, 44, 46–7, 82–8

Cohen, Calman, 42
COLC, 211
Collins International Trading Corps, 17
Commercial Trademark Service Ltd, 119, 179, 218
Commodore Computers, 134
computers:
  counterfeiting, 109–17
  illegal exporting, 9–92
  software, 226–8
Comx World Operation, 134
Concine, 160–1
Continental Engineering Products Co., 132
Continental Technology Corp., 26
Conze, Henri, 82
Cooper, Allen, 163
Cooper, McDougall and Robertson, 228
Coordinated Requests for Technological Information, 9–11
Copam Electronics Corp., 127
Counterfeiting Intelligence Bureau, 125
Crossman, David, 129–30
Crown Wallpaper, 124–5
Crown Wallpaper Industrial Co., 125
Cruise missiles, 58
Cunningham, John, 52

Dadourian, Jack, 189–90
Dan Control, 13, 17
Dar El Maaref, 175
DARPA, 57
Datasaab, 38
Deacons, 138–9, 215–16
Dean, Linsey, 195–6
DeGeyter, Marc Andre, 26
Deighton, Len, 121
DeLauer, Richard, 29–32
Delta-Avia Fluggerate, 87
Demerol, 185
Dennison, Maria, 202, 203, 205
Dewan Bahasa, 171
Digital Equipment Corp. (DEC), 17, 19, 20, 43
Dionysus Enterprises Co., 127
Dior, Christian, 144, 145, 211, 212, 222
disinformation, 45–8
Disney, Walt, 215–16
Domenico, 66
drugs, 177–86
DST, 82
Du Guozhen, 217–18